Praise for *The Leadership Challenge*

"Kouzes and Posner continue to strengthen and widen our definition of leadership. They make the role of the leader and the process of leadership understandable and accessible to anyone who wants to improve on their own abilities and guide others in significant ways."

— Beverly Kaye, founder and CEO, Career Systems International and coauthor, *Love 'Em or Lose 'Em: Getting Good People to Stay*

"This new edition of *The Leadership Challenge* shall be mandatory reading for any individual or organization that cares about the future. Evidence-based from the authors' twenty-five years of global research, this fully practical and inspirational book will provide the tools and the motivation both to select and develop the exceptional leaders we need so much all around the world."

— Claudio Fernández-Aráoz, partner and global executive committee member, Egon Zehnder International; author of *Great People Decisions*

"A timely, practical update of the definitive book on leadership. If you haven't read this work, do it now ... before your competitors get their hands on it. If you've already read the book, the new edition is certainly worth another read. It truly enhances the groundbreaking work of these preeminent leadership thinkers."

— Adrian Gostick, *New York Times* bestselling author of *The Carrot Principle*

"Leadership is the one central and most important element of successful management teams—be it in a start-up company, a growth phase of an established organization, or as key for a successful turnaround. During their extensive research on leadership, Kouzes and Posner have worked with many successful leaders around the world. Their research results and the many different leadership examples are the basis of this most comprehensive and inspiring book on leadership. *The Leadership Challenge* is the classic, and yet the most updated, publication on leadership—the best I have seen."

— Chris Muntwyler, CEO, DHL Express UK & Ireland

"*The Leadership Challenge* is a revealing guide to 'liberating the leader in you.' Kouzes and Posner prove that effective leadership can be learned and each chapter is a step on the journey to bringing the best from yourself and others. Their book offers practical, research-based lessons that are at the core of our corporate leadership development program."

— Debra L. Lyons, chief human resources officer, Westfield Group

"Even the most seasoned executive or veteran manager will find much to learn from these two authors. More than any other leadership book in my collection, their work provides an introspective look at the opportunities we all have to improve our skills and cast a more inspirational and influential shadow in our organizations. Take the challenge!"
— Ken Wilcox, president and CEO, SVB Financial Group

"*The Leadership Challenge* is a profound and inspiring blueprint for building leadership capacity that should be read by all. In this latest edition, Kouzes and Posner once again bring us the insight and wisdom of ordinary people in everyday situations that have produced extraordinary results. These leaders are living examples of the power of leadership. By understanding their stories and the lessons they have learned, you will embrace The Five Practices and the Ten Commitments of Exemplary Leadership to improve your own leadership skills as well as inspire a new generation of future leaders. Take The Leadership Challenge. I guarantee you will not be disappointed!"
— Dan Warmenhoven, CEO, Network Appliance, Inc.

"Kouzes and Posner created a classic book that is essential reading, with a message that has become increasingly poignant for leaders for generations to come."
— Mark C. Thompson, coauthor of the international bestseller *Success Built to Last: Creating a Life that Matters*

"*The Leadership Challenge* is packed with great stories of leadership and leadership challenges from all walks of life. In today's world, we need leaders with integrity. Kouzes and Posner have laid out a simple plan to help develop those leaders. Reading the book feels like speaking to a mentor on leadership."
— Stephen E. Almassy, global vice chair of technology, Ernst & Young LLP

"This is the most timeless and practical work of modern management thinking on how to be a leader of people. Solid research, great storytelling, and useful practices—this book has it all. This new edition is packed with leading-edge research and great ways to become a leader."
— John Izzo, Ph.D., author of *Awakening Corporate Soul*

"Whether you've worked in a professional environment for decades or you're just stepping into the business world for the first time, *The Leadership Challenge* is the book for you. It's a perfect resource for people looking for information on leadership, personal development, and change. This book is an invaluable tool to find the true leader in each and every one of us."
— Bob Moles, chairman, Intero Real Estate Services

"The first edition was seminal and totally original. It became a modern classic on leadership practically overnight. With new cases and concepts and action steps that are even riper and more important, Kouzes and Posner go way beyond their earlier work and have made yet another brilliant contribution to leadership studies. This new book, a product of an unusual collaboration, is essential reading for everyone involved or concerned with leading."

— Warren Bennis, distinguished professor of business administration at the University of Southern California and author of *On Becoming a Leader*

"From the Ten Commitments of Leadership to the emphasis on actions and relationships, this valuable book is full of enduring wisdom and practical insights essential for success in changing times."

— Rosabeth Moss Kanter, professor, Harvard Business School, and bestselling author of *Confidence: How Winning & Losing Streaks Begin & End*

"For twenty-five years I have written about and taught leadership. *The Leadership Challenge* is one of the five best books I have ever read. I continually recommend it to others."

— John C. Maxwell, founder, The INJOY Group, and author, *The 21 Irrefutable Laws of Leadership*

"Based upon evidence collected from around the world and over decades, *The Leadership Challenge* provides practical guidance on how to lead and inspiration to make the effort."

— Jeffrey Pfeffer, professor, Stanford Business School, and author of *The Human Equation: Building Profits by Putting People First*

"This is perhaps the most comprehensive field guide ever written for leaders. The principles are powerful, and have been a key part of my personal journey as a leader for years."

— Patrick Lencioni, president, The Table Group, and bestselling author of *The Five Dysfunctions of a Team*

"*The Leadership Challenge* answers the greatest challenge leaders face—knowing what to do to deliver value. Kouzes and Posner turn research into practical ideas that leaders at all levels can use. Full of practical tools and wonderful cases, it offers easy access to concepts that will build personal and organizational leadership depth. When the book first came out, it affected my thinking on leadership, and it continues to do so."

— Dave Ulrich, professor at the Ross School of Business, University of Michigan, and coauthor of *The HR Value Proposition*

"If you can have only one book on leadership, *The Leadership Challenge* has to be it. Kouzes and Posner reinforce their timeless principles with the stories of people who are actually leading in today's world."
— Terry Pearce, founder of Leadership Communication and author of
Leading Out Loud

"If you read only one book on leadership, this is the one to read. If you read it more than a year ago, you need to read it again. It will stimulate new thoughts and (more important) inspire you to action. A true classic, extraordinarily well written."
— David H. Maister, author of *Practice What You Preach* and coauthor of
The Trusted Advisor

"Want to increase your professional and personal ROI? Then read this book, use this book, and give this book to others. The ROI on your leadership will be significant, visible, and bankable."
— Sharon A. Winston, senior vice president, Lee Hecht Harrison

JB JOSSEY-BASS

THE LEADERSHIP CHALLENGE

FOURTH EDITION

JAMES M. KOUZES

BARRY Z. POSNER

John Wiley & Sons, Inc.

Published by Jossey-Bass
A Wiley Imprint
989 Market Street, San Francisco, CA 94103-1741—www.josseybass.com

Library of Congress Cataloging-in-Publication Data

Kouzes, James M., 1945–
    The leadership challenge / James M. Kouzes, Barry Z. Posner. — 4th ed.
      p. cm.
    Includes bibliographical references and index.
    ISBN-13: 978-0-7879-8491-5
    1. Leadership. 2. Executive ability. 3. Management. I. Posner, Barry Z. II. Title.
  HD57.7.K68 2007
  658.4'092—dc22
                                                    2006103359

Printed in the United States of America
FIRST EDITION
HB Printing   10 9 8 7 6 5 4 3 2

CONTENTS

6 ENCOURAGE THE HEART

7 LEADERSHIP FOR EVERYONE

We dedicate this book, with love,

to the two leaders we admire most,

Tae Moon Kouzes and Jackie Schmidt-Posner,

and to the upcoming generation of leaders,

Nicholas Lopez and Amanda Posner.

PREFACE

Getting Extraordinary Things Done in Organizations

The Leadership Challenge is about how leaders mobilize others to want to get extraordinary things done in organizations. It's about the practices leaders use to transform values into actions, visions into realities, obstacles into innovations, separateness into solidarity, and risks into rewards. It's about leadership that creates the climate in which people turn challenging opportunities into remarkable successes.

There are no shortages of challenging opportunities. In these extraordinary times, the challenges seem only to be increasing in number and complexity. All generations confront their own serious threats and receive their own favorable circumstances. The abundance of challenges is not the issue. It's how we respond to them that matters. Through our responses to challenges, we all have the potential to seriously worsen or profoundly improve the world in which we live and work. With the kinds of leadership excellence we've observed in over twenty-five years of research, we're going to bet on the latter.

There are countless opportunities for each of us to make a difference. For instance, there are opportunities to

- Provide direction and support to our teams during uncertain times
- More fully utilize the talents of our colleagues
- Set a positive example of what honesty and ethics mean in daily life

- Find a better balance in our always-on, 24/7/365 lives
- Apply knowledge to products and services, creating extraordinary value for the customer
- Put the innocence and wisdom of different generations into our workplace and into our products and services
- Use the tools of technology to weave a web of human connection
- Tap the wealth of scientific knowledge to create a safer and more sustainable world
- Rebuild a sense of community and increase understanding among diverse peoples
- Turn information into knowledge and improve the collective standard of living
- Bring peace to a world tired of war
- Restore hope and create a deeper sense of meaning in our lives

More than ever there is need for people to seize these opportunities to lead us to greatness. *The Leadership Challenge* is about those who do. It is about how traditional systems of rewards and punishments, control and scrutiny give way to innovation, individual character, and the courage of convictions. It offers a set of leadership practices based on the real-world experiences of thousands of people who have answered the call for leadership.

What we have discovered, and rediscovered, is that leadership is not the private reserve of a few charismatic men and women. It is a process ordinary people use when they are bringing forth the best from themselves and others. When the leader in everyone is liberated extraordinary things happen.

THE PURPOSE OF THIS BOOK

The fundamental purpose of *The Leadership Challenge* is to assist people—managers and individual contributors alike—in furthering their abilities to lead others to get extraordinary things done. Whether you're in the private sector or public, an employee or a volunteer, on the front line or in the senior echelon, a student or a parent, we have written this book to help you develop your capacity to guide others to places they have never been before. We believe that you are capable of developing yourself as a leader far more than tradition has ever assumed possible.

The Leadership Challenge is written both to strengthen your abilities and to uplift your spirits. We intend it to be practical and inspirational. We also make you a promise: everything in this book is *evidence-based.* Everything we write about, everything we advise is solidly based in research—our own and others'. If you engage in the practices we describe in this book, you *will* improve your performance and the performance of your team. There is a catch, of course. You have to do it with commitment and consistency. Excellence in anything—whether it's leadership, music, sports, or engineering—requires disciplined practice.

This book has its origins in a research project we began over twenty-five years ago. We wanted to know what people did when they were at their "personal best" in leading others. The personal bests were experiences in which our respondents, in their own perception, set their individual leadership standards of excellence. We started with an assumption that we didn't have to interview and survey star performers in excellent companies to discover best practices. Instead, we assumed that by asking ordinary people to describe extraordinary leadership experiences we would find patterns of success. And we did.

When they are doing their best, leaders exhibit certain distinct practices, which vary little from industry to industry, profession to profession, community to community, and country to country. Good leadership is an understandable and universal process. Though each leader is a unique individual, there are shared patterns to the practice of leadership. And these practices can be learned.

This book is about how ordinary people exercise leadership at its best. There are a few CEOs mentioned in *The Leadership Challenge,* but you probably won't recognize their names. This is *not* a book about famous people or about people in positions of high power—as if leadership were based on rank and place. Instead, the stories you will read are those of regular people, from all walks of life—people like you—who get bigger-than-life results. It's a book about people who have the courage and spirit to make a significant difference.

The leaders we've worked with and learned from have asked us many questions about enhancing their leadership capabilities:

- What values should guide my actions as a leader?
- How do I best set an example for others?
- How do I articulate a vision of the future when things are so unpredictable?
- How do I improve my ability to inspire others toward a common purpose?
- How do I create an environment that promotes innovation and risk?
- How do I build a cohesive and spirited team?
- How do I share power and information and still maintain accountability?
- How do I put more joy and celebration into our efforts?
- What is the source of self-confidence required to lead others?
- How do I go about improving my leadership abilities?

In *The Leadership Challenge,* we offer guidance on these questions, and others.

A FIELD GUIDE FOR LEADERS

Think of *The Leadership Challenge* as a field guide to take along on your leadership journey. We begin the expedition with two chapters that introduce you to our point of view about leadership. In Chapter One we describe The Five Practices of Exemplary Leadership revealed in our research.[1] But you can't do justice to leadership without also talking about what constituents want, so in Chapter Two we describe the results of our research on the characteristics that people most admire in their leaders.

In Chapters Three through Twelve we explore The Five Practices in depth. We have designed each chapter to describe one of the Ten Commitments of

Leadership—the essential behaviors—that leaders employ to get extraordinary things done, and to explain the fundamental principles that support the leadership practices. We offer evidence from our research and that of others to support the principles, provide actual case examples of real people who demonstrate each practice, and prescribe specific recommendations on what you can do to make each practice your own and to continue your development as a leader. Every chapter from Three to Twelve concludes with suggested steps to take, alone or with others, to build specific skills in implementing the practice. Each of our suggestions is a "small win." Whether the focus is your own learning or the development of your constituents—your direct reports, team, peers, manager, community members, and the like—you can take immediate action on every one of our recommendations. They require little or no budget, discussion, and consensus among peers, nor approval of top management. They just require your personal commitment and discipline.

In our closing chapter, Chapter Thirteen, we offer a call to action, a call to everyone to accept personal responsibility to be a role model for leadership. Over the past twenty-five years we kept relearning that leadership is everyone's business. The first place to look for leadership is within yourself. We will ask you in our closing chapter to consider the difference you want to make, the legacy you want to leave. And we promise that if you read to the very end of this book, we'll tell you the secret to success in life.

Those familiar with our previous three editions of *The Leadership Challenge* will notice that the practices and the commitments have remained the same over more than a quarter century. Nothing in our continuing research has told us that there is a magical sixth practice that will revolutionize the conduct of leadership, and nothing in our research suggests that any of the Five Practices are now irrelevant. But we did decide we needed to go on a diet. Each succeeding edition tended to put on a little weight—feature creep, as they say in the technology business. We decided that we needed to trim down to our original size, so this edition is more like the first edition in terms of length. There are still lots of stories and lots of research, we just focus more intently on the essentials and keep it simple. The other noticeable change from the previous edition is the inclusion of more cases from outside the United States. *The Leadership Challenge* has been translated into twelve other languages, and we wanted to bring leaders from around the globe more prominently into this new edition.

Short of starting with Chapters One and Two, there is no sacred order to this book. Go wherever your interests are. We wrote this material to support you in your leadership development. Just remember that each practice is essential. Although you might skip around in the book, you can't skip any of the fundamentals of leadership.

Finally, for those who wish to know more about how we conducted our research, detailed information on our methodology, statistical data, and highlights of validation studies by other scholars of our leadership paradigm are available on the Web at www.leadershipchallenge.com.

THE FUTURE OF LEADERSHIP

The domain of leaders is the future. The leader's unique legacy is the creation of valued institutions that survive over time. The most significant contribution leaders make is not simply to today's bottom line; it is to the long-term development of people and institutions so they can adapt, change, prosper, and grow. We hope this book contributes to the revitalization of organizations, to the creation of new enterprises, to the renewal of healthy communities, and to greater respect and understanding in the world. We also fervently hope that it enriches your life and that of your community and your family.

Leadership is important, not just in your career and within your organization, but in every sector, in every community, and in every country. We need more exemplary leaders, and we need them more than ever. There is so much extraordinary work that needs to be done. We need leaders who can unite us and ignite us.

In the end, we realize that leadership development is self-development. Meeting the leadership challenge is a personal—and a daily—challenge for all of us. We know that if you have the will and the way to lead, you can. You have to supply the will. We'll do our best to supply the way.

June 2007

James M. Kouzes
Orinda, California
Barry Z. Posner
Santa Clara, California

THE LEADERSHIP CHALLENGE

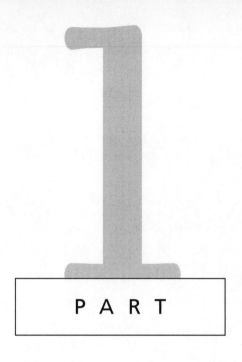

PART

1

WHAT LEADERS
DO AND WHAT
CONSTITUENTS
EXPECT

- THE FIVE PRACTICES OF EXEMPLARY
  LEADERSHIP

- CREDIBILITY IS THE FOUNDATION
  OF LEADERSHIP

THE FIVE PRACTICES
OF EXEMPLARY
LEADERSHIP

*"Leadership is ultimately about creating a way for people to
contribute to making something extraordinary happen."*
Alan Keith, Genentech

"When I walked in the door on my first day," Dick Nettell told us, "we had
four hundred people working really, really hard, but they weren't winning. We
had people who were walking around looking like they ran over their dogs on
the way to work. It was very, very sad." As the new site executive for Bank of
America's Consumer Call Center in Concord, California, Dick found "rep

scores" (the key performance measure) 21 percentage points behind the top performing call center and 18 points behind the next lowest performer. Fifty-five percent of employees felt that they were in an environment in which they could not speak their minds, and 50 percent believed that nothing was going to happen even if they did.[1]

It's Dick's firm belief that "everybody wants to win. Everybody wants to be successful. Everybody comes to work trying to make a difference." But the call center employees suffered from "management whiplash." The constant turnover in leadership and changes in priorities had been sending them down the path of poor performance. Dick said that when he started asking about the comparisons with other centers, "All I heard were the reasons why we couldn't do this or that. If there were an Olympic excuse-making team, we would be gold medallists. People were very disempowered." So Dick set out to change all that.

Dick set aside three entire days just for talking and listening to people. He gathered as much data as he could from these interviews and elsewhere. "If you keep your eyes open and periodically actually shut your mouth, and you have the courage to turn the mirror around on yourself," said Dick, "it's amazing what you can learn and how you can change things."

He met with the call center's senior managers and support staff in a large basement conference room and presented his findings. Then he handed out stacks of Post-it notepads and asked the group to write down five adjectives that described the center at that time. He repeated this process two more times, asking them to write down five adjectives that described how they thought their peers would describe the center and what they thought the associates, or customer service representatives, would say. Each time, their responses were written on an easel. It was a bleak picture. Words such as *demotivated, volatile, imprecise, failing, disorganized, frustrating, not fun, constantly changing priorities, lack of appreciation, too many changes,* and *not enough coaching* appeared on the lists. Even so, there were some positive comments about the people, such as *dedicated, energetic,* and *supportive.*

Then Dick asked them to go through the process once more, this time describing how they would *like* the call center to look in the future. "If you could wave a magic wand," he asked the group, "in three to five years how would you like the center to be described?" The language they used to express their hopes, dreams, and aspirations painted a dramatically different picture from the one Dick found when he came aboard: *amazing results, world class, a model for others to follow, a unique place to work, partnership, opportunities to learn and grow, true passion for our customers.* Armed with this list of aspirations Dick and the management team began to craft a vision, mission, and set of values (which they called commitments). The resulting vision and mission read as follows:

OUR VISION OF THE FUTURE . . .

- We will be seen as a *World Class Call Center* and the standard against which others are measured—one with true passion for our customers.
- We will be acknowledged across the franchise as a model to follow, where every associate truly feels like a partner, has an equal opportunity to learn and grow, and understands their personal impact on our overall success.
- We will be viewed as a unique place to work, an organization that drives amazing results while having fun along the way.

OUR MISSION IS . . .

- To provide an experience that consistently "delights" our customers every single minute of every single day.

Over the next six weeks Dick held twenty-two forty-five minute state-of-the-center meetings with every team in the call center. "Here's our vision, here's what we're committed to," Dick would say to begin raising awareness of the issues, and then he'd ask, "Does this make sense to you? Is there something we need to change?" Then Dick told them about his own beginnings in Bank of America. He told them about how he started as a garage helper, worked his way up to be an automobile fleet manager, and eventually found his way into senior management. He told them, "I'm here at the call center because I want to be here," and then related the story of how he had retired as the bank's corporate services executive and decided to come back.

He said he woke up early one morning and realized that something was missing in his life. "At four in the morning you can't lie to yourself," he told them. "I realized that I'm really passionate about working with folks to get them to think differently about themselves. What was missing in my life was the ability to make a difference in people's lives. It may sound corny, but I love to be able to work with people so that they can be the best they can be." So Dick reached out to an executive he admired at the bank and asked about the chance of coming back. He got his wish when the opportunity to take on the Concord Call Center came along. Everyone in those state-of-the-center meetings, when they heard Dick's story, realized that they had a champion on their side, a genuine leader who would enable them to turn their aspirations into actuality. They understood that Dick was there because he wanted to be there, not because the call center was on some career path to a higher position.

At those meetings Dick challenged everyone to take the initiative to make the new vision a reality. "You've lost the right to suffer in silence," he said. "If you have an issue, open your mouth. I want you to talk to your managers, talk to my communications person, talk to me, or visit AskDick.com. Think about sitting in my chair. Give me ideas and proposals that I have the authority to approve." Dick made it clear that from then on changing the call center was everybody's business. "You have to be a part of this," he said. "You want to be like a partner, then you've signed up for some responsibility in the process." Dick's challenge made it clear that things were going to change, and that the associates were empowered to act. "Everybody should have that equal opportunity to succeed and learn and know what it feels like to win," Dick said, and "once you've done that—you've got people well positioned—get the hell out of their way and watch them rock and roll."

To maintain the momentum, Dick began holding monthly "town hall" meetings. To make that happen he had to challenge the way things are normally done—it's tough to pull call center people off the phone, even once a month. So they do two half-hour town halls each month, with half the center attending one, and the other half coming to the other. At each one, Dick constantly reiterates the mission, commitments, and vision—that's a ritual with him. He gives a "you said, we did" report. Then there's a discussion of current initiatives. For example, the month that we visited Dick, the new-hire onboarding process, the upcoming associate survey, and clothing guidelines were the topics of discussion. Following the initiative discussion is a report on the month's performance. Each town hall concludes with "Celebrating Heroes," a time for individuals who have made significant contributions to the center to be publicly recognized. And it's not just Dick and his managers doing the recognizing. Associates also get time on the agenda to celebrate peers for living the values of the bank and keeping the commitments they've made to each other.

Recognition and celebration are a big deal to Dick. When he arrived at the Concord Call Center, very little of either was going on, so Dick put it on the agenda. Every Wednesday, for example, is "Pride Day," when people wear company logo merchandise and you see a lot of red, blue, and white bank shirts. Although Pride Day was started before Dick arrived, he added new dimensions to the ritual. For starters, there's the fifteen-minute spirit huddle; once a month every one of the team managers has to bring at least one associate with them, and in the huddles the managers recognize their local heroes. You'll also see people wearing spirit beads. Dick came up with the idea because he wanted something really visible yet inexpensive enough that they could do a lot of it. The beads come in different colors, but on every string hangs a medallion with the same word: PRIDE.

PRIDE is Dick's motto; it stands for Personal Responsibility In Delivering Excellence. That medallion suspended from the gold, blue, and green beads symbolizes what all the values, vision, and mission are about to Dick. They're about taking pride in what you do. And when Dick conducts quarterly coaching sessions with each of his direct reports, they talk about PRIDE, and mission, and vision, and values. Another thing they talk about is how other people see them as leaders. "When we turn that mirror around," he asks, "is there a match to what we're saying? How do we spend our time every day? Do our goals match our commitments?" It's in these discussions that Dick gets down to aligning actions with the values of the center.

Despite the tremendous progress they've made in becoming a model call center, and toward keeping the commitments that they've made to each other, Dick still believes that "every day is opening day." He said, "It doesn't matter what you did yesterday. Each and every decision and action is a moment of truth. You say something and what do people see? The two have to be aligned. It's all about the video matching the audio."

And for Dick the challenge continues, for he knows that every day will present him and the organization with some wonderful chance to try something new: "In today's environment, if you want to be successful, doing things the same way just won't get it done, period. Expectations continue to be raised, by our shareholders, by our managers, and by our customers. And if we're not willing to be innovative and do things differently, we're going to have the competition pass us like we're sitting still on the freeway."

Dick demonstrates exemplary leadership skills, and he shows us how leaders can seize the opportunities to bring out the best in others and guide them on the journey to accomplishing exceptionally challenging goals. He serves as a role model for leaders who want to get extraordinary things done in organizations.

LEADERSHIP OPPORTUNITIES ARE EVERYWHERE

Leadership can happen anywhere, at any time. It can happen in a huge business or a small one. It can happen in the public, private, or social sector. It can happen in any function. It can happen at home, at school, or in the community. The call to lead can come at four o'clock in the morning, or it can come late at night. The energy and motivation to lead can come in ways you'd least expect. While Dick Nettell's most recent personal-best leadership grew out of a need to again challenge himself, Claire Owen's leadership best grew out of necessity.

Claire Owen is founder and Leader of Vision & Values of the SG Group in London, England, a 110-person firm that's a collection of four businesses designed to meet the marketing and human resource recruitment needs of agencies and corporations. Stopgap, the United Kingdom's first specialist freelance marketing agency and the SG Group's original business, began because the marketing agency Claire was working in at

Leadership can happen any- where, at any time.

the time went into receivership. She had a four-week-old baby and a huge mortgage, and was wondering what was going to happen next. But Claire was also worried about what would happen to her client, with whom they were midway through an important promotion. Her concern for her client overrode her personal concerns, so she called her contacts there, told them what was happening, and agreed on what they were going to do.

"I said to the client, 'Look, you are up you-know-where without a paddle, but don't panic. I will provide you with a stopgap.' So the account manager and I provided them with a temporary solution, and finished off running the promotion. I thought at the end of that, gosh, there is something here, providing people with a temporary marketing solution. But I knew *I* didn't want to be that temporary solution. I had had enough of printers, and creatives, and copywriters, so I thought maybe I could find other people to do the doing and I would just put them together with the client."

When Stopgap opened its doors there wasn't another business out there that was doing what Claire proposed. "We created the marketplace that we operate in," she said. "When we started up, nobody was providing freelance marketers. You could get locum (temporary) doctors, teachers, lawyers, dentists, and vets. In most professions you could get a temp, interim, whatever you like, but you couldn't in marketing." The fact that there was no other business like hers was fine with Claire. "I hate the predictable," she told us. "I hate doing things the way everyone else does. Whatever I do I like to do something different. I never wanted to be a me-too company from day one."

Claire is very outspoken about her lack of respect for the traditional ways the recruitment industries have been run. "I had been a candidate myself, and I had been so mistreated by the recruitment consultancy that I wanted to challenge the rules the recruitment industry was playing by," she told us. "If I could change those practices then I'd be proud to work in this field, and that is what I did."

For Claire the most fundamental rules had to do with how they operated. "I wanted an open and transparent business that people could trust," she said. "Whether it was about our fee structure, or the fact that we never send a candidate to a job before telling them everything about the organization, we operate by the principle of total transparency. We might say to a candidate, 'This looks like a great job for your career, but the location is terrible.'"

The early days were tough. There were a lot of naysayers. Because Claire was so outspoken about her views of the industry, competitors were particularly harsh. Claire remembers one time when a competitor looked at her, wagged his finger, and told her that she would never be a success in the business. She just laughed and said, "You don't know how wrong you are."

Success for Claire is not defined by a specific revenue amount or a specific head count. Quite simply, Claire said, "I wanted to run a business that had a phenomenal reputation." Her vision was that there would be Stopgaps all over the country, as there are Reeds (the U.K. leader in specialist recruitment, training, and HR consultancy)—an outlet on every corner so to speak. She knew they were never going to be a High Street recruitment consultancy, but she wanted Stopgap to be everywhere and to be a company that people wanted to do business with. Claire said that she's not a dreamer, but closer to the truth is that she is living her dream every day. For her the future is now.

Rather than waiting to run the business the way she thinks it should be run, she's bringing it to life every day of the week.

A clear set of values guides the daily decisions and actions that Claire and her staff make. These values came from walking in the shoes of her staff and their candidates. These wouldn't work, however, if they weren't shared values. As Claire told us, "People have said to me time and time again, 'I wouldn't work for any other recruitment consultancy. The only reason I'm sitting here is because I like these values. They're the same as mine.'"

"That's music to my ears," Claire said. "We're not everybody's cup of tea. People come and work for us because they want to make a difference to people. They want to help people. It's what they do."

"We are a very, very candidate-driven business," Claire told us. But even more important to her than the candidate is her staff. She fervently believes that if you take care of your staff, they will take care of the candidate; if the staff takes care of the candidate, the candidate will take care of the client; and if the candidate takes care of the client, the client will return to the SG Group for more business. Claire puts her staff first, knowing that they are the ones that ultimately determine the reputation of the company.

As you'd expect, staff turnover at the SG Group is extremely low. People rarely leave the business, and if they do they are always welcomed back should they choose to return. "Friendship is the glue that keeps people here. Why would I want to leave when my best mates work with me? Someone once said to me, 'Don't take this the wrong way, Claire, but coming to work is a bit like going to a coffee morning.' I asked her what she meant, and she said, 'I am with people I like, and we can socialize. And yes, we do the job.' I thought that was wonderful. They love coming to work because of the people that are here."

The values of helping and caring for clients and staff are by no means permission to coddle people and allow them to do whatever they want. Claire is very clear that she expects the values to be lived, not just talked about. They are as much a discipline as any other operational values. "If you want customers to have a certain experience," says Claire, "you have got to have people who can deliver on that experience. It's a darn sight easier if you employ people who have the values that you want to give your customers."

Clearly the SG Group values aren't just posters on the wall—they are the guidelines the group uses in everything they do. For example, there is the "First Tuesday in the Month" meeting. It's actually never held on the first Tuesday, but that's what it was called when they were first held and the name has stuck. It happens once a month from 9:00 A.M. to 10:00 A.M., and everybody comes. In that meeting they share the company's financials. Everybody learns what the business turned over, and the profit made or loss taken. They talk about where the business has come from, so people don't forget about their important clients. They share any marketing that's going on. They share a lot of people things—who's joining, who's leaving, who's got an anniversary this month, and anything else that affects staff. And they always have the "grapevine"—a time when people can ask about things they might have heard about and want to know if it's really happening. They film the meeting, so if someone has to miss it they can watch it on DVD.

Then there's the Friday meeting. It's a look back at the week, a sharing of good things and bad things that went on during the week. There's also the Thursday Breakfast Club, which happens every other Thursday. That's a forum for consultants to talk about candidates and clients, and to just share in depth the issues they're having. Notes from these meetings are often posted in the lavatory so that they are visible at all times—you never know when you might come up with a solution to someone's problem. Finally, there is a staff newsletter that goes out every other week for more personal needs, like someone wanting details of a great Mexican restaurant, a good plumber, or a flatmate.

Being physically present is important for Claire. She asked her staff what they wanted from her, and they told her "that they just wanted to see more of me, to have time to talk to me, to see me wandering around." Claire radiates energy. When you're around her you have no doubt that she cares deeply about the business, and, in particular, about the people in the business. Claire fully understands the potency of her physical presence. "You see that I get excited about things," she pointed out to us—not that there was any doubt—"and people go, 'Well, Claire is excited by it, so I'm going to get excited by it. She believes it and she thinks it is going to be great—well I think it's going to be great.' That's really all I do."

Claire also realizes that if her enthusiasm isn't genuine, it's going to have a negative effect. "If it's an act," she said, "they'll see right through it. People really respect you for who you are, and they don't want you to be someone you are not. They prefer to see who you are, the real you."

The SG Group has a positively charged atmosphere that is fueled by numerous recognitions and celebrations. These are the informal kinds at which people toast personal successes, anniversaries, and births of babies. Every month staff members nominate people who have gone the extra mile. Anybody can nominate anybody. Every month all the nominations are considered, 99 percent are approved, and every winner gets a silver envelope placed on their desk thanking them for going the extra mile and presenting usually between 25 and 50 Stopgap Points. Each point is worth about £1, and they can convert the points into whatever they want to spend it on. The SG Group also has a very flexible benefits scheme called "Mind, Body, Soul." Nothing is formal, and staff create things for themselves. The whole idea is that each person is different and they can customize the plan to fit their needs. For some it's a gym membership, for others it's health insurance, and for others it's personal coaching. The entire scheme celebrates the individuality of each person.

The marketplace for freelance marketers has grown more and more competitive.[2] "You can never get complacent," Claire said. "As a business we are always, always thinking, 'What else can we do to stay ahead?'" But something that won't change is Claire Owen's leadership philosophy. "We are human beings," she said. "We don't have employees. We don't have staff. We have people, and people have emotions, and people have needs. If you are happy you do a better job. If you are excited about the business, and if you are excited about where it is going and what is happening in it, then there is a buzz, a physical buzz. It's my job to create that kind of place."

THE FIVE PRACTICES OF EXEMPLARY LEADERSHIP

Since 1983 we've been conducting research on personal-best leadership experiences, and we've discovered that there are countless examples of how leaders, like Dick and Claire, mobilize others to get extraordinary things done in virtually every arena of organized activity. We've found them in profit-based firms and nonprofits, manufacturing and services, government and business, health care, education and entertainment, and work and community service. Leaders reside in every city and every country, in every position and every place. They're employees and volunteers, young and old, women and men. Leadership knows no racial or religious bounds, no ethnic or cultural borders. We find exemplary leadership everywhere we look.

From our analysis of thousands of personal-best leadership experiences, we've discovered that ordinary people who guide others along pioneering journeys follow rather similar paths. Though each experience we examined was unique in expression, every case followed remarkably similar patterns of action. We've forged these common practices into a model of leadership, and we offer it here as guidance for leaders as they attempt to keep their own bearings and steer others toward peak achievements.

As we looked deeper into the dynamic process of leadership, through case analyses and survey questionnaires, we uncovered five practices common to personal-best leadership experiences. When getting extraordinary things done in organizations, leaders engage in these Five Practices of Exemplary Leadership:

- Model the Way
- Inspire a Shared Vision
- Challenge the Process
- Enable Others to Act
- Encourage the Heart

The Five Practices—which we discuss briefly in this chapter and then in depth in Chapters Three through Twelve—aren't the private property of the people we studied or of a few select shining stars. Leadership is not about personality; it's about behavior. The Five Practices are available to anyone who accepts the leadership challenge. And they're also not the accident of a unique moment in history. The Five Practices have stood the test of time, and our most recent research confirms that they're just as relevant today as they were when we first began our investigation more than twenty-five years ago.

Leadership is not about personality; it's about behavior.

Model the Way

Titles are granted, but it's your behavior that wins you respect. As Tom Brack, with Europe's SmartTeam AG, told us, "Leading means you have to be a good example, and live what you say." This sentiment was shared across all the cases that we collected. Exemplary leaders know that if they want to gain commitment and achieve the highest standards, they must be models of the behavior they expect of others. *Leaders model the way.*

To effectively model the behavior they expect of others, leaders must first be clear about guiding principles. They must *clarify values.* As Lindsay Levin, chairman for Whites Group in England, explained, "You have to open up your heart and let people know what you really think and believe. This means talking about your values." Leaders must find their own voice, and then they must clearly and distinctively give voice to their values. As the personal-best stories illustrate, leaders are supposed to stand up for their beliefs, so they'd better have some beliefs to stand up for. But it's not just the leader's values that are important. Leaders aren't just representing themselves. They speak and act on behalf of a larger organization. Leaders must forge agreement around common principles and common ideals.

Eloquent speeches about common values, however, aren't nearly enough. Leaders' deeds are far more important than their words when one wants to determine how serious leaders really are about what they say. Words and deeds must be consistent. Exemplary leaders go first. They go first by *setting the example* through daily actions that demonstrate they are deeply committed to their beliefs. As Prabha Seshan, principal engineer for SSA Global, told us, "One of the best ways to prove something is important is by doing it yourself and setting an example." She discovered that her actions spoke volumes about how the team needed to "take ownership of things they believed in and valued." There wasn't anything Prabha asked others to do that she wasn't willing to do herself, and as a result, "while I always trusted my team, my team in turn trusted me." For instance, she wasn't required to design or code features but by doing some of this work she demonstrated to others not only what she stood for but also how much she valued the work they were doing and what their end user expected from the product.

The personal-best projects we heard about in our research were all distinguished by relentless effort, steadfastness, competence, and attention to detail. We were also struck by how the actions leaders took to set an example were often simple things. Sure, leaders had operational and strategic plans. But the examples they gave were not about elaborate designs. They were about the power of spending time with someone, of working side by side with colleagues, of telling stories that made values come alive, of being highly visible during times of uncertainty, and of asking questions to get people to think about values and priorities.

Modeling the way is about earning the right and the respect to lead through direct involvement and action. People follow first the person, then the plan.

Inspire a Shared Vision

When people described to us their personal-best leadership experiences, they told of times when they imagined an exciting, highly attractive future for their organization. They had visions and dreams of what *could* be. They had absolute and total personal belief in those dreams, and they were confident in their abilities to make extraordinary things happen. Every organization, every social movement, begins with a dream. The dream or vision is the force that invents the future. *Leaders inspire a shared vision.* As Mark D'Arcangelo, system memory product marketing manager at Hitachi Semiconductor, told us about his personal-best leadership experience, "What made the difference was the vision of how things could be and clearly painting this picture for all to see and comprehend."

Leaders gaze across the horizon of time, imagining the attractive opportunities that are in store when they and their constituents arrive at a distant destination. They *envision exciting and ennobling possibilities.* Leaders have a desire to make something happen, to change the way things are, to create something that no one else has ever created before. In some ways, leaders live their lives backward. They see pictures in their mind's eye of what the results will look like even before they've started their project, much as an architect draws a blueprint or an engineer builds a model. Their clear image of the future pulls them forward. Yet visions seen only by leaders are insufficient to create an organized movement or a significant change in a company. A person with no constituents is not a leader, and people will not follow until they accept a vision as their own. Leaders cannot command commitment, only inspire it.

Leaders have to *enlist others in a common vision.* To enlist people in a vision, leaders must know their constituents and speak their language. People must believe that leaders understand their needs and have their interests at heart. Leadership is a dialogue, not a monologue. To enlist support, leaders must have intimate knowledge of people's dreams, hopes, aspirations, visions, and values. Evelia Davis, merchandise manager for Mervyns, told us that while she was good at telling people where they were going together, she also needed to do a good job of explaining why they should follow her, how they could help reach the destination, and what this meant for them. As Evelia put it, "If you don't believe enough to share it, talk about it, and get others excited about it then it's not much of a vision!"

Leaders breathe life into the hopes and dreams of others and enable them to see the exciting possibilities that the future holds. Leaders forge a unity of purpose by showing constituents how the dream is for the common good. Leaders stir the fire of passion in others by expressing enthusiasm for the compelling vision of their group. Leaders communicate their passion through vivid language and an expressive style.

Whatever the venue, and without exception, the people in our study reported that they were incredibly enthusiastic about their personal-best projects. Their own enthusiasm was catching; it spread from leader to constituents. Their belief in and enthusiasm for the vision were the sparks that ignited the flame of inspiration.

Challenge the Process

Every single personal-best leadership case we collected involved some kind of challenge. The challenge might have been an innovative new product, a cutting-edge service, a groundbreaking piece of legislation, an invigorating campaign to get adolescents to join an environmental program, a revolutionary turnaround of a bureaucratic military program, or the start-up of a new plant or business. Whatever the challenge, all the cases involved a change from the status quo. Not one person claimed to have achieved a personal best by keeping things the same. All leaders *challenge the process.*

Leaders venture out. None of the individuals in our study sat idly by waiting for fate to smile upon them. "Luck" or "being in the right place at the right time" may play a role in the specific opportunities leaders embrace, but those who lead others to greatness seek and accept challenge. Jennifer Cun, in her role as a budget analyst with Intel, noted how critical it is for leaders "to always be looking for ways to improve their team, taking interests outside of their job or organization, finding ways to stay current of what the competition is doing, networking, and taking initiative to try new things."

Leaders are pioneers. They are willing to step out into the unknown. They *search for opportunities to innovate, grow, and improve.* But leaders aren't the only creators or originators of new products, services, or processes. In fact, it's more likely that they're not: innovation comes more from listening than from telling. Product and service innovations tend to come from customers, clients, vendors, people in the labs, and people on the front lines; process innovations, from the people doing the work. Sometimes a dramatic external event thrusts an organization into a radically new condition. Leaders have to constantly be looking outside of themselves and their organizations for new and innovative products, processes, and services. "Mediocrity and status quo will never lead a company to success in the marketplace," is what Mike Pepe, product marketing manager at O3 Entertainment, told us. "Taking risks and believing that taking them is worthwhile," he went on to say, "are the only way companies can 'jump' rather than simply climb the improvement ladder."

When it comes to innovation, the leader's major contributions are in the creation of a climate for experimentation, the recognition of good ideas, the support of those ideas, and the willingness to challenge the system to get new products, processes, services, and systems adopted. It might be more accurate, then, to say that leaders aren't the inventors as much as they are the early patrons and adopters of innovation.

Leaders know well that innovation and change involve *experimenting and taking risks.* Despite the inevitability of mistakes and failures leaders proceed anyway. One way of dealing with the potential risks and failures of experimentation is to approach change through incremental steps and small wins. Little victories, when piled on top of each other, build confidence that even the biggest challenges can be met. In so doing, they strengthen commitment to the long-term future. Not everyone is equally comfortable with risk and uncertainty. Leaders must pay attention to the capacity of their constituents to take control of challenging situations and become fully committed to change. You can't exhort people to take risks if they don't also feel safe.

It would be ridiculous to assert that those who fail over and over again eventually succeed as leaders. Success in any endeavor isn't a process of simply buying enough lottery tickets. The key that unlocks the door to opportunity is learning. Claude Meyer, with the Red Cross in Kenya, put it to us this way: "Leadership is learning by doing, adapting to actual conditions. Leaders are constantly learning from their errors and failures." Life is the leader's laboratory, and exemplary leaders use it to conduct as many experiments as possible. Try, fail, learn. Try, fail, learn. Try, fail, learn. That's the leader's mantra. Leaders are learners. They learn from their failures as well as their successes, and they make it possible for others to do the same.

Enable Others to Act

Grand dreams don't become significant realities through the actions of a single person. It requires a team effort. It requires solid trust and strong relationships. It requires deep competence and cool confidence. It requires group collaboration and individual accountability. To get extraordinary things done in organizations, leaders have to *enable others to act.*

After reviewing thousands of personal-best cases, we developed a simple test to detect whether someone is on the road to becoming a leader. That test is the frequency of the use of the word *we.* In our interviews, we found that people used *we* nearly three times more often than *I* in explaining their personal-best leadership experience. Hewlett-Packard's Angie Yim was the technical IT team leader on a project involving core team members from the United States, Singapore, Australia, and Hong Kong. In the past, Angie told us, she "had a bad habit of using the pronoun *I* instead of *we,*" but she learned that people responded more eagerly and her team became more cohesive when people felt part of the *we.* "This is a magic word," Angie realized. "I would recommend that others use it more often."

Leaders *foster collaboration and build trust.* This sense of teamwork goes far beyond a few direct reports or close confidants. They engage all those who must make the project work—and in some way, all who must live with the results. In today's virtual organizations, cooperation can't be restricted to a small group of loyalists; it must include peers, managers, customers and clients, suppliers, citizens—all those who have a stake in the vision.

Leaders make it possible for others to do good work. They know that those who are expected to produce the results must feel a sense of personal power and ownership. Leaders understand that the command-and-control techniques of traditional management no longer apply. Instead, leaders work to make people feel strong, capable, and committed. Leaders enable others to act not by hoarding the power they have but by giving it away. Exemplary leaders *strengthen everyone's capacity* to deliver on the promises they make. As Kathryn Winters learned working with the communications department at NVIDIA Corporation, "You have to make sure that no one is outside the loop or uninvolved in all the changes that occur." She continually ensures that each person has a sense of ownership for his or her projects. She seeks out the opinions of others and uses the ensuing discussion not only to build up their capabilities but also to educate and update her own information and perspective. "Inclusion (not exclusion)," she finds, "ensures that everyone feels and thinks that they are owners and leaders—this makes work much easier." Kathryn realized that when people are trusted and have more discretion, more authority, and more information, they're much more likely to use their energies to produce extraordinary results.

In the cases we analyzed, leaders proudly discussed teamwork, trust, and empowerment as essential elements of their efforts. A leader's ability to enable others to act is essential. Constituents neither perform at their best nor stick around for very long if their leader makes them feel weak, dependent, or alienated. But when a leader makes people feel strong and capable—as if they can do more than they ever thought possible—they'll give it their all and exceed their own expectations. Authentic leadership is founded on trust, and the more people trust their leader, and each other, the more they take risks, make changes, and keep organizations and movements alive. Through that relationship, leaders turn their constituents into leaders themselves.

Encourage the Heart

The climb to the top is arduous and long. People become exhausted, frustrated, and disenchanted. They're often tempted to give up. Leaders *encourage the heart* of their constituents to carry on. Genuine acts of caring uplift the spirits and draw people forward. In his personal-best leadership experience, Ankush Joshi, the service line manager with Informix USA, learned that "writing a personal thank-you note, rather than sending an e-mail, can do wonders." Janel Ahrens, marcom manager with National Semiconductor, echoed Ankush's observation. Janel would make notes about important events in other people's lives and then follow up with them directly after or simply wish them luck prior to an important event. Every person was "genuinely touched that I cared enough to ask them about how things are going." She told us that in her organization "work relationships have been stronger since this undertaking." Janel's and Ankush's experiences are testimony to the power of a "thank you."

Recognizing contributions can be one-to-one or with many people. It can come from dramatic gestures or simple actions. One of the first actions that Abraham Kuruvilla took upon becoming CEO of the Dredging Corporation of India (a government-owned private-sector company providing services to all ten major Indian ports) was to send out to every employee a monthly newsletter (*DCI News*) that was full of success stories. In addition, he introduced, for the first time, a public-recognition program through which awards and simple appreciation notices were given out to individuals and teams for doing great work. Abraham made sure that people were recognized for their contributions, because he wanted to provide a climate in which "people felt cared about and genuinely appreciated by their leaders."

It's part of the leader's job to show appreciation for people's contributions and to create a culture of *celebrating values and victories*. In the cases we collected, we saw thousands of examples of individual recognition and group celebration. We've heard and seen everything from handwritten thank-yous to marching bands and "This Is Your Life"–type ceremonies.

Recognition and celebration aren't about fun and games, though there is a lot of fun and there are a lot of games when people encourage the hearts of their constituents. Neither are they about pretentious ceremonies designed to create some phony sense of camaraderie. When people see a charlatan making noisy affectations, they turn away in disgust. Encouragement is, curiously, serious business. It's how leaders visibly and behaviorally link rewards with performance. When striving to raise quality, recover from disaster, start up a new service, or make dramatic change of any kind, leaders make sure people see the benefit of behavior that's aligned with cherished values. Leaders also know that celebrations and rituals, when done with authenticity and from the heart, build a strong sense of collective identity and community spirit that can carry a group through extraordinarily tough times.

LEADERSHIP IS A RELATIONSHIP

Our findings from the analysis of personal-best leadership experiences challenge the myth that leadership is something that you find only at the highest levels of organizations and society. We found it everywhere. These findings also challenge the belief that leadership is reserved for a few charismatic men and women. Leadership is not a gene and it's not an inheritance. Leadership is an identifiable set of skills and abilities that are available to all of us. The "great person"—woman or man—theory of leadership is just plain wrong. Or, we should say, the theory that there are only a few great men and women who can lead others to greatness is just plain wrong. Likewise, it is plain wrong that leaders only come from large, or great, or small, or new organizations, or from established economies, or from start-up companies. We consider the women and men in our research to be great, and so do those with whom they worked. They are the everyday heroes of our world. It's because there are so many—not so few—leaders that extraordinary things get done on a regular basis, especially in extraordinary times.

To us this is inspiring and should give everyone hope. Hope, because it means that no one needs to wait around to be saved by someone riding into town on a white horse. Hope, because there's a generation of leaders searching for the opportunities to make a difference. Hope, because right down the block or right down the hall there are people who will seize the opportunity to lead you to greatness. They're your neighbors, friends, and colleagues. And you are one of them, too.

There's still another crucial truth about leadership. It's something that we've known for a long time, but we've come to prize even more today. In talking to leaders and reading their cases, there was a very clear message that wove itself throughout every situation and every action. The message was: *leadership is a relationship.* Leadership is a relationship between those who aspire to lead and those who choose to follow. It's the quality of this relationship that matters most when we're engaged in getting extraordinary things done. A leader-constituent relationship that's characterized by fear and distrust will never, ever produce anything of lasting value. A relationship characterized by mutual respect and confidence will overcome the greatest adversities and leave a legacy of significance.

> *Leadership is a relationship.*

Evidence abounds for this point of view. For instance, in examining the critical variables for executive success in the top three jobs in large organizations, Jodi Taylor and Valerie Sessa at the Center for Creative Leadership found the number one success factor to be "relationships with subordinates."[3] We were intrigued to find that even in this nanosecond world of e-everything, opinion is consistent with the facts. In an online survey, respondents were asked to indicate, among other things, which would be more essential to business success in five years—social skills or skills in using the Internet. Seventy-two percent selected social skills; 28 percent, Internet skills.[4] Internet literati completing a poll online realize that it's not the web of technology that matters the most, it's the web of people.

Similar results were found in a study by Public Allies, an AmeriCorps organization dedicated to creating young leaders who can strengthen their communities. Public Allies sought the opinions of eighteen- to thirty-year-olds on the subject of leadership. Among the items was a question about the qualities that were important in a good leader. Topping the respondents' list is "Being able to see a situation from someone else's point of view." In second place is "Getting along well with other people."[5]

Success in leadership, success in business, and success in life have been, are now, and will continue to be a function of how well people work and play together. Success in leading will be wholly dependent upon the capacity to build and sustain those human relationships that enable people to get extraordinary things done on a regular basis.

THE TEN COMMITMENTS OF LEADERSHIP

Embedded in The Five Practices of Exemplary Leadership are behaviors that can serve as the basis for learning to lead. We call these The Ten Commitments of Leadership (Table 1.1). These ten commitments serve as the guide for our discussion of how leaders get extraordinary things done in organizations and as the structure for what's to follow. We'll fully explore each of these commitments in Chapters Three through Twelve. Before delving into the practices and commitments further, however, let's consider leadership from the vantage point of the constituent. If leadership is a relationship, as we have discovered, then what do people expect from that relationship? What do people look for and admire in a leader? What do people want from someone whose direction they'd be willing to follow?

TABLE 1.1 THE FIVE PRACTICES AND TEN COMMITMENTS OF LEADERSHIP.

Practice	Commitment
Model the Way	1. Clarify values by finding your voice and affirming shared ideals.
	2. Set the example by aligning actions with shared values.
Inspire a Shared Vision	3. Envision the future by imagining exciting and ennobling possibilities.
	4. Enlist others in a common vision by appealing to shared aspirations.
Challenge the Process	5. Search for opportunities by seizing the initiative and by looking outward for innovative ways to improve.
	6. Experiment and take risks by constantly generating small wins and learning from experience.
Enable Others to Act	7. Foster collaboration by building trust and facilitating relationships.
	8. Strengthen others by increasing self-determination and developing competence.
Encourage the Heart	9. Recognize contributions by showing appreciation for individual excellence.
	10. Celebrate the values and victories by creating a spirit of community.

CREDIBILITY IS THE FOUNDATION OF LEADERSHIP

"Leadership is in the eyes of other people;
it is they who proclaim you as a leader."
Carrie Gilstrap, Hewlett-Packard

Model the way, inspire a shared vision, challenge the process, enable others to act, and encourage the heart: these are the leadership practices that emerge from thousands of personal-best cases. But they paint only a partial picture. Leaders don't get extraordinary things done all by themselves! The portrayal can be completed only when we add in what constituents expect from their leaders. With these brush strokes the picture takes on depth and vitality.

What leaders say they do is one thing; what constituents say they want and how well leaders meet these expectations is another. Because leadership is a reciprocal process between leaders and their constituents, any discussion of leadership must attend to the dynamics of this relationship. Strategies, tactics, skills, and practices are empty without an understanding of the fundamental human aspirations that connect leaders and constituents.

To balance our understanding of leadership, we investigated the expectations that constituents have of leaders. We asked constituents to tell us what they look for in a person that they would be *willing* to follow, someone who had the personal traits, characteristics, and attributes they wanted in a leader. Their responses both affirm and enrich the picture that emerged from our studies of personal leadership bests.

WHAT PEOPLE LOOK FOR AND ADMIRE IN LEADERS

We began our research on what constituents expect of leaders more than twenty-five years ago by surveying thousands of business and government executives. We asked the following *open-ended* question: "What values, personal traits, or characteristics do you look for and admire in a leader?"[1] In response to that question, respondents identified several hundred different values, traits, and characteristics. Subsequent content analysis by several independent judges, followed by further empirical analyses, reduced these items to a list of twenty characteristics (each grouped with several synonyms for clarification and completeness).

From this list of twenty characteristics, we developed a survey questionnaire called "Characteristics of Admired Leaders." We've administered this questionnaire to over seventy-five thousand people around the globe, and we update the findings continuously. We distribute a one-page checklist and ask respondents to select the seven qualities that they "most look for and admire in a leader, someone whose direction they would willingly follow." We tell them that the key word in this question is *willingly*. What do they expect from a leader they would follow, not because they have to, but because they want to?

The results have been striking in their regularity over the years, and they do not significantly vary by demographical, organizational, or cultural differences. Wherever we've asked the question, it's clear, as the data in Table 2.1 illustrate, that there are a few essential "character tests" someone must pass before others are willing to grant the designation *leader*.

What people most look for in a leader has been constant over time.

Although every characteristic receives some votes, and therefore each is important to some people, what is most striking and most evident is that only four over time (with the exception of Inspiring in 1987) have always received over 60 percent of the votes. And these same four have consistently been ranked at the top *across different countries,* as shown by the data in Table 2.2.

What people most look for in a leader (a person that they would be willing to follow) has been constant over time. And our research documents this consistent pattern across countries, cultures, ethnicities, organizational functions and hierarchies, gender, educational, and age groups. For people to follow someone willingly, the majority of constituents believe the leader must be

- Honest
- Forward-looking
- Inspiring
- Competent

These investigations of desired leader attributes demonstrate consistent and clear relationships with the stories we heard people tell us about their personal-best leadership experiences. The Five Practices of Exemplary Leadership and the behaviors of people whom others think of as exemplary leaders are complementary perspectives on the same subject. When they're

TABLE 2.1 CHARACTERISTICS OF ADMIRED LEADERS.

Characteristic	Percentage of Respondents Selecting Each Characteristic			
	2007 edition	2002 edition	1995 edition	1987 edition
HONEST	89	88	88	83
FORWARD-LOOKING	71	71	75	62
INSPIRING	69	65	68	58
COMPETENT	68	66	63	67
Intelligent	48	47	40	43
Fair-minded	39	42	49	40
Straightforward	36	34	33	34
Broad-minded	35	40	40	37
Supportive	35	35	41	32
Dependable	34	33	32	33
Cooperative	25	28	28	25
Courageous	25	20	29	27
Determined	25	23	17	17
Caring	22	20	23	26
Imaginative	17	23	28	34
Mature	15	21	13	23
Ambitious	16	17	13	21
Loyal	18	14	11	11
Self-Controlled	10	8	5	13
Independent	4	6	5	10

Note: These percentages represent respondents from six continents: Africa, North America, South America, Asia, Europe, and Australia. The majority of respondents are from the United States. Since we asked people to select seven characteristics, the total adds up to more than 100 percent.

TABLE 2.2 CROSS-CULTURAL COMPARISONS OF THE CHARACTERISTICS OF ADMIRED LEADERS.

Country	Percentage of Respondents Selecting Each Characteristic			
	Honest	Forward-Looking	Inspiring	Competent
Australia	93	83	73	59
Canada	88	88	73	60
Japan	67	83	51	61
Korea	74	82	55	62
Malaysia	95	78	60	62
Mexico	85	82	71	62
New Zealand	86	86	71	68
Singapore	72	76	69	76
Sweden, Denmark	84	86	90	53
United States	89	71	69	68

performing at their peak, leaders are doing more than just getting results. They're also responding to the expectations of their constituents.[2]

As we weave the themes of being honest, forward-looking, inspiring, and competent into the text of the subsequent chapters on The Five Practices, you'll see in more detail how exemplary leaders respond to the expectations of their constituents. For example, leaders cannot Model the Way without being seen as honest. The leadership practice of Inspire a Shared Vision involves being forward-looking and inspiring. When leaders Challenge the Process, they also enhance the perception that they're dynamic. Trustworthiness, often a synonym for honesty, plays a major role in how leaders Enable Others to Act, as does the leader's own competency. Likewise, leaders who recognize and celebrate significant accomplishments—who Encourage the Heart—show inspiration and positive energy, which increases their constituents' understanding of the commitment to the vision and values. When leaders demonstrate capacity in all of The Five Practices, they show others they have the competence to get extraordinary things done.

Let's take a closer look at each of the four attributes that have been selected by the majority of respondents since the early 1980s.

Honest

In almost every survey we've conducted, honesty has been selected more often than any other leadership characteristic; overall, it emerges as the single most important factor in the leader-constituent relationship. The percentages vary, but the final ranking does not. Since the very first time we conducted our studies honesty has been at the top of the list.

It's clear that if people anywhere are to willingly follow someone—whether it's into battle or into the boardroom, the front office or the front lines—they first want to assure themselves that the person is worthy of their trust. They want to know that the person is truthful, ethical, and principled. When people talk to us about the qualities they admire in leaders, they often use the terms *integrity* and *character* as synonymous with honesty. No matter what the setting, everyone wants to be fully confident in their leaders, and to be fully confident they have to believe that their leaders are individuals of strong character and solid integrity.[3]

We—all of us—don't want to be lied to or deceived. We want to be told the truth. We want a leader who knows right from wrong. Sure, we want our team to win, but we don't want to be led—better to say, *misled*—by someone who cheats in the process of attaining victory. It lowers our current and future motivational levels; we just won't work as hard for a person or a cause once we've been tricked.

We want our leaders to be honest because their honesty is also a reflection upon our own honesty. Of all the qualities that people look for and admire in a leader, honesty is by far the most personal. More than likely this is also why it consistently ranks number one. It's the quality that can most enhance or most damage our own personal reputations. If we follow someone who's universally viewed as having an impeccable character and strong integrity, then we're likely to be viewed the same. But if we willingly follow someone who's considered dishonest, our own images are tarnished. And there's perhaps another, more subtle, reason why honesty is at the top. When we follow someone we believe to be dishonest, we come to realize that we've compromised our own integrity. Over time, we not only lose respect for the leader, we lose respect for ourselves.

Honesty is strongly tied to values and ethics. We appreciate people who know where they stand on important principles. We resolutely refuse to follow those who lack confidence in their own beliefs. We simply don't trust people who can't or won't disclose a clear set of values, ethics, and standards and live by them.

Forward-Looking

A little more than 70 percent of our most recent respondents selected the ability to look ahead as one of their most sought-after leadership traits. People expect leaders to have a sense of direction and a concern for the future of the organization. This expectation directly corresponds to the ability to envision the future that leaders described in their personal-best cases. Whether we call that ability vision, a dream, a calling, a goal, or a personal agenda, the message is clear: leaders must know where they're going if they expect others to willingly join them on the journey. They have to have a point of view about the future envisioned for their organizations, and they need to be able to connect that point of view to the hopes and dreams of their constituents.

By *forward-looking*, people don't mean the magical power of a prescient visionary. The reality is far more down to earth. It's the ability to imagine or discover a desirable destination toward which the company, agency, congregation, or community should head. Vision reveals the beckoning summit that provides others with the capacity to chart their course toward the future. As constituents, we ask that a leader have a well-defined orientation toward the future. We want to know what the organization will look like, feel like, and be like when it arrives at its destination in six quarters or six years. We want to have it described to us in rich detail so that we can select the proper route for getting there and know when we've arrived.

Clarity of vision into the distant future may be difficult to attain, but it's essential that leaders seek the knowledge and master the skills necessary to envision what's across the horizon. Compared to all the other leadership qualities constituents expect, this is the one that most distinguishes leaders from other credible people. Expecting leaders to be forward-looking doesn't mean constituents want their leaders to set out on a solitary vision quest; people want to be engaged in the search for a meaningful future, as we will discuss in Chapters Five and Six. But this expectation does mean that leaders have a special responsibility to attend to the future of their organizations.[4]

Inspiring

People expect their leaders to be enthusiastic, energetic, and positive about the future. It's not enough for a leader to have a dream. A leader must be able to communicate the vision in ways that encourage people to sign on for the duration and excite them about the cause. Although the enthusiasm, energy, and positive attitude of an exemplary leader may not change the content of work, they certainly can make the context more meaningful. Whatever the circumstances, when leaders breathe life into peoples' dreams and aspirations, those people are much more willing to enlist in the movement.

Leaders must uplift their constituents' spirits and give them hope if they're to voluntarily engage in challenging pursuits. Enthusiasm and excitement are essential, and they signal the leader's personal commitment to pursuing a dream. If a leader displays no passion for a cause, why should anyone else?

Inspiring leadership also speaks to constituents' need to have meaning and purpose in their lives. Being upbeat, positive, and optimistic about the future offers people hope. This is crucial at any time, but in times of great uncertainty, leading with positive emotions is absolutely essential to moving people upward and forward.[5] When people are worried, discouraged, frightened, and uncertain about the future, the last thing needed is a leader who feeds those negative emotions. Instead, they need leaders who communicate in words, demeanor, and actions that they believe their constituents will overcome. Emotions are contagious, and positive emotions resonate throughout an organization and into relationships with other constituents. To get extraordinary things done in extraordinary times, leaders must inspire optimal performance—and that can only be fueled with positive emotions.

Competent

To enlist in a common cause, people must believe that the leader is competent to guide them where they're headed. They must see the leader as having relevant experience and sound judgment. If they doubt the person's abilities, they're unlikely to join in the crusade.

Leadership competence refers to the leader's track record and ability to get things done. This kind of competence inspires confidence that the leader will be able to guide the entire organization, large or small, in the direction in which it needs to go. It doesn't refer specifically to the leader's abilities in the core technology of the operation. In fact, the type of competence demanded seems to vary more with the leader's position and the condition of the organization. Although people demand a base level of understanding of the fundamentals of the industry, market, or professional service environment, they also know that leaders can't be expected to be the most technically competent in their fields. Organizations are too complex and multifunctional for that ever to be the case. This is particularly true as people reach the more senior levels. For example, those who hold officer positions are definitely expected to demonstrate abilities in strategic planning and policymaking. If a company desperately needs to clarify its core competence and market position, a CEO who is savvy in competitive marketing may be perceived as a fine leader. But in the line function, where people expect guidance in technical areas, these same strategic marketing abilities will be insufficient. A leader on the line or at the point of customer or client contact will typically have to be more technically competent than someone less engaged in providing services or making products. What's often most significant is that the leader takes the time to learn the business and to know the current operation.

Relevant experience is a dimension of competence, one that is different from technical expertise. Experience is about active participation in situational, functional, and industry events and activities and the accumulation of knowledge derived from participation. Experience correlates with one's track record, and the broader one's experience, the more likely he or she is to be successful across organizations and industries. An effective leader in a high-technology company, for example, may not need to be a master programmer but must understand the business implications of electronic data interchange, networking, and the Internet. A health care administrator with experience only in the insurance industry is more than likely doomed; the job needs extensive experience in the delivery of human services. There may be notable exceptions, but it is highly unlikely that a leader can succeed without both relevant experience and, most important, exceptionally good people skills.

PUTTING IT ALL TOGETHER: CREDIBILITY IS THE FOUNDATION

Honest, forward-looking, inspiring, and competent: these are the characteristics that have remained constant over more than twenty years of economic growth and recession, the surge in new technology enterprises, the birth of the World Wide Web, the further globalization of business and industry, the ever-changing political environment, and the expansion, bursting, and regeneration of the Internet economy. The relative importance of the most desired qualities has varied somewhat over time, but there has been no change in the fact that these are the four qualities people want most in their leaders. Whether they believe their leaders are true to these values is another matter, but what they would like from them has remained constant.

This list of four consistent findings is useful in and of itself—but there's a more profound implication revealed by our research. Three of these four key characteristics make up what communications experts refer to as "source credibility." In assessing the believability of sources of communication—whether newscasters, salespeople, physicians, or priests; whether business managers, military officers, politicians, or civic leaders—researchers typically evaluate them on three criteria: their perceived *trustworthiness,* their *expertise,* and their *dynamism.* Those who are rated more highly on these dimensions are considered to be more credible sources of information.[6]

Notice how strikingly similar these three characteristics are to the essential leader qualities of being honest, competent, and inspiring—three of the top four items selected in our survey. What we found in our investigation of admired leadership qualities is that more than anything, people want to follow leaders who are credible. *Credibility is the foundation of leadership.*

> *Credibility is the foundation of leadership.*

Above all else, we as constituents must be able to believe in our leaders. We must believe that their word can be trusted, that they're personally passionate and enthusiastic about the work that they're doing, and that they have the knowledge and skill to lead.

We also must believe that they know where we're headed and have a vision for the future. Adding *forward-looking* to what we expect from our leaders is what sets leaders apart from other credible individuals. Compared to other sources of information (for example, news anchors), leaders must do more than be reliable reporters of the news. Leaders make the news, interpret the news, and make sense of the news. We expect our leaders to have a point of view about the future. We expect them to articulate exciting possibilities. We want to be confident that our leaders know where they're going.

Even so, although compelling visions are necessary for leadership, if the leader is not credible the message rests on a weak and precarious foundation.

Leaders therefore must be ever-diligent in guarding their credibility. Their ability to take strong stands, to challenge the status quo, and to point us in new directions depends on their being highly credible. Leaders must never take their credibility for granted, regardless of the times or their positions. If leaders ask others to follow them to some uncertain future—a future that may not be realized in their lifetime—and if the journey is going to require sacrifice, isn't it reasonable that constituents should believe in them? To believe in the exciting future possibilities leaders present, constituents must first believe in their leaders.

Because these findings about the characteristics of admired leaders—people we would willingly follow—have been so pervasive and so consistent, we've come to call this "The Kouzes-Posner First Law of Leadership":

> If you don't believe in the messenger, you won't believe the message.

Credibility Matters

At this point, some people might well say, "So what? I know people who are in positions of power, and I know people who are enormously wealthy, and I don't find them credible. Does credibility really matter? Does it make a difference?"

It's a legitimate concern, so we decided to study the question of whether or not credibility mattered. But rather than ask about the credibility of "top management" or "elected officials," we decided to ask questions about people closer to home. We asked people to rate their immediate managers. As part of our quantitative research, using a behavioral measure of credibility, we asked organization members to think about the extent to which their immediate manager exhibited credibility-enhancing behaviors. In our studies we found that when people perceive their *immediate manager* to have high credibility, they're significantly more likely to

- Be proud to tell others they're part of the organization
- Feel a strong sense of team spirit

- See their own personal values as consistent with those of the organization
- Feel attached and committed to the organization
- Have a sense of ownership of the organization

When people perceive their manager to have low credibility, however, they're significantly more likely to

- Produce only if they're watched carefully
- Be motivated primarily by money
- Say good things about the organization publicly but criticize it privately
- Consider looking for another job if the organization experiences problems
- Feel unsupported and unappreciated

This evidence of the significant impact of leadership credibility on employee attitudes and behavior certainly provides clear dictates for organizational leaders. Credibility makes a difference, and leaders must take it personally. Loyalty, commitment, energy, and productivity depend on it.

Credibility goes far beyond employee attitudes. It influences customer and investor loyalty as well as employee loyalty. In an extensive study of the economic value of business loyalty, Frederick Reichheld and his Bain & Company colleagues found that businesses concentrating on customer, employee, and investor loyalty generate superior results compared with those engendering disloyalty. They found further that disloyalty can dampen performance by a stunning 25–50 percent.[7] Loyalty is clearly responsible for extraordinary value creation. So what accounts for business loyalty? When they investigated this question, the researchers found that "The center of gravity for business loyalty—whether it be the loyalty of customers, employees, investors, suppliers, or dealers—is the personal integrity of the senior leadership team and its ability to put its principles into practice."[8] And what's true for bricks-and-mortar companies is just as true for the clicks companies. "In fact, when Web shoppers were asked to name the attributes of e-tailers that were most important in earning their business, the number one answer was 'a Web site I know and trust.' All other attributes, including lowest cost and broadest selection, lagged far behind. Price does not rule the Web; trust does."[9]

What Is Credibility Behaviorally?

The data confirm that credibility is the foundation of leadership. But what is credibility behaviorally? How do you know it when you see it?

We've asked this question of tens of thousands of people around the globe, and the response we get is essentially the same, regardless of how it may be phrased in one company versus another or one country versus another. Here are some of the common phrases people use to describe how they know credibility when they see it:

- "They practice what they preach."
- "They walk the talk."
- "Their actions are consistent with their words."
- "They put their money where their mouth is."
- "They follow through on their promises."
- "They do what they say they will do."

The last is the most frequent response. When it comes to deciding whether a leader is believable, people first listen to the words, then they watch the actions. They listen to the talk, and then they watch the walk. They listen to the promises of resources to support change initiatives, and then they wait to see if the money and materials follow. They hear the promises to deliver, and then they look for evidence that the commitments are met. A judgment of "credible" is handed down when words and deeds are consonant. If people don't see consistency, they conclude that the leader is, at best, not really serious, or, at worst, an outright hypocrite. If leaders espouse one set of values but personally practice another, people find them to be duplicitous. If leaders practice what they preach, people are more willing to entrust them with their livelihood and even their lives.

This realization leads to a straightforward prescription for leaders on how to establish credibility. This is "The Kouzes-Posner Second Law of Leadership":

DWYSYWD: Do What You Say You Will Do

This commonsense definition of credibility corresponds directly to one of The Five Practices of Exemplary Leadership identified in the personal-best cases. DWYSYWD has two essential elements: say and do. To be credible in action, leaders must be clear about their beliefs; they must know what they stand for. That's the "say" part. Then they must put what they say into practice: they must act on their beliefs and "do." The practice of Model the Way links directly to these two dimensions of people's behavioral definition of credibility. This practice includes the clarification of a set of values and being an example of those values to others. This consistent living out of values is a behavioral way of demonstrating honesty and trustworthiness. People trust leaders when their deeds and words match.

To gain and sustain the moral authority to lead, it's essential to Model the Way. Because of this important connection between words and actions, we've chosen to start our discussion of The Five Practices with a thorough examination of the principles and behaviors that bring Model the Way to life.

PART 2

MODEL THE WAY

- CLARIFY VALUES
- SET THE EXAMPLE

CLARIFY VALUES

"Having faith in my principles and beliefs gave me the courage to navigate difficult situations and make tough decisions."
Tim Avila, CMP Media Electronics Group

Name an historical leader whom you greatly admire—a well-known leader from the distant or recent past whom you could imagine following willingly. Who is that leader?

In our research we've asked thousands of people to do this. Although no single leader receives a majority of the nominations, in the United States the two most frequently mentioned are Abraham Lincoln and Martin Luther King

Jr. Other historical leaders who've made the list include Aung San Suu Kyi, Susan B. Anthony, Benazir Bhutto, César Chávez, Winston Churchill, Mahatma Gandhi, Mikhail Gorbachev, Miguel Hidalgo, Nelson Mandela, Golda Meir, His Holiness the Dalai Lama, J. Robert Oppenheimer, His Holiness Pope John Paul II, Eleanor Roosevelt, Franklin D. Roosevelt, Mother Teresa, Margaret Thatcher, and Archbishop Desmond Tutu.

What do leaders such as these have in common? Among these most admired leaders, one quality stands out above all else. The most striking similarity we've found—and surely it's evident to you—is that the list is populated by people with *strong beliefs about matters of principle.* They all have, or had, unwavering commitment to a clear set of values. They all are, or were, passionate about their causes. The lesson from this simple exercise is unmistakable. People admire most those who believe strongly in something, and who are willing to stand up for their beliefs. If anyone is ever to become a leader whom others would willingly follow, one certain prerequisite is that they must be someone of principle. Famous figures from history, of course, aren't the only leaders with strong beliefs on matters of principle. All exemplary leaders share this quality no matter what status they may have achieved. It could be a leader in your local community, one down the hall from you, one next door—and also you. The personal-best leadership cases we've collected are, at their core, the stories of individuals who remained true to deeply held values. For Nevzat Mert Topcu, who with his cousin successfully started a magazine about PC games in Turkey, becoming a leader meant "getting in touch with my core values." If you want to lead others, he told us, "you have to open up your heart. . . . you have to be able to be honest with yourself in order to be honest with others." For Walt Shaw, working as associate director of business development for Visto Corporation, the crucial lesson was "understanding what you deeply believe because people won't follow you, or even pay much attention to you, if you don't have strong beliefs." One mid-level manager poignantly explained to us that because of her cultural heritage and gender stereotyping, she had not always stood for her principles.

I ignored my heart and didn't listen to my own voice. I was a walking corpse. But I've come to understand that everyone has beliefs and values, and that in order for people to lead they've got to connect with them and be able to express them. This means that I have to let people know and understand what my thoughts are so that I can become a good leader. How can others follow me if I'm not willing to listen to my own inner self? Now, I let others know what I think is important and how hard I'm willing to fight for my values.

People expect their leaders to speak out on matters of values and conscience. But to speak out you have to know what to speak about. To stand up for your beliefs, you have to know what you stand for. To walk the talk, you have to have a talk to walk. To do what you say, you have to know what you want to say. To earn and sustain personal credibility, you must first be able to clearly articulate deeply held beliefs.

That is why Clarify Values is the first of the leader commitments we discuss in this book. It's where it all begins. To Clarify Values as a leader you must engage in these two essentials:

- **Find your voice**
- **Affirm shared values**

Remember the Kouzes-Posner First Law of Leadership?

If you don't believe in the messenger, you won't believe the message.

The observation that people most admire those leaders with clear and strong beliefs leads to the following two corollaries to our First Law:

- You can't believe in the messenger if you don't know what the messenger believes.
- You can't be the messenger until you're clear about what you believe.

To become a credible leader you have to comprehend fully the deeply held beliefs—values, principles, standards, ethics, and ideals—that drive you. You have to freely and honestly choose the principles you will use to guide your decisions and actions. Then you have to genuinely express yourself. You must authentically communicate your beliefs in ways that uniquely represent who you are.

But leaders aren't just speaking for themselves when they talk about the values that should guide decisions and actions. When leaders passionately express a commitment to quality or innovation or service or some other core value, those leaders are not just saying, "I believe in this." They're making a commitment for an entire organization. They're saying, "We all believe in this." Therefore, leaders must not only be clear about their own personal values but also make sure that there's agreement on a set of shared values among everyone they lead.

FIND YOUR VOICE

We all know deep down that people can only speak the truth when speaking in their own true voice. The techniques and tools that fill the pages of management and leadership books—including this one—are not substitutes for who and what you are.

Max De Pree, former chairman and CEO of Herman Miller, the Michigan furniture maker, tells a moving story that well illustrates this principle:

Esther, my wife, and I have a granddaughter named Zoe, the Greek word for "life." She was born prematurely and weighed one pound, seven ounces, so small that my wedding ring could slide up her arm to her shoulder. The neonatologist who first examined her told us that she had a 5 to 10 percent chance of living three days. When Esther and I scrubbed up for our first visit and saw Zoe in her isolette in the neonatal intensive care unit, she had two IVs in her navel, one in her foot, a monitor on each side of her chest, and a respirator tube and a feeding tube in her mouth.

To complicate matters, Zoe's biological father had jumped ship the month before Zoe was born. Realizing this, a wise and caring nurse named Ruth gave me my instructions. "For the next several months, at least, you're the surrogate father. I want you to come to the hospital every day to visit Zoe, and when you come, I would like you to rub her body and her legs and her arms with the tip of your finger. While you're caressing her, you should tell her over and over how much you love her, because she has to be able to connect your voice to your touch."

Ruth was doing exactly the right thing on Zoe's behalf (and, of course, on my behalf as well), and without realizing it she was giving me one of the best possible descriptions of the work of a leader. At the core of becoming a leader is the need always to connect one's voice to one's touch.[1]

In this poignant story, Max eloquently illustrates the power we all have to shape a life—even save a life—when we connect what we do to what we say. But Max goes on. He articulates another important leadership lesson he learned from this traumatic experience: "There is of course a prior task—finding one's voice in the first place."[2]

Before you can become a credible leader—one who connects "say" and "do"—first you have to find your voice. If you can't find your voice, you'll end up with a vocabulary that belongs to someone else, mouthing words that were written by some speechwriter or mimicking the language of some other leader who's nothing like you at all. If the words you speak are not your words but someone else's, you will not, in the long term, be able to be consistent in word and deed. You will not have the integrity to lead.

Explore Your Inner Territory

Once, when discussing the origins of leadership, our conversation went something like this:

Jim: I think leadership begins with discontent.

Barry: That's too dismal a view for me. I think leadership begins with caring.

Jim: Okay, then, let's look up *caring* in the dictionary.

We grabbed one off the shelf, and opened it to *care*. The first meaning was "suffering of mind: GRIEF."[3] There it was. Suffering and caring, discontent and concern, all come from one source. Deep within us all there is something we hold dear, and if it's ever violated we'll weep and wail. We'll fight to the death to secure it, grieve if we lose it, and shriek with joy when we achieve it.

To act with integrity, you must first know who you are.

We realized that what we were both saying is that leadership begins with something that grabs hold of you and won't let go. This is where you must go to find your voice. To find your voice, you have to explore your inner territory. You have to take a journey into those places in your heart and soul where you bury your treasures, so that you can carefully examine them and eventually bring them out for display.

You must know what you care about. If you don't care, how can you expect others to do so? If you don't burn with desire to be true to something you hold passionately, how can you expect commitment from others? And until you get close enough to the flame to feel the heat, how can you know the source? You can only be authentic when you lead according to the principles that matter most to you. Otherwise you're just putting on an act.

The answers to the question of values will come only when you're willing to take a journey through your inner territory—a journey that'll require opening doors that are shut, walking in dark spaces that are frightening, and touching the flame that burns. But at the end is truth.

This is the common lesson we must all learn. To act with integrity, you must first know who you are. You must know what you stand for, what you believe in, and what you care most about. Clarity of values will give you the confidence to make the tough decisions, to act with determination, and to take charge of your life.

Values Guide Us

Lillas Brown Hatala was recruited to be the director of Business and Leadership Programs, a start-up operation in the University of Saskatchewan's (Canada) Extension Division. She'd had a successful career as a corporate human resource development manager at Federated Co-operatives Limited, a large retailer and wholesaler, but decided to make the switch to have an expanded role in working with people in a different setting. "I wanted to make a difference," says Lillas, "in the lives of leaders and their constituents in the workplace."

Lillas was new to the university system, and, she says now, "Like any new leader, I had to earn credibility. In any organization, credibility building is a process that takes time, hard work, devotion, and patience." But coming in as an outsider can be especially trying. There's more skepticism about your intentions and your abilities. This was even truer in Lillas's case, because one of the projects she initially took on was a leadership development program for department chairs. You can just hear the rumblings: "How can someone from retailing possibly help develop the skills of those in academia?"

"In the early years," Lillas says, "some naysayers dismissed my work, saying, 'This is a business model,' or 'You can't herd cats,' or 'Watch the fluff,' and so on. Painful as some of this was at the time, it not only contributed to my challenge but caused me to persevere. . . . It reinforced my intent to contribute to a more encouraging and nurturing culture than what I was experiencing."

Throughout this process Lillas turned to a simple method to aid her in staying the course. Every day she used personal journal writing for reflection and contemplation. "I use my journal to dialogue with the small still voice within," Lillas says. "Every evening I ask, 'What have I done today that demonstrates this value that is near and dear to me? What have I done inadvertently to demonstrate this is not a value for me? What do I need to do more of to more fully express my values?'" By daily clarifying and reaffirming her values in those first difficult years at the university, Lillas was able to strengthen her resolve to contribute. Increasingly, Lillas was able to win over even the most hardened skeptics and "accomplish what really mattered to the University and me while being more able to enjoy my life."

As Lillas's story illustrates, values are guides. They supply us with a moral compass by which to navigate the course of our daily lives. Clarity of values is essential to knowing which way, for each of us, is north, south, east, and west. The clearer we are about our values, the easier it is to stay on the path we've chosen. This kind of guidance is especially needed in difficult and uncertain times. When there are daily challenges that can throw us off course, it's crucial that we have some signposts that tell us where we are.

The late Milton Rokeach, one of the leading researchers and scholars in the field of human values, referred to a value as an enduring belief. He noted that values are organized into two sets: means and ends.[4] In the context of our work on modeling, we use the term *values* to refer to our here-and-now beliefs about how things should be accomplished—what Rokeach calls *means* values. We will use *vision* in Chapters Five and Six when we refer to the long-term *ends* values that leaders and constituents aspire to attain. Leadership takes both. When sailing through the turbulent seas of change and uncertainty, crewmembers need a vision of the destination that lies beyond the horizon, and they also need to understand the principles by which they must navigate their course. If either of these is absent, the journey is likely to end with the crew lost at sea.

Values influence every aspect of our lives: our moral judgments, our responses to others, our commitments to personal and organizational goals. Values set the parameters for the hundreds of decisions we all make every day. Options that run counter to our value systems are seldom acted upon; and if they are, it's done with a sense of compliance rather than commitment. Values constitute our personal "bottom line."

Values also serve as guides to action. They inform our decisions as to what to do and what not to do; they tell us when to say yes, or no, and help us really understand why we mean it.[5] If you believe, for instance, that diversity enriches innovation and service, then you should know what to do if people with differing views keep getting cut off when they offer up fresh ideas. If you value collaboration over individualistic achievement, then you'll know what to do when your best salesperson skips team meetings and refuses to share information with colleagues. If you value independence and initiative over conformity and obedience, you'll be more likely to challenge something your manager says if you think it's wrong.

Radha Basu, cofounder of SupportSoft, explained how being clear about her personal values regarding career provided her the ability to make choices among competing demands, requests, and claims on her time and attention. "Knowing who I am, and what's important to me," she told us, "gives me focus and also enables me to keep juggling more balls in the air than I otherwise could. If you are clear about your values, and your actions are aligned, it makes all the hard work worth the effort."[6]

Values serve as guides to action.

Values are empowering. We are much more in control of our own lives, as Radha found, when we're clear about our personal values. When values are clear we don't have to rely on direction from someone in authority. By knowing which means and ends are most important, we can act independently. We can also recognize a conflict between our own values and the values of the organization or society, and we can exercise choice about how to respond.

Values also motivate. They keep us focused on why we're doing what we're doing and on the ends toward which we're striving. Values are the banners that fly as we persist, as we struggle, as we toil. We refer to them when we need to replenish our energy.

For example, John Siegel, M.D., described the impact of values on a particular discussion at Valley Medical Center about a proposal to restructure their department:

As sometimes happens during any spirited discussion, the conversation turned away from worrying about the educational experience of our residents to comments on all kinds of side issues, general frustrations, worries about the overall medical system, and the like.

I raised my hand and, in a calm steady voice, reminded everyone that our first priority is to deliver excellent care for our patients, and a restructuring plan that assured that as our primary goal would necessarily allow an excellent learning experience for the residents and may even show them what it's like to care passionately about something like quality of care and see the satisfaction we derive from providing it. Without actually saying it, I pushed the button that was in each of us, reminding us of the values we are living and the dream we all have for where we work.

I had the least seniority of anyone, but I could say what I believed in, with confidence and a strength that comes from that personal commitment to values, and they listened. The mood changed, we were constructively engaged again, and eventually settled on a restructure plan that will improve how our department works.

John's story is a reminder of how well values can keep you—and your colleagues—on course, especially when you become engaged in conflicts or controversies. Just reminding yourself of the principles that are most important often can refocus your attention on the things that really matter.

Personal Values Clarity Drives Commitment

It's one thing to expect that leaders are clear about their values and beliefs, but it's another to prove that it really matters if they are. What's the evidence for this assertion? How much difference does being clear about values really make? We set out to empirically investigate the relationship between personal values clarity, organizational values clarity, and a variety of outcomes such as commitment and job satisfaction.[7] The results of our research clearly indicate that personal values clarity makes a significant difference in behavior at work. Figure 3.1 shows what we discovered about values clarity and commitment to organizations, for example.

Along the vertical axis is the extent to which people report being clear about their organization's values. Along the horizontal axis is the extent to which these same people report being clear about their own personal values. We then correlated these responses with the extent to which people said they were committed to the organization as measured on a scale of 1 (low) to 7 (high). We've organized the data into four cells, each representing a level of clarity from low to high on personal and organizational values. The numbers in each of the four cells represent the average level of commitment people have to their organizations as it relates to the degree of their clarity about personal and organizational values.

Take a look at where the highest level of commitment is. The people who have the greatest clarity about both personal and organizational values have the highest degree of commitment to the organization.

Now, take another look. Where's the lowest level of commitment to the organization? It's in the upper left corner—high clarity about organizational

FIGURE 3.1 THE IMPACT OF VALUES CLARITY ON COMMITMENT.

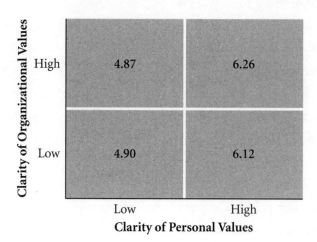

values but low clarity about personal values. It shows that people can be very clear about the organization's values and *not* be highly committed. And indeed these folks are not significantly more committed than those with lower levels of organizational values clarity. Doesn't this make you a bit curious? It did us. Initially it seemed inconsistent with the messages we'd been hearing about strong organizational cultures. So we looked again at the data to see if we could understand what people were telling us.

Take a look at the second-highest level of commitment (which, by the way, is not statistically different from the highest level). It's in the bottom right corner—high clarity about personal values but low clarity about organizational values. The people who are clear about their personal beliefs but can't recite the corporate credo are significantly more likely to stick around than are those people who've heard the organizational litany but have never listened to their own inner voice. In other words, *personal values drive commitment.* Personal values are the route to loyalty and commitment, *not* organizational values.

> *Personal values drive commitment.*

How can this be? How can people who are very clear about their own values be committed to a place that has never posted its organizational values? Think about it. Have you ever had the feeling that "This place is not for me?" Have you ever walked into a place, immediately gotten the sense that "I don't belong here," and just walked right out? In contrast, have you ever just known that you belong, can be yourself, and that "This is the right place for me"? Of course you have. We've all had those experiences.

It's the same way in the workplace. There comes a point when we just know whether it is or isn't a good fit with our values and beliefs, even if there was no lecture on the organization's values. We won't stick around a place for very long when we feel in our heart and in our soul that we don't belong.

Clarity about personal values is more important in your attitude about work than is clarity about organizational values alone. Ultimately it's the individual who decides if the organization is a great place to work. Those individuals who are clearest about personal values are better prepared to make choices based on principle—including deciding whether the principles of the organization fit with their own!

The data also establish that sending the executive team off on a retreat to chisel out the organization's values, making videos about them, conducting seminars on them, or handing out laminated wallet cards imprinted with the values all matter very little until leaders also make sure that they help individuals understand their own values and beliefs.

Say It in Your Own Words

Once you have the words you want to say, you must also give voice to those words. You must be able to express your voice so that everyone knows that you are the one who's speaking.

In this book we present a lot of scientific data to support our assertions about each of the five leadership practices. But leadership is also an art. And just as with any other art form—whether it's painting, playing music, dancing, acting, or writing—leadership is a means of personal expression. To become a credible leader you have to learn to express yourself in ways that are uniquely your own. As author Anne Lamott tells would-be writers in her classes:

> And the truth of your experience can only come through in your own voice. If it is wrapped in someone else's voice, we readers are suspicious, as if you are dressed up in someone else's clothes. You cannot write out of someone else's big dark place; you can only write out of your own. Sometimes wearing someone else's style is very comforting, warm and pretty and bright, and it may loosen you up, tune you into the joys of language and rhythm and concern. But what you say will be an abstraction because it will not have sprung from direct experience; when you try to capture the truth of your experience in some other person's voice or on that person's

terms, you are removing yourself one step further from what you have seen and what you know.[8]

What's true for writers is just as true for leaders. You cannot lead through someone else's values, someone else's words. You cannot lead out of someone else's experience. You can only lead out of your own. Unless it's your style, your words, it's not you—it's just an act. People don't follow your position or your technique. They follow you. If you're not the genuine article, can you really expect others to want to follow?

One route to a true and genuine voice is in being more conscious about the words you choose and the words you use. Words matter. They're as much a form of expression for leaders as they are for poets, singers, and writers. Words send signals, and, if you listen intently, you just may hear the hidden assumptions about how someone views the world.

Take the following examples from an after-lunch speech we heard a bank manager give to his employees. His intent was to motivate, but as we listened we heard more than that. We heard a fundamental belief system about how business functioned and what he believed to be important. Have a listen for yourself:

- "You've got to watch out for the headhunters."
- "Safeguard your capital and keep it dry."
- "We will act like SWAT teams."
- "We are going to beat their brains out."
- "Get the moccasins and the tom-tom going."
- "We won't tolerate the building of little fiefdoms."
- "There will be only a few survivors."

What is the main metaphor in these direct quotes from his speech? War. What this manager is saying is, "Business is a bloody war, and we're going to have to behave that way. It's kill or be killed."

Contrast the bank manager's speech with the following words from Louis (Tex) Gunning, who heads the Southeast Asia and Australia regions for Unilever, the global foods, home care, and personal care manufacturer:

- "The business needs to be grounded in deep human values, and you need to have integrity in your actions."
- "We have to have a social meaning that resonates with the people who volunteer to work here, and with the people we serve."
- "The core insight about great leadership comes down to service. Somehow it humanizes us."
- "It's our souls that give us guidance and wisdom, and it is our souls that animate human qualities of love, compassion, and humility."
- "People want to live meaningful lives; . . . they want to grow and they want to be part of an organization that helps them to contribute to something that is far bigger than they could ever create on their own."
- "Caring for community needs to be in the heart of all our actions. Once we get this right, then the rest will come into place."[9]

The organizational and business world that Tex paints with his words contrasts dramatically with that of the bank manager. His is not about business as war, but about business as service and love. Tex and the bank manager are speaking in entirely different voices.

What's most important to understand is that Tex absolutely could not deliver the bank manager's words, and the bank manager could not deliver Tex's. Their words are internally congruent for each of them. Each would be disingenuous and inauthentic if they spoke like the other.

To be a leader, you've got to awaken to the fact that you don't have to copy someone else, you don't have to read a script written by someone else, and you don't have to wear someone else's style. Instead, you are free to choose what you want to express and the way you want to express it. In fact, we'd argue that you have a responsibility to your constituents to express yourself in an authentic manner—in a way they would immediately recognize as yours.

AFFIRM SHARED VALUES

Shared values are the foundations for building productive and genuine working relationships. Although credible leaders honor the diversity of their many constituencies, they also stress their common values. Leaders build on agreement. They don't try to get everyone to be in accord on everything—this goal is unrealistic, perhaps even impossible. Moreover, to achieve it would negate the very advantages of diversity. But to take a first step, and then a second, and then a third, people must have some common core of understanding. After all, if there's no agreement about values, then what exactly is the leader—and everyone else—going to model? If disagreements over fundamental values continue, the result is intense conflict, false expectations, and diminished capacity.

Shared Values Are an Organization's Promises

Important as it is that leaders forthrightly articulate the principles for which they stand, what leaders say must be consistent with the aspirations of their constituents. Leaders who advocate or stand for values that aren't representative of the collective won't be able to mobilize people to act as one. Leaders set an example for all constituents based on a shared understanding of what's expected. Leaders must be able to gain consensus on a common cause and a common set of principles. They must be able to build and affirm a community of shared values.

For Michael Ryan, Network Appliance's manager of systems integration, the company's core values—Trust and Integrity, Leadership, Simplicity, Teamwork and Synergy, Go Beyond, and Get Things Done—were the glue that held his team together, especially as they partnered with several other companies in building a customer data-management solution. As Michael put it,

When things seemed like they were falling apart and splintering, I went back to core NetApp values: I cast the effort as a means of using new technology to *Simplify* the solution, that we had to *Trust* each other, that the *Teamwork* was critical, that the *Synergy* of our partners was required for success because we definitely had to *Go Beyond* to get this thing done so quickly.

Michael held "value quizzes" in his staff meetings. He asked various team members to recall the NetApp values and provide examples of them at work. "We would then comment about our current project," he recalled, "and discuss how well these values were or were not being upheld, and what to do about any misalignments."

A leader's promise, as Michael knows, is really an organization's promise—regardless of whether the organization is a team of two, an agency of two hundred, a school of two thousand, a company of twenty thousand, or a community of two hundred thousand. Unless there's agreement about which promises can be kept, leaders, constituents, and their organizations risk losing credibility.

Recognition of shared values provides people with a common language. Tremendous energy is generated when individual, group, and organizational values are in synch. Commitment, enthusiasm, and drive are intensified. People have reasons for caring about their work. When individuals are able to care about what they are doing, they are more effective and satisfied. They experience less stress and tension. Shared values are the internal compasses that enable people to act both independently and interdependently.

As noted earlier in this chapter, employees are more loyal when they believe that their values and those of the organization are aligned. The quality and accuracy of communication and the integrity of the decision-making process increase when people feel part of the same team. They are more creative because they become immersed in what they are doing.

Across a wide range of companies and industries, people whose personal values match those of their company feel significantly more strongly attached to their work and organization than do those who see little relationship in values. Not surprisingly, these two groups differ in the extent to which they find their management to be credible.[10] Studies across the globe yield similar results.[11]

Shared Values Make a Difference

In our own research, we've carefully examined the relationship between personal and organizational values. Our findings clearly reveal that when there's congruence between individual values and organizational values, there's significant payoff for leaders and their organizations.[12] Shared values do make a significant positive difference in work attitudes and performance:

- They foster strong feelings of personal effectiveness.
- They promote high levels of company loyalty.
- They facilitate consensus about key organizational goals and stakeholders.
- They encourage ethical behavior.
- They promote strong norms about working hard and caring.
- They reduce levels of job stress and tension.
- They foster pride in the company.
- They facilitate understanding about job expectations.
- They foster teamwork and esprit de corps.

When leaders seek consensus around shared values, constituents are more positive. People who report that their senior managers engage in dialogue regarding common values feel a significantly stronger sense of personal effectiveness than do those individuals who feel that they're wasting energy trying to figure out what they're supposed to be doing.[13] France's Bongrain, one of the world's largest cheese companies, doing business in 150 countries, understands that shared values matter. "I see the value of values every day," says Thomas Swartele, president. "The communications, the innovation, the adaptability, the coherence: those are the value of values. Because you are approaching markets, problems, and business opportunities from a shared basic-belief system, a values-based business approach becomes extremely efficient and powerful."[14] That's the point: people tend to drift when they're unsure or confused about how they should be operating. The energy that goes into coping with, and possibly fighting about, incompatible values takes its toll on both personal effectiveness and organizational productivity.

Research confirms that organizations with a strong corporate culture based on a foundation of shared values outperformed other firms by a huge margin.[15]

> *Shared values make a significant positive difference in work attitudes and performance.*

- Their revenue grew more than four times faster.
- Their rate of job creation was seven times higher.
- Their stock price grew twelve times faster.
- Their profit performance was 750 percent higher.

Studies of adaptive corporate cultures—organizations with consistent guiding values, a shared purpose, teamwork, innovation, and learning—showed similar powerful results. Compared with nonadaptive cultures, over a ten-year period, the organizations with strong values

- Experienced nearly ten times the growth in net income
- Had three times the growth in stock price[16]

Studies of public sector organizations also support the importance of shared values to organizational effectiveness.[17] Within successful agencies and departments, considerable agreement, as well as intense feeling, is found among employees and managers about the importance of their values and about how those values could best be implemented.

Periodically taking the organization's pulse in regard to the clarity and consensus of its values is well worthwhile. It renews commitment. It engages the institution in discussing values (such as diversity, accessibility, sustainability, and so on) that are more relevant to a changing constituency. Once people are clear about the leader's values, about their own values, and about shared values, they know what's expected of them, can manage higher levels of stress, and can better handle the conflicting demands of work and their personal lives.

Which Shared Values Are Important?

Is there some particular value or set of values that fuels organizational vitality? Consider this example of three electronics companies, each of which has a strong set of values.[18] The first company prides itself on technical innovation and has a culture dominated by engineering values; it informally encourages and rewards activities such as experimentation and risk taking. The second company is much flashier; its important organizational values are associated with marketing, and the company gears itself toward providing outstanding customer service. The third company does things "by the numbers"; accounting standards dominate its key values, and energies are directed toward making the organization more efficient (by cutting costs, for example).

Successful companies may have very different values.

Each of these companies operates by a different set of values. Is one more successful than the other? No, not really. All three companies compete in the same market, and all are successful, each with a different strategy and culture. It's apparent, then, that successful companies may have very different values— and that the specific set of values that serves one company may hurt another.

This view is supported by the research on companies that are "built to last." Each high-performing organization, compared with a like company in its industry, had a very strong "core ideology" but didn't share the *same* core ideology.[19] The source of sustained competitive advantage for organizations begins with a values-based foundation on which management and leadership practices are built.

Although there may not be one best set of values, you can find some guidance from the research on central themes in the values of highly successful, strong-culture organizations.[20] There are three central themes in the values of these organizations:

- High performance standards
- A caring attitude about people
- A sense of uniqueness and pride

High-performance values stress the commitment to excellence, *caring* values communicate how others are to be treated, and *uniqueness* values tell people inside and outside how the organization is different from all the others. These three common threads seem to be critical to weaving a values tapestry that leads to greatness.

Unity Is Forged, Not Forced

Questions such as "What are our basic principles?" and "What do we believe in?" are far from simple. Even with commonly identified values, there may be little agreement on the meaning of values statements. One study, for example, uncovered 185 different behavioral expectations about the value of integrity alone.[21] The lesson here is that leaders must engage their constituents in a dialogue about values. A common understanding of values emerges from a process, not a pronouncement.

This is precisely what Michael Lin discovered when he became the technical support manager for a small wireless company. Although he felt that it was important "to clarify my personal values from the onset, at the same time I needed to give each of my fellow technical support engineers an opportunity to express what individual values were important to them." He noted that it was not so important what the particular value was called or labeled but that everyone agreed on the importance and meaning of the values. One of his initial actions was to bring people together just for that purpose, so that they could arrive at common and shared understandings of what their key priorities and values were and what these meant in action:

> The last thing I wanted them to feel was that my values were being imposed on them. So each person talked about their own values, the reasoning behind them. In this fashion we were able to identify the common values that were important to us as a group. The key values that the team and I felt were most important to model were honesty, responsibility, customer focus, and teamwork. This led us to drafting a team credo: Do whatever it takes to satisfy the customer. The process of deciding on one common set of values was an extremely valuable unifying and clarifying experience.

Experience has taught us that no matter how extensive top management's support of shared values is, leaders can't impose their values on organizational members. Instead they must be proactive in involving people in the process of creating shared values. Imagine how much ownership of values there would be if leaders actively engaged a wide range of people in their development. We encourage leaders to invite everybody—or if that's not feasible, a representative group of constituents—to discuss the organization's values and see what critical themes emerge. Shared values are the result of listening, appreciating, building consensus, and practicing conflict resolution. For people to understand the values and come to agree with them, they must participate in the process: unity is forged, not forced.

Someone who knows all about resolving conflict and building consensus around a unifying set of values is Pat Christen, president of HopeLab, a nonprofit organization that combines rigorous research with some very innovative solutions to improving the health and quality of life of young people with chronic illnesses. HopeLab's first product was Re-Mission, a videogame for young people with cancer. Pat found that shared values were critical guide-posts when difficulties arose:

> Our staff and external collaborators have competencies that were really critical to our success with Re-Mission, but their different perspectives were often in conflict with one another in terms of how we should move forward with the project. Our leadership role was to manage these tensions to bring out the best in everyone. It was an extraordinary challenge, but I believe that when you reach difficult crossroads in an organization, you go back to your core values and you constantly ask how you should be behaving and what path you should be taking in order to align your values with actions. The manner in which the staff rose to the occasion in producing such a high-quality product is a real testament to having a set of core values and using them to guide how you act and behave in the world.

For values to be truly shared, they must be more than advertising slogans. They must be deeply supported and broadly endorsed beliefs about what's important to the people who hold them. Constituents must be able to enumerate the values and must have common interpretations of how those values will be put into practice. They must know how the values influence their own jobs and how they directly contribute to organizational success.

One word of caution: shared values should never be used as an excuse for the suppression of dissent. When dissenting voices are silenced, and when shared values become unquestioned doctrine, freedom of expression is lost—and with it goes innovation, creativity, and talent. And sometimes people's lives. Freedom of expression is essential to creating a culture of contribution and commitment. If leaders desire long-term sustainable growth and development, then freedom just may be that value that makes possible all the others.

A unified voice on values results from discovery and dialogue. Leaders must provide a chance for individuals to engage in a discussion of what the values mean and how their personal beliefs and behaviors are influenced by what the organization stands for. Leaders must also be prepared to discuss values and expectations in the recruitment, selection, and orientation of new members. Better to explore early the fit between person and organization than to have members find out at some key juncture that they're in violent disagreement over matters of principle.[22]

REFLECTION AND ACTION: CLARIFYING VALUES

The very first step on the journey to credible leadership is clarifying your values—discovering those fundamental beliefs that will guide your decisions and actions along the path to success and significance. That journey involves an exploration of the inner territory where your true voice resides. It's essential that you take yourself on this voyage because it's the only route to authenticity and because your personal values drive your commitment to the organization and to the cause. You can't do what you say if you don't know what you believe. And, you can't do what you say if you don't believe in what you're saying.

Although personal values clarity is essential for all leaders, it's insufficient alone. That's because leaders don't just speak for themselves, they speak for their constituents as well. There must be agreement on the *shared values* that everyone will commit to upholding. Shared values make a significant and positive difference in work attitudes and performance, and a common understanding of those values emerges from a process, not a pronouncement. Unity comes about through dialogue and debate. And, finally, to make sure that people can act on the values they share, it's essential to build competence. Credibility, both individual and organizational, is not just a promise—it's also the ability to deliver on the promise.

We talk throughout this book about building your competence to lead in each of The Five Practices of Exemplary Leadership. As mentioned in the Preface, we close each chapter with suggestions on actions you can take, alone or with others, to build skills for implementing the practice in question. As you will see, we designed our suggestions to be "small wins." Whether the focus is your own learning or the development of your constituents (such as direct reports, team, peers, manager, community), small wins are things you can do on your own immediately—they take little or no budget, nor do they require consensus among peers or approval of top management.

Here are three actions that you can use to Clarify Values for yourself and others.

Write a Tribute to Yourself

Begin the process of clarifying your values by reflecting on your ideal image of yourself—how you would most like to be seen by others. Try this exercise: Imagine that tonight you'll be honored as Leader of the Year. Hundreds of people will gather to pay tribute to your contributions to your family, your colleagues, your organization, or your community. Several people will make speeches praising your performance and your character.

What words or phrases would you most like to hear others say about you? How would you like to be remembered tonight? What descriptions would make you feel the proudest? If you could write these tributes yourself, what would you want them to say? These descriptive adjectives and phrases may well be lofty and ideal. That's exactly the point: the greater the clarity of, belief in, and passion for our personal standards of excellence, the greater the probability we'll act in concert with them.

If you have trouble writing your tribute, you might start by recording your answers to some of these questions:

- What do you stand for? Why?
- What do you believe in? Why?
- What are you discontented about? Why?
- What brings you suffering? Why?
- What makes you weep and wail? Why?

- What makes you jump for joy? Why?
- What are you passionate about? Why?
- What keeps you awake at night? Why?
- What's grabbed hold and won't let go? Why?
- What do you want for your life? Why?
- Just what is it that you really care about? Why?

To write your tribute, and to lead, you'll need to be able to answer these questions.

Write Your Credo

Imagine that your organization has afforded you the chance to take a six-month sabbatical, all expenses paid. You will not be permitted to communicate to anyone at your office or plant while you are away. Not by letter, phone, fax, e-mail, or other means.

But before you depart, those with whom you work need to know the principles that you believe should guide their decisions and actions in your absence. They need to know the values and beliefs that you think should steer the organization while you're away. After all, you'll want to be able to fit back in on your return.

You are not to write a long report, however. Just a one-page "Credo Memo." Get a single sheet of paper and write that memo.

It usually takes about five to ten minutes to write a Credo Memo. We do not pretend that this exercise is a substitute for more in-depth self-discovery, but it does provide a useful starting point for articulating your guiding principles. To deepen the clarification process, identify the values you listed in your memo (usually they appear as key words or phrases) and put them in order of priority. Or rank them from low to high. Or place them on a continuum. Forcing yourself to express preferences enables you to see the relative potency of each value.

Engage in a Credo Dialogue

Start by gathering together the people you lead for a dialogue about shared values. Tell them what you've learned about personal values and about shared values. Tell them that you've written a Credo Memo that you'd like to share with them, but before doing it you'd like them to do the same thing. Explain the Credo Memo process to them (see previous action) and give them each time to write something—five to ten minutes should be sufficient.

Once they have all written their own Credo Memos, ask each person to share with a few colleagues in small groups what he or she wrote. Ask them to describe both what they wrote and why they selected the values they recorded in the memo. Before they begin, you can model the process by reading your memo to them and telling them why you prize the values you chose.

Remind your team that the objective of this activity is clarity. You want them to understand what each other values; there's no need for consensus at this stage. Suggest that they ask each other clarifying questions if they don't understand something, and follow-up questions if they still aren't clear.

Once each person has had a chance to express key values, ask the groups to reflect on what was discussed. Was each person's set of guiding values in the Credo Memo idiosyncratic, or were there some similar values being expressed? (If your experience is similar to ours, you'll hear that there were a number of commonalities.) Ask, What are the common values that were expressed?

There's a lot more you can do with this list—you can turn it into a formal document for everyone to sign, you can form a committee to write a group credo, or you can just have everyone keep their own notes. The critical thing is that you begin to build consensus around a common set of values that emerges from the group and not one that is imposed from the top.

COMMITMENT NUMBER 1

Clarify Values

Essentials of Clarifying Values

- Find your voice
- Affirm shared values

Taking Action

- Write a tribute to yourself
- Write your credo
- Engage in a credo dialogue

SET THE EXAMPLE

"The action that made the most difference was
setting a personal example."
Idan Bar-Sade, BridgeWave

"It all starts," explains Juan Gonzalez, industry solution manager at IBM, "with understanding yourself and identifying the driving forces within in order to have the courage and consistency to engage successfully as a leader." With this realization Juan started getting involved more personally, and emotionally, in activities that he once would have handled at arm's length. "I started by taking the time to go a little beyond the required level of interaction with others," he says, "like making that extra phone call and showing interest in others' day-to-day activities, rather than simply focusing on the job to be done." The pay-off, says Juan, is that "now I find our achievements, big or small, more rewarding than before. This in turn has had an effect on my mood, and I can see how this is also reflected in the ways others perceive me at work. Understanding my values allows me to be more passionate about my work and gives a focus for what everyone on the team should be striving for."

But sometimes one's values are tested, and that's when leaders have to make sure they demonstrate through personal example what it means to be passionately committed. That's exactly what happened to Juan. While his company was applying a product upgrade to the live system of one of their customers, something went terribly wrong. It was quite a mess, and, wouldn't you know it, the problem became apparent the Saturday morning of a long holiday weekend. This was a critical process for their customer, and there was simply no way they could wait until the next regular workday to work on the problem. Says Juan, "I found that I could drive myself harder by letting my voice—my clarity about my values—remind me of the importance of my actions. This voice was fundamental in my decisions about getting personally involved in taking action and pulling the team together on a weekend." He started by calling each member of the team, rather than sending an "SOS" to their pagers. He described the situation, and learned that it helped immensely that he had already spent several hours testing the scope of the issue. "I had been working to figure out a solution before calling them," he explains. "Showing them the way by going in in advance gave enormous credibility to my request, and I got them signed up."

Time was short, and they scrambled to make the needed fixes. "We would implement each fix and test thoroughly. If it didn't work, we were all available to troubleshoot," Juan tells us. "If it worked, we moved on to the next problem." Juan was right in the middle of things with everyone: "There wasn't anything I was asking them to do that I wasn't already doing myself. They knew that I was willing to do whatever it took to get this solved, including running errands or handling grunt work for those working on a particular application, and they picked up the same attitude."

Juan says that he could have just ordered the team back to the office on Saturday (even on a holiday weekend), because it was an emergency. "It's their job anyway, and they get paid for that," he explains. And he also notes that there wasn't any company requirement or expectation for him to come in. But he clearly understood that even if the situation had been handled successfully, the wounds to morale and motivation would probably have been deep. More important, Juan points out, "I had to show others by my actions that we were serious about our values and commitments. My credibility would have been shattered if I hadn't pitched in, and I would definitely have had a difficult time getting help from them in future situations."

No down time was experienced by their customer. Before the team departed, Juan went to each team member, one by one, and thanked them personally for all their hard work. Then he sat down and followed up. "I sent a very detailed e-mail, copying anyone who might listen, describing what a great job the team had done in the relentless pursuit of customer satisfaction (our key value) and how their actions directly impacted our bottom line." Each team member received a thank-you note from the CEO and compensatory time off—all arranged by Juan. And, Juan notes with amused surprise, "The team members really thanked me for that, even though it was I who disrupted their holiday weekend in the first place! This was indeed very rewarding."

Juan's story illustrates the central message in this chapter—leaders take every opportunity to show others by their own example that they're deeply committed to the values and aspirations they espouse. No one will believe you're serious until they see you doing what you're asking of others. Leading by example is how leaders make visions and values tangible. It's how they provide the evidence that they're personally committed.

Setting the Example is all about execution. It's about *putting* your money where your mouth is. It's about *practicing* what you preach. It's about *following through* on commitments. It's about *keeping* promises. It's about *walking* the talk. It's about *doing* what you say. And because you're leading a group of people—not just leading yourself—it's also about what those who are following you are doing. How consistent are they in deed and word? How well are they practicing what's preached? As the leader you're held accountable for their actions, too.

There are two essentials necessary to Set the Example, one that's focused on you and one that's focused on your constituents. To Set the Example you need to

- **Personify the shared values**
- **Teach others to model the values**

In practicing these essentials leaders become role models for what the whole team (the group, the organization, or the company) stands for, and they also create a culture in which everyone commits to aligning themselves with shared values.

PERSONIFY THE SHARED VALUES

We were talking with Gary McBee, who at the time was executive vice president with a regional telecommunications company. He shared a personal story with us that clearly communicated how powerful modeling is, at home as well as at work.

"When my son was seven years old," he said, "I thought it was time to bring him to the place where I worked and show him my office. I sat him down in that big chair behind my desk. He peeked up over the top and said, 'Dad. Call somebody in here and fire him.'"

We all laughed. It was that kind of laughter that appreciates the story's irony but also recognizes its bittersweet truth. We all send signals about what's important to us. Sometimes we may not be completely aware of the signals we're sending, just as Gary wasn't, but we send them nonetheless. We send them through the daily choices we make. We send them in a wide variety of settings and media. We send them verbally and nonverbally. Leaders just happen to be more visible signal senders than others of us, and they know that people are always watching, trying to determine what's important. Leaders recognize that they have to be mindful of and accountable for the choices they make, because they're setting the example of what's appropriate and inappropriate, what's exemplary and what's second-rate.

Mary Godwin became acutely aware of the messages she was sending as vice president of operations of a company that creditors were threatening to put into bankruptcy. At first, Mary was trying to figure out how she was going to keep herself from resigning, never mind keep the operations team together while the company worked its way out of a $70 million debt. Acknowledging that it would have been a lot easier to leave, she explained, "It came to me that if I wanted everyone else to be committed, then I had to be totally, 100 percent, without doubt, committed personally." Mary realized that before she could ask others to change she had to be willing to make those same changes and sacrifices herself. What's more, she understood that it would be only through her actions that people would come to know the depth of her convictions:

I had to follow through on commitments and show others by my actions how serious we were about our values and standards. My credibility depended upon this, and so I had to set the example for others to follow. For example, if there was "bad news" to be delivered to the company, I would be the one to deliver it. If we needed to work on weekends, then I'd be there. If something didn't work out as planned, I'd never let anyone on the team get "blamed" for it.

In the end, they met the deadline from their creditors and kept the company from going into bankruptcy; most important to Mary, the entire operations team stayed on board through the whole process. Those accomplishments wouldn't have been possible without Mary's leadership by example.

We can't stress enough the power of the leader's personal example. Cornell professor Tony Simons offers telling evidence of this. In his research on behavioral integrity, for instance, he found that organizations "where employees strongly believed [that] their managers followed through on promises and demonstrated the values they preached were substantially more profitable than those whose managers scored average or lower [on follow through]."[1] In other words, if you want to get better results, make sure you practice what you preach. What you do speaks more loudly than what you say.

Sometimes the greatest distance we have to travel is the distance from our mouths to our feet.

Leaders are their organizations' ambassadors of shared values. Their mission is to represent the values and standards to the rest of the world, and it is their solemn duty to serve the values to the best of their abilities. Here are a few signal-sending actions to consider as you work to personally exemplify the shared values in your organization.[2]

- Spend your *time and attention* wisely. Spend this precious nonrenewable resource on the most important values.
- Watch your *language.* Use words and phrases that best express the culture you want to create.
- Ask purposeful *questions.* Raise questions that intentionally stimulate people to think more purposefully about values.
- Seek *feedback.* Ask others about the impact of your behavior on their performance.

Each of these signal-sending opportunities offers a chance to make visible and tangible to others your personal commitment to a shared way of being. Each affords the chance to show where you stand on matters of principle. Simple though they may appear, we should all remember that sometimes the greatest distance we have to travel is the distance from our mouths to our feet. Exemplary leaders are very mindful of the signals they send and how they send them.

Spend Your Time and Attention Wisely

How you spend your time is the single clearest indicator, especially to other people, of what's important to you. If you say, for example, that your top priority is your customers (or clients, patients, students, voters, or parishioners), then how much of your daily time do you spend with them? What's the connection between how you schedule your time and what you consider to be priorities and key values? If an independent auditor were to compare your daily calendar to what you say is important to you, what would it say in the audit report?

At one of our client engagements—the annual sales meeting for the company's largest region—we were scheduled to speak right after the company's CEO. Account reps from all over the United States, Latin America, and Canada were in the audience. When the show started, we fully expected to see the CEO walk out onto the stage with all the fanfare that goes with the role. Instead, the lights dimmed and a video began playing. There he was, larger than life all right, but instead of being live-and-in-person he was prerecorded.

Now we don't know how you'd react to something like this, but we were shocked. Here were some of the most important people in the company— the folks who call on customers and prospects every day—getting the cold shoulder from their chief. The employees who had invited us to speak said they felt slighted. They were upset that their leader hadn't made a personal appearance. We're willing to cut the CEO some slack. He, like all his colleagues, is a very busy person, he has lots of demands on his time, and he can't be everywhere, especially when the company has multiple offices in many different countries. But we just can't fathom how this guy could skip out on something as important as the annual gathering of the salesforce, and neither could those who were with us. Leaders make choices about where they spend their time and attention. They send signals by their presence and their absence. In this case, by his absence the message the CEO sent, most likely unintentionally, was "You're not important enough to me." Sometimes leadership is just showing up.

Setting an example means arriving early, staying late, and being there to show you care. It's about being the first to do something that everyone should value. Whether the value is family, teamwork, hard work, or fun, the truest measure of what leaders deeply believe is how they spend their time. Constituents look to this metric and use it to judge whether a leader measures up to espoused standards. Visibly spending time on what's important shows that you're putting your time and money where your mouth is. For example, by attending operating meetings in the field, leaders provide visible evidence of their concerns and the direction they want to pursue. That's why Logitech's vice president of worldwide human resources, Roberta Linsky, traveled halfway around the world (from Fremont, California) to attend Lunar New Year celebrations in the company's manufacturing facility in Suzhou, China. Being there in person said more about how much Roberta values her constituents than any e-mail message, telegram, card, or video could ever do.

Watch Your Language

Harvard professor Shoshana Zuboff has observed that people are "prisoners" of their organizational vocabulary.[3] Zuboff's choice of words is deliberate and none too strong. If you disagree, try talking about an organization for even a day without using the words *employee, manager, boss, supervisor, subordinate,* or *hierarchy.* You may find this exercise nearly impossible unless you've gotten comfortable with the language some organizations use today, such as *associates, crew, cast members, team members, partners,* or even *constituents.* We've all come to accept certain words we use as the reality of organizational life. Those words can trap us into a particular way of thinking about our roles and relationships.

One company that clearly understands how to consciously use a different vocabulary to reflect its unique set of values is DaVita, the largest independent provider of dialysis services in the United States for patients suffering from chronic kidney failure. "All the words and phrases we use," Joe Mello, chief operating officer, told us, "evolved over time and have ended up being symbolic of the messages we're trying to send and the real environment we're trying to create. . . . You have to make sure that everybody has a good understanding of what the beliefs are and a good understanding of what the expected behaviors are. Part of that belief system is encompassed in our language, and we have to be more deliberate about our language than we have been in the past." It begins with the choice of the company name. DaVita is definitely a name that fits the nature of their work. Roughly translated from the Italian, the phrase means "he or she gives life." Every day in every clinic, DaVitans—that's what they call themselves—work hard to give life to those suffering from renal disease.

At DaVita, memorable catchphrases infuse the daily conversation and reinforce the company's values and management practices. The *Three Musketeers* maxim "one for all, and all for one," for example, permeates the culture of the company and reinforces the idea that everyone in DaVita is in it together, looking out for each other. Corporate headquarters is called "Casa DaVita" (house of DaVita). Employees are all "teammates"—be prepared to put a buck in a glass on the meeting table if you should ever use the "E word." The company is called the "Village," and DaVita's CEO, Kent Thiry, is its "mayor," signaling that DaVita is really more like the small town in Wisconsin that Kent grew up in—the kind of place where, as Joe explained, "People don't just go to work and come home. They take people casseroles when they're sick. They take care of each other. They watch out for each other." Teammates become "citizens" of the Village when they are willing to "cross the bridge" and make a public commitment to the community. Every member of the senior leadership crossed the bridge as part of their symbolic rite of passage into those roles. The company's long-standing emphasis on execution and operational excellence is embodied in the slogan "GSD" (get stuff done); the highest compliment to pay a teammate is to say he or she is "good at GSD." Another key motto is "We said, we did," because, as Joe pointed out, "You have to go beyond just doing it, you have to make sure you publicize that you did it."[4]

Leaders understand and are attentive to language. They know the power of words. The words people choose to use are metaphors for concepts that define attitudes and behaviors, structures and systems. Words don't just give voice to one's own mind-set and beliefs, they evoke images of what people hope to create with others and how they expect people to behave, as evident in the comparison of the bank manager and the Unilever executive in Chapter Three.

Paying attention to the way you use language isn't one of those ideas-of-the-month that's the trendy thing to do. Researchers have documented the power of language in shaping thoughts and actions. Just a few words from someone can make the difference in the beliefs that people articulate. For example, at an East Coast university where there was a publicized incidence of hate mail sent to an African American student, researchers randomly stopped students walking across campus and asked them what they thought of the occurrence. Before the subject could respond, however, a confederate of the researchers would come up and answer. One response was something like "Well, he must have done something to deserve it." As you might expect, the subject's response was more often than not just like the confederate's. Then the researchers would stop another student and ask the same question. This time the confederate gave an alternative response that was something like "There's no place for that kind of behavior on our campus." The subject's response again replicated the confederate's.[5]

This study dramatically illustrates how potent language is in influencing people's responses to what's going on around them. Language helps to build the frame around people's views of the world, and it's essential for leaders to be mindful of their choice of words. If you want people to act like citizens of a village you have to talk about them that way, not as subordinates in a hierarchy. If you want people to appreciate the rich diversity in their organizations, you have to use language that's inclusive. If you want people to be innovative, you have to use words that spark exploration, discovery, and invention. "Watch your language" has come to take on a whole new meaning from when your teacher scolded you in school for the use of an inappropriate word. It's now about setting an example for others of how they need to think and act.

Ask Purposeful Questions

The questions you ask can also be quite powerful in focusing attention. When leaders ask questions, they send constituents on mental journeys—"quests"—in search of answers. The questions that a leader asks send messages about the focus of the organization, and they're indicators of what is of most concern to the leader. They're one more measure of how serious we are about our espoused beliefs. Questions direct attention to the values that should be attended to and how much energy should be devoted to them.

You need to be intentional and purposeful about the questions that you ask. You need to make sure that the questions you ask are directly related to the values that you hold dear. Barbara Goretsky, corporate director of leadership development at Northrop Grumman Corporation, points out the importance of asking people questions such as "What evidence exists that we are living by our values and making decisions consistent with these values?" Although this question can take many different forms, what's critical is that leaders ask about the evidence. What questions should you be asking, for example, if you want people to focus on integrity? On trust? On customer or client satisfaction? On quality? On innovation? On growth? On personal responsibility?

Questions frame the issue and set the agenda. In one of our workshops, we suggested that participants who wanted their constituents to stay focused on continuous improvement ask this simple question of every person attending their next group meeting: "What have you done in the past week to improve so that you're better this week than last?" We then recommended that they repeat this question for the next four weeks or more, predicting that it would take at least that many repetitions to sustain the focus.

About a month later, we heard from a participant in the workshop who had done what we recommended. He told us that the first time he asked the question, people looked at each other skeptically, apparently thinking, "Oh, this guy's just been to a seminar." The second time, some of his team members took him seriously and about 30 percent had a response. The third time, about 70 percent reported what they had done. And the fourth? Something very interesting happened: "They asked me what I had done in the last week to improve myself so I was better than I was last week." Questions can indeed be very effective tools for change.

> *Questions can be very effective tools for change.*

Questions can also develop people. They help others escape the trap of their own paradigms by broadening their perspectives and taking responsibility for their own viewpoints. Asking good questions, rather than giving answers, forces you to listen attentively to your constituents and what they are saying. This action demonstrates your respect for their ideas and opinions. If you are genuinely interested in what other people have to say then you need to ask their opinion, especially before giving your own. Asking what others think facilitates participation in whatever decision will ultimately be determined and consequently increases support for that decision. Asking good questions reduces the risk that a decision might be undermined by either inadequate consideration or unexpected opposition.

Seek Feedback

Feedback comes from a variety of sources. For example, some of the feedback that Seang Wee Lee received when he was promoted at Cisco Systems was from his own management about the need to change the engagement model that his team used with internal organizations and external vendors. He decided right away that he also needed to have an open dialogue with the team, as he told us, "to understand their perception about what was going on and to obtain feedback on my role as their leader." Seang Wee explained that he had done this throughout his career:

> I have enlisted feedback from those that I work with very closely with the hope of understanding how I can further improve. I utilize this feedback to further improve my leadership skills, identify shortfalls, and open up communications with the team. This promotes trust in my leadership and creates a climate of trust within the team and with me. I almost always learn about some things I can do to help develop each individual as well as the team, and also me.

Another benefit, according to Seang Wee, is that "my seeking feedback and listening in turn encourages my team to maintain open communication with other groups through enlisting their feedback and understanding the impact they can make to make their work more efficient." Leaders realize that while they may not always like the feedback, it is the only way they can really know how they are doing as someone's leader. Seeking feedback provides a powerful statement about the value of self-improvement and how everyone can be even better than they are today.

As critical as feedback is to assessing and improving our performance as leaders, leaders don't seem to ask for much of it. In our most recent analysis of data from over seventy thousand individuals who completed the *Leadership Practices Inventory*, our thirty-item behavioral assessment, we've found that the statement that ranks the lowest from the observers' perspective, and the next to lowest from the leaders' perspective, is this item:

> 16. (He or she) asks for feedback on how his/her actions affect other people's performance.

When we related this finding to the director of leadership development for one of the world's largest technology companies, he told us that the same was true for his organization. The lowest-scoring item on its internal leadership assessment was the one on seeking feedback. We hear the same thing from other executive coaches.

Let's think about this for a moment. Credibility, which is at the foundation of leadership, from a *behavioral* perspective is about doing what you say you will do. But how can you know that you're doing what you say if you never ask for feedback on your behavior and on how your behavior affects how others are doing? How can you really expect to align your words and your actions over the long haul?

There's solid evidence that the best leaders are highly attuned to what's going on inside themselves as they are leading and to what's going on with others.[6] They're very self-aware, and they're very socially aware. They can tell in short order whether they've done something that has enabled someone to perform at a higher level or whether they've sent motivation heading south.

Troy Hansen was vice president of AgDirect and Leasing, Farm Credit Services (FCS) of America, a leading financial services provider in Omaha, Nebraska, when he illustrated how his team learned that feedback is essential to both personal and professional development.[7] Although Troy knew the importance of regular performance reviews, his team members held some rather negative attitudes about these appraisals. "The performance evaluation had this big negative tone to it," he said. "It just doesn't sound like a real positive experience in most cases." Troy wanted to change that. He did something that had never been done before at FCS. To kick off the initial round of performance appraisals, Troy asked his team members to evaluate his performance first.

After a brief orientation, Troy left the group members alone to evaluate his performance in private. This was the first time the team members had given a performance review on a team leader, and quite naturally they were initially reluctant, particularly in front of other team members and without Troy present. The process was very challenging at first, but eventually the team completed their review and then, at Troy's request, delivered it to him face-to-face in the presence of all his team members.

"The feedback that I received was kind of hard to hear," Troy admitted. But then he added, "And that was really one of the benefits to the group. To take that personal risk; to model for the group that it's okay to place yourself at personal risk and take that honest feedback. What I hoped the team members would come away with was a sense that it's okay to be in that environment, that feedback is necessary for growth, and then to see how you accept that feedback and then what you do with it."

Because of Troy's ability to model his commitment to the value of personal feedback—and of not asking someone to do something he wouldn't do first—his team gained a newfound respect for the performance review process itself. Preston Kranz, an AgDirect Representative and a member of Troy's team, commented, "After having the opportunity to go through this performance review, the individual review that I received meant more to me. I placed more value on Troy's feedback." And then Preston added, "He's asking the question, 'How can I do this better?' The performance review shows his commitment to do that. He used that feedback and information to make a difference."

Often leaders fear the exposure and vulnerability that accompanies direct and honest feedback. Those giving the feedback can often feel a bit exposed themselves and may even fear retribution or hurting someone. Troy admits that it's a risk, but also recognizes that the upside of learning and growth are far more beneficial than the downside of being nervous or embarrassed. Learning to be a better leader requires great self-awareness, and it requires making ourselves vulnerable. Modeling that for others makes it easier for them to do the same when it comes their turn.

TEACH OTHERS TO MODEL THE VALUES

People are not watching only you, they're watching everyone else in your organization. They're paying attention to what others say and do, and so should you. It's not just what you do that demonstrates consistency between word and deed. Everyone—every team member, partner, and colleague—is a sender of signals about what's valued, and they also set an example. Part of leadership is making sure that their actions are also aligned with shared values. Here are a few things you can do to *teach others* what's expected so they can hold themselves accountable for living the values of the organization.

- *Confront critical incidents.* Respond to those disruptive occurrences in the life of your organization in ways that reinforce core values.
- *Tell stories.* Publicly give examples of what team members do to live the values, and make sure to mention "the moral at the end of the story."
- *Reinforce the behavior you want repeated.* Keep score and measure performance to determine consistency with values. Tangibly and intangibly recognize performance that's consistent with espoused values.

Confront Critical Incidents

Consciously choosing how you spend your time, the language you use, and how you get feedback on your performance are essential for sending the signal that you're serious about an issue. But you can't plan everything about your day. Even the most disciplined leaders can't stop the intrusion of the unexpected. Critical incidents—chance occurrences, particularly at a time of stress and challenge—offer significant moments of learning for leaders and constituents. Critical incidents present opportunities for leaders to teach important lessons about appropriate norms of behavior.

For example, as Jennifer Tran, content manager at PayPal, found out, being part of a team doesn't automatically mean that everyone has the same set of priorities. While working on a project developing a new technology that would have a huge impact on the way consumers would pay for purchases, she discovered a problem with the documentation that would require further work. The team's copyeditor had already edited the documentation several times and was hesitant to step back and review it yet again. Jennifer pushed back, reminding her teammate about the possibility of not creating a "great user experience"—a core shared value among all groups in their company. With that, the copyeditor reconsidered, and Jennifer's team came up with a solution that satisfied everyone. "The fact that I stood up for this common value," Jennifer told us, "was instrumental in both mitigating potential conflict and encouraging greater team spirit." Jennifer saw in this situation not simply another problem to be dealt with but an opportune moment to remind her colleagues about the importance of living up to their shared values.

Critical incidents present opportunities for leaders to teach important lessons.

Having shared values may not always be sufficient to ensure that everyone's actions are aligned. There are critical moments when leaders have to take action to put values squarely on the table and in front of others so that they can return to this common ground for working together. In the process, leaders make clear how their actions are compelled by shared values. In this way they set an example for what it means to take actions on the basis of values. By standing up for values, leaders demonstrate that having shared values requires a mutual commitment to aligning words and deeds for everyone.

Critical incidents aren't planned. They are those events in the lives of leaders (and organizations) that offer the chance to improvise while still staying true to the script. Although they can't be explicitly planned, it's useful to keep in mind, as Jennifer did, that the way you handle these incidents—how you link actions and decisions to shared values—speaks volumes about what's really important.

Tell Stories

Critical incidents create important teachable moments. They offer leaders the occasion in real time to demonstrate what's valued and what's not. Stories are another way that leaders pass on lessons about shared values and get others working together.

Steve Denning knows firsthand how stories can change the course of an organization. When Steve was program director of knowledge management for the World Bank, one day he was sitting with a colleague over lunch and swapping work stories. Steve's colleague, who had been working on a project in Zambia with the goal of improving health services to families, talked about a health worker in Kasama, six hundred kilometers from the capital city of Lusaka, who had logged on to the Web site for the Centers for Disease Control in Atlanta, Georgia, and found the answer to a question on how to treat malaria. His colleague thought this was a neat illustration of how knowledge sharing on the Web was working, even in one of the poorest countries on earth. Steve didn't realize it at the time, but this very simple story was ultimately going to change his whole approach to persuading others about the vital role knowledge management could play within the World Bank.[8]

Steve had been having little success up to this point in convincing others in the World Bank that they had a role other than just a financial one, so he decided to incorporate the Zambia anecdote into his presentations. In the weeks that followed, Steve saw the Zambia story starting to have unexpectedly positive results. He noticed that when he began his presentations with the Zambia story, something was "beginning to click" with his audiences. When he didn't use the Zambia story, Steve found that the conversation ended up "in a tangle of debates about various aspects of the feasibility of the change idea."

Over the ensuing years Steve learned how truly vital stories were to communicating essential messages within the World Bank, and within all organizations. Why storytelling? He says, "Nothing else worked. Charts left listeners bemused. Prose remained unread. Dialogue was just too laborious and slow. Time after time, when faced with the task of persuading a group of managers or frontline staff in a large organization to get enthusiastic about a major change, I found that storytelling was the only thing that worked."[9]

Steve's experience with storytelling, in fact, is not remarkable, though the method is seriously underused. Why tell stories? For one simple reason: they are powerful tools for teaching people about what's important and what's not, what works and what doesn't, what is and what could be.[10]

David Armstrong, president and chief executive officer at Armstrong International, is so convinced of the critical impact of storytelling that he has written several books that include hundreds of stories direct from the factory and office of the company. On the basis of his personal experience with storytelling, David offers a dozen reasons why telling stories is such an effective leadership practice. Among them are these: stories are simple, timeless, and can appeal to everybody regardless of age, gender, or race. They're fun, a useful form of training, and a good method for empowering people. They're also great as a recognition device, a recruiting and hiring tool, a sales technique, and an excellent way to pass along corporate traditions.[11]

David says that you become a different kind of leader when you tell stories. "For one thing, you create an environment where people are receptive to change and new ideas," he writes. "Just think about what happens when you yell at people or order them about. They pull back. They get upset. They withdraw. But telling stories is friendly and enjoyable. People want to hear what you have to say."[12]

David's and Steve's reports about the impact of stories on attitude and behavior are well supported by the data. Research on stories shows that when leaders want to communicate standards, stories are a much more effective means of communication than are corporate policy statements, data about performance, and even a story plus the data.[13] Information is more quickly and accurately remembered when it is first presented in the form of an example or story.[14]

As Jack Little explains, "Storytelling is more compelling than just giving rules, guidelines, and policies. It gives you an actual example that people can remember a lot better. Storytelling can be tied to people and names and events that are much more relevant." And this comes from the CEO of The Math Works, a Massachusetts-based developer of engineering software. Despite the company's high-tech focus, leaders at all levels of the organization use stories to communicate organizational values and practices.

Telling stories has another lasting benefit. It forces leaders to pay close attention to what their constituents are doing. Peers—"people like me"—generally make better role models for what to do at work than famous people or ones several levels up in the hierarchy. When others hear or read a story about someone with whom they can identify, they are much more likely to see themselves doing the same thing. People seldom tire of hearing stories about themselves and the people they know. These stories get repeated, and the lessons of the stories get spread far and wide.

Reinforce the Behavior You Want Repeated

Leaders need feedback to help keep them on track. So do their constituents. Feedback is a way of telling them how successful they are at doing what they say they'll do. It's a way of reinforcing what they're doing right, and helping them correct what they're doing wrong. Research indicates clearly that measurement and feedback are absolutely essential to increasing efforts to improve performance.[15] Score-keeping systems are essential to knowing how people are doing.

But you don't need a lot of research to understand how behavior changes when you measure performance. We all know about keeping score from the games and sports we've played. Imagine what it'd be like if you didn't have a way of keeping track of your performance in soccer, tennis, golf, basketball, or football. Imagine what it'd be like if you never got information on how well you did at bridge, poker, Scrabble, or Monopoly. And it's not just the numbers themselves that are important. It's what you get points for. For instance, the game of hockey was altered forever when the league changed the rules so that players got points for assists and not just for goals. All of a sudden team members started passing the puck to each other rather than trying to be the one that put it through the net.

Brian Coleman knows firsthand about the impact of scorekeeping. When he was tool-and-die manager with Ford Motor Company in the United Kingdom, he led a turnaround effort at one of their plants.[16] One of the tools that he and his team of union employees, based in Dagenham, England, developed was a simple device to measure car quality: "The workers would mark a tick on the outline of a car indicating the location of every defect that came down the line."

When they put the device to use, reports Brian, "I was shocked by the result. After only five hours there were more than fourteen hundred ticks on our drawing! I asked the team where we should begin, and they pointed to the area with the densest mass of ticks. Why? 'Because that's where we'll have the greatest impact,' they said."

What you choose to reinforce is what people will choose to value.

For Brian and his team, that simple measuring device was a major factor in reducing the number of defects by over 70 percent and nearly doubling productivity in three months. In Brian's case, the value of quality, the specific goal of reducing defects, and the scoring mechanism all converged to produce results.

Leaders can easily influence outcome by providing the tools for measuring progress. For example, if the organization's performance-appraisal system fails to measure how well people perform against the standards of excellence set by corporate values, leaders can add clear performance measures that evaluate how well people are doing on quality, customer service, innovation, respect for others, contribution to profitability, fun, or whatever else is of critical value to the organization.

Rewards and recognition are other tangible means of reinforcing values (and we'll discuss recognition more thoroughly in Chapter Eleven). The important message to keep in mind is that what you choose to reinforce is what people will choose to value. You have to reinforce the key values important to building and sustaining the kind of culture you want.

The leader who places a premium on innovation and risk taking, for example, must be willing to "promote" in a variety of ways those who innovate. Leaders must be attentive to how people are made to feel when they take risks and fail. Are people rewarded or punished when they fail? Are positive or negative stories told about failure? Is the leader's energy funneled into searching for the culprit or assessing what has been learned from the experience? The leader's actions set the tone for innovation and risk taking.

Who is rewarded, who is promoted—as well as who is given a "time out"—and why are among the clearest ways in which leaders demonstrate their seriousness to a specific set of principles. Leaders literally can "put their money where their mouths are" with financial rewards and put their hearts where their good intentions are with more personalized recognition. The same goes for all other support systems—incentive, recruitment, training, information, and the like. They all send signals about what you value and what you don't, and they must be aligned with the shared values and standards that you're trying to instill.

REFLECTION AND ACTION: SETTING THE EXAMPLE

Leaders demonstrate their intense commitment to the values they espouse by setting an example. It's how they earn and sustain credibility over time. Setting the Example is all about execution and action. It's all about *doing* what you say. Leaders who are seen as practicing what they preach are more effective than those leaders who don't.

Leaders send signals in a variety of ways and in all kinds of settings, and constituents read those signals as indicators of what's okay and what's not okay to do. How leaders spend their time is the single best indicator of what's important. Time is a precious asset, because once passed it can never be recovered. But if invested wisely, it can earn returns for years. The language leaders use and the questions they ask are other powerful ways that shape perceptions of what they value. Leaders also need feedback in order to know if they're doing what they say. They need others to let them know if they're on or off track.

But it's not just what leaders do that matters. Leaders are also measured by how consistent their constituents' actions are with the shared values, so leaders must teach others how to set an example. Critical incidents—those chance occurrences in the lives of all organizations—offer marvelous teachable moments. They offer leaders the opportunity to pass along lessons in real time, not just in the classroom. Sometimes critical incidents become stories, and stories are among the most influential tools leaders have to teach values. And leaders also have to remember that what gets reinforced gets done. Leaders have to keep score in order for people to know how they're doing and to improve how they're doing it. They also have to reward the appropriate behavior if they expect it to get repeated.

One of the toughest parts about being a leader is that you're always onstage. People are always watching you, always talking about you. They're always testing your credibility. That's why setting the *right* example is so important, and why it's essential to make use of all the tools you have available to you to set the example.

Here's a series of action steps that you can use to improve and apply your capacity to Set the Example.

Do a Personal Audit

To set the example, you need to really know what example you're setting. To see how you're modeling the way, have an audit of your actions completed by someone other than yourself.

Audit your daily routines. Are you spending sufficient time on matters consistent with your shared values? Use your shared values as the basis for planning your weekly schedule. Let values be your guide, not old habits or the in-basket.

Audit your daily calendar. How much time are you spending modeling shared values? How do your appointments contribute to communicating and reinforcing shared values?

Audit the agendas for your meetings. What topics are discussed? What issue is first on the agenda? What signal does that issue send about what people should consider to be important? Audit your questions. What questions do you typically ask in meetings, one-on-ones, telephone calls, and interviews? How do these questions help to clarify and gain commitment to shared values? Make a list of searching questions that correspond to each of the shared values.

Audit how you deal with critical incidents. How did you respond to the most recent incident? To what extent did your actions teach lessons about the most important shared values? Audit your rewards and recognitions. Who's being recognized? Do these people exemplify the values you want reinforced? When someone gets recognized have you made clear the value (or standard) on which the reward is based?

Make the audit results public. Explain what's right and working. Disclose what is not working. Set in motion changes that will realign your actions and behaviors to be more consistent with shared values. Your personal audit will help you discover the example that you're really setting. Be sure it's what you intend.

Develop a Routine for Questioning

In our daily lives at work we ask a lot of questions, often for more information, clarification, and greater understanding. Leaders should ask their constituents questions not just for these reasons, but also because every question is a potential teaching opportunity. The key to good questions from a leader's perspective is to think about the "quest" in your question: Where do you want to take this person (or group, unit, organization) with your question? What value or values are you trying to reinforce with your questions? Rather than "what do I want to know?" leaders ask questions to get others to know and become more aware of certain critical factors, perspectives, and beliefs. You need to come up with a routine set of questions that will get people to reflect on the core values and what they have done each day to act on those values. And they ought to be questions that they will *expect* you to ask, and not be surprised by. Why? Because you want them to be thinking about them well before you ask them. You want people to routinely ask themselves these questions, knowing that you will be expecting an answer to them the next time you see them. In one way or another, the questions you ask are all a variation on a single theme: What have you done to live out our values?

What would you ask if the value were innovation? How about, What's the most creative idea you heard today? Or, What's the best suggestion you got from our customers today about how we can improve our products and services? Or, If our competitors were going to put us out of business, what weakness of ours would they exploit? The possibilities are many, and the list can be quite fun.

What would you like each of your constituents to think about each day? What would you like each of your constituents to pay attention to each day? Developing a questioning routine forces you to understand what you are trying to teach and achieve. Consider carefully the key (two or three) questions you want to ask about each and every action and decision that takes place. The point is not to ask rhetorical questions (ones which have obvious answers or responses) but to get others to think about how their own actions are consistent with shared values. Your questions help to keep others focused and paying attention to what really matters in your workplace.

Put Storytelling on Your Meeting Agendas

Think of yourself as the CSO—Chief Story Officer—for your team. Be on the lookout for good stories! Capture as many examples of exemplary behavior in your organization as you can. The practice of observing and recording is important to building your skills in storytelling.

Then put it on the weekly meeting agenda. Start each meeting with a story about something someone on your team did to demonstrate a cherished value. If possible, figure out a way to reenact the incident. If you're a virtual team and can't do it in a meeting, then use voicemail and e-mail as media for telling stories. In these formats shorter stories are generally more useful than longer ones, but they're still helpful ways to disseminate good news.

Also keep in mind that the "memorability" of stories is in direct proportion to their "vividness."[17] To be vivid, a story should be about a real person, have a strong sense of time and place, and be told in colorful and animated language.[18] It helps immensely if you can talk from a first-person perspective. Allow your emotions to surface as you speak; this brings excitement to your voice and increases your natural tendency to use gestures and to smile. If you are feeling truly excited about a particular activity or goal, show it. If you are deeply concerned about competitive threats, show it. Start your story by relating an "above-and-beyond-the-call" deed. Think of a clever title for the story that will capture people's attention and help them to remember (catalogue) it. Give your story a theme. Be willing to repeat this theme. Keep the story short. Use people's names. Verify all facts. Be sure to end your message or story with a conclusion that demonstrates concretely the intended message or lesson to be learned. The old storytellers had good reasons for calling the ending "the moral of the story."

Finally, in setting the example through storytelling, provide opportunities for others to share a story or two—not necessarily about themselves but about a colleague who took an action that exemplified the organization's values.

Don't be worried about either telling too many stories or repeating the same theme (moral, lesson, or value) too often. People simply like good stories—and they are a great way to learn!

COMMITMENT NUMBER 2
Set the Example

Essentials of Setting the Example

- Personify the shared values
- Teach others to model the values

Taking Action

- Do a personal audit
- Develop a routine for questioning
- Put storytelling on your meeting agendas

PART

INSPIRE A SHARED VISION

- ENVISION THE FUTURE

- ENLIST OTHERS

ENVISION
THE FUTURE

*"You begin with the end in mind, by knowing what you dream
about accomplishing, and then figure out how to make it happen."*
Jim Pitts, Northrop Grumman Corporation

"Be an enzyme" is a refrain that Pam Omidyar, founder of HopeLab, often repeats. The idea of "be an enzyme" evolved out of her love of science—her graduate training is in plant molecular genetics—and it conveys her strong belief in the power of people to make a difference. "I love the concept of catalysts, in science and life," she says. "Enzymes are the catalysts that make possible biochemical reactions. Enzymes increase the rate of a reaction, but are not themselves consumed by the reaction. . . . In short, enzymes are nature's activists."

Pam has been an enzyme for a lot of positive change, and the creation of Re-Mission™ has been one of her most extraordinary innovations. The idea for Re-Mission was born while Pam was a research assistant in the cellular immunology lab at Stanford University. After a typical day of doing experiments on cancer cells, she was at home playing videogames, and she thought, "Wouldn't it be great if there were a game where kids could blast away at their cancer cells and also learn about what goes on in their bodies during treatment?"

Like a lot of wonderfully creative ideas, Pam's inspiration of a cancer-fighting videogame didn't immediately take flight. But eleven years later, after a stint as a consultant in the pharmaceutical industry and some serendipitous encounters, Pam founded HopeLab to turn her dream into reality.[1]

Pam's initial aspiration for HopeLab was the development of Re-Mission as a form of visualization therapy. The goals for the game evolved on the basis of the development team's belief that a well-designed videogame could improve health outcomes for adolescents with cancer by actually changing behavior, Pam tells us.

> We know that compliance to medications is often a problem for adolescents. We also know that reporting treatment complications and communication in general is a challenge for adolescents. We hypothesized that through a videogame, we might be able to help them understand why taking their meds and reporting symptoms is important and, ultimately, change their behavior. Most importantly, we wanted the game to be really fun to play—otherwise, kids would choose to play something else. We wanted to reach kids in a way that was accessible to them and at their pace, and videogames are a powerful medium in both regards.

As the work with Re-Mission progressed, the dream for HopeLab broadened. "We wanted to show that it is possible to combine top-quality product design with the best science to produce an intervention that kids find truly engaging," Pam explains. Re-Mission was the first proof that the dream was possible. Today HopeLab envisions applying the Re-Mission model to other interventions and innovations. It is taking different approaches to identify innovative solutions that will address obesity, sickle cell disease, autism, and major depressive disorders. "It's an exciting time for HopeLab," Pam says. "I want HopeLab to be a leader in a customer-centered approach to innovative solutions, tested with scientific rigor."

Pam's story illustrates how organized efforts—whether those of a company, a project, or a movement—begin in the mind's eye. Call it what you will—*vision, purpose, mission, legacy, dream, aspiration, calling,* or *personal agenda*—the point is the same. If we are going to be catalytic leaders in life, we have to be able to imagine a positive future. When we envision the future we want for ourselves and others, and when we feel passionate about the legacy we want to leave, then we are much more likely to take that first step forward. If we don't have the slightest clue about our hopes, dreams, and aspirations, then the chance that we'll take the lead is nil. In fact, we may not even see the opportunity that's right in front of us.

Exemplary leaders are forward-looking. They are able to *envision the future,* to gaze across the horizon of time and imagine the greater opportunities to come. They see something out ahead, vague as it might appear from a distance, and they imagine that extraordinary feats are possible and that the ordinary could be transformed into something noble. They are able to develop an *ideal and unique image of the future for the common good.*

But it's not just the leader's vision. It's a shared vision. We all have dreams and aspirations. We all think about the future; we all want tomorrow to be better than today. Leaders have to make sure that what they see is also something that others can see. When visions are shared they attract more people, sustain higher levels of motivation, and withstand more challenges than those that are singular.

Leaders develop the capacity to Envision the Future for themselves and others by mastering two essentials:

- Imagine the possibilities
- Find a common purpose

IMAGINE THE POSSIBILITIES

"The human being is the only animal that thinks about the future," (italics his) writes Daniel Gilbert, professor of psychology at Harvard University. "The greatest achievement of the human brain is its ability to imagine objects and episodes that do not exist in the realm of the real, and it is this ability that allows us to think about the future. . . . the human brain is an 'anticipation machine,' and 'making future' is the most important thing it does."[2]

Leaders are dreamers. Leaders are idealists. Leaders are possibility thinkers. All enterprises, big or small, begin with imagination and with the belief that what's merely an image today can one day be made real in the future. It's this belief that sustains leaders through the difficult times.[3] Turning possibility thinking into an inspiring vision—and an inspiring vision that is shared—is the leader's challenge.

Turning possibility thinking into an inspiring vision is the leader's challenge.

When we ask people to tell us where their visions come from they often have great difficulty in describing the process. And when they do provide an answer, typically it's more about a feeling, a sense, a gut reaction. Clarifying your vision, like clarifying your values, is a process of self-exploration and self-creation. It's an intuitive, emotional process. There's often no logic to it. You just feel strongly about something, and that sense, that intuition, has to be fully explored.[4] Visions are reflections of one's fundamental beliefs and assumptions about human nature, technology, economics, science, politics, art, and ethics.

A vision of the future is much like a literary or musical theme. It's the broad message that you want to convey, it's the primary melody that you want people to remember, and whenever it's repeated it reminds the audience of the entire work. Every leader needs a theme, something on which they can structure the rest of his or her performance. What's *your* central message? What's *your* theme?

Fortunately for all of us there are ways we can improve our capacity to imagine exciting possibilities and to discover the central theme for our lives. Improvement comes when you engage in conscious introspection. You need to do more to *reflect* on your past, *attend* to the present, *prospect* the future, and *feel* your passion.

Reflect on Your Past

As surprising as it might seem, in aiming for the future you need to look back into your past. Looking backward can actually enable you to see farther than if you only stare straight ahead.

Revealing research reported by University of Southern California Professor Omar A. El Sawy extends our understanding of the relevance of past experience to envisioning the future.[5] El Sawy studied chief executive officers, dividing them into two equal groups. The CEOs were asked to look ahead into their personal futures—to "think of things that might (or will) happen to you in the future." They were also asked to look into their personal pasts—to "think of the things that have happened to you in the past." In each case, they were asked to list ten events and to date each event.

One group listed the past events first; the other group listed the future events first. El Sawy then compared the past and future time horizons for the two groups. The two groups had similar past time horizons, both with a maximum of about twenty years. But, as illustrated in Table 5.1, the CEOs who listed their past events first had significantly longer future time horizons than the CEOs who listed future events first. El Sawy refers to the difference in future horizons as "the Janus Effect," after the two-faced Roman god of beginnings.

Of several plausible explanations for the Janus Effect, El Sawy supports the "one-way-mirror hypothesis." This hypothesis states, "We make sense of our world retrospectively, and all understanding originates in reflection

TABLE 5.1   THE JANUS EFFECT.

	Looked Toward Future First	Reviewed Past First
Mean time in future	1.8 years	3.2 years
Maximum time in future	5.1 years	9.2 years
Minimum time in future	0.2 years	0.4 years

and looking backward. . . . We construct the future by some kind of ex-trapolation, in which the past is prologue, and the approach to the future is backward-looking."[6]

When we gaze first into our past, we elongate our future. We also enrich our future and give it detail as we recall the richness of our past experiences.

Search your past to find the recurring theme in your life.

So to be able to envision the possibilities in the distant future, to enhance your ability to be forward-looking, look first into the past. When you do, you're likely to find that your central theme didn't just occur to you this morning. It's been there for a long time. Search your past to find the recurring theme in your life.

In addition to identifying lifelong themes, there's another benefit to looking back before looking ahead: you can gain a greater appreciation for how long it can take to fulfill aspirations. You also realize that there are many, many avenues to pursue, and that there may actually be no end in sight.

None of this is to say that the past *is* your future. Adopting this extremely dangerous perspective would be like trying to drive to the future while look-ing only in the rearview mirror. With that point of view, you'd drive yourself and your organization right off a cliff. What the Janus Effect does tell us is that it's difficult, if not impossible, to imagine going to a place we've never experienced, either actually or vicariously.

Attend to the Present

We're quite proud of the fact that we wrote *Credibility: How Leaders Gain and Lose It, Why People Demand It* through use of the Internet, thinking we were rather cool and *avant-garde*. At the time Barry was in Perth on sabbatical at the University of Western Australia; Jim was living and working in Northern California. We needed a fast and efficient way to send chapter drafts back and forth to each other. Express mail service was prohibitively expensive, and still would have taken at least a week. The regular postal service, though affordable, was agonizingly slow and would've added several months to our schedule. The Internet was our best option. Today, no one would give it a second thought, but when we did it the Internet was not available to the general public. It was available only to research institutions, government agencies, and educational institutions, thanks to ARPANET. We thought of ourselves as real pioneers as we attached files to e-mail messages and, using a program called Kermit, sent chapters halfway around the world.

Yet there was something we missed entirely—something that could have changed the course of our lives, the lives of our families, and who knows what else. If we'd been paying attention, if we'd really been seeing what was right in front of us, one of us would have jumped up and yelled, "WOW! Do you see what we're doing here? In seconds what we've composed on one desktop computer arrives on another computer half a world away. This is awesome! I bet there're millions of other people around the world who'd love to be able to do this. Why don't we write a business plan for a company that connects people virtually and allows them to communicate 24/7/365? And then let's find investors willing to take a risk on this wacky idea." But that didn't happen. In a way, our eyes were closed, leaving us blind to the possibilities. We were using a tool to do our jobs, but we didn't see its potential, we didn't envision the possibilities. The future can be right in front of us, and yet we might not even see it.

To be able to have a vision of the future, you have to be able to see the big picture—to see trends and patterns and not just one-off or one-time occurrences. John Naisbitt, the futurist best known for his book *Megatrends*, recently wrote, "In the stream of time, the future is always with us. The directions and turns the world will take are embedded in the past and in the present. We often recognize them retrospectively, but our purpose is to anticipate what lies ahead."[7] Leaders peek behind the curtain to see what is hiding there. They see the future as a picture puzzle and figure out how all the pieces fit together. They rummage through the bits and bytes of data that accumulate daily and notice how they relate to each other. Envisioning the future is not about gazing into a fortune-teller's crystal ball; it's about paying attention to the little things that are going on all around them and being able to recognize patterns that point to the future.

Prospect the Future

Even as you stop, look, and listen to messages you're being sent in the present, you also need to raise your head and gaze out toward the horizon. Being forward-looking is not the same as meeting the deadline for your current project. Leaders have to prospect the future. They have to be on the lookout for emerging developments in technology, demographics, economics, politics, arts, and all aspects of life inside and outside the organization. They have to anticipate what might be coming just over the hill and around the corner.

As one of the leaders we interviewed told us, "I'm my organization's futures department." We think all leaders should view themselves this way. Leaders need to spend considerable time reading about, thinking about, and talking about the long-term view, not only for their specific organization, but also for the environment in which they operate.

Yet despite the expectation that leaders need to spend time thinking about the future, the attention that senior management tends to devote to building a collective perspective on the future is woefully inadequate. Researchers estimate that the time spent by senior managers on being forward-looking is only about 3 percent of their total time.[8] That's a pathetic percentage given the responsibility they have for the future of their organizations. Leaders need to be much more proactive in thinking about the future than they are currently, and this imperative increases with the leader's scope and level of responsibility. Naturally, all roles require attention to the present and the future; it's only the ratio that varies.

As we illustrate in Figure 5.1, when a leader's role is strategic (as it is for a CEO, president, or research director, for example), the time orientation is longer term and more future-oriented than it is for a leader whose role is more tactical (for example, a production supervisor or operations manager). There is no hard and fast rule as to how far into the future a leader should look. For those on the front lines of supervision, the future might be a year from now. For those in middle levels it might be three to five years. At the more senior levels it should be at least ten, and executive leaders responsible for entire organizations in the national and international arenas have to look out twenty years and beyond.

Dan Schwab is director of training and organizational development for The Trust for Public Land, and he's always searching for ways to get people to think more about influencing the future. With an organizational mission to conserve land for human use across the United States you might think that every one of the Trust's 450-member staff in forty-five locations would be

FIGURE 5.1 MIX OF PRESENT-FUTURE TIME ORIENTATIONS OF LEADERS.

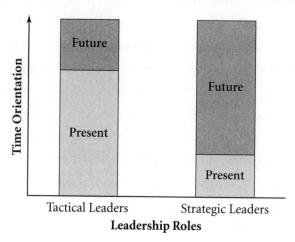

thinking long term. But, just as in lots of other organizations, that's not always the case. "What we do is about helping people create a more livable future for their communities, and that is a very powerful thing," says Dan. "But it's surprising how little skill people have in being forward-looking, or how little effort most of us invest in learning to do this." Dan, like many of us, knows that it's very hard to think long term. "Humans are hardwired to live in the here and now. When we were living on the savannah millions of years ago, I don't think we had the luxury to be looking very far ahead. It was all about 'today.' We don't have examples around us of people saying, 'Here's a vision of where we can be in ten years.' In the modern world, much of the problem is workload, of course—we're all really busy—but it's more than that. You have to discipline yourself to look over the horizon."

That's why Dan is always looking for ways to extend people's vision. "I like to send around articles from publications like *The Futurist* and get people to pay closer attention to the demographic changes taking place in America. Things are changing dramatically and unpredictably all around us." He also spends a lot of time connecting people—in person or in Web conferences—to talk to each other about how the future is coming to us faster all the time.

At new hire orientations he asks those who've just joined, "Where do you want to see this organization in five years? In ten years? What is your vision of what we could be?" He also helps people to think big. "In our regional retreats and other training sessions, I say to people 'What would happen if you got an unsolicited call from a major donor saying he would match us 50 percent to double public shoreline access to Puget Sound? Would you be ready to respond?' You have to think big to attract big resources." Why does Dan spend so much energy and effort building skills in envisioning the future? Because, says Dan, "One of the greatest gifts you can give others is the understanding that they can think bigger things than they believe they can. It's contagious. What limits vision in an organization is nobody being willing to speak up for one. But once you do, there is a sort of avalanche or landslide factor; it just keeps rolling."

Visions are future-oriented and are made real over different spans of time. It may take three years from the time you decide to climb a mountain until you actually reach the summit. It may take a decade to build a company that is one of the best places to work. It may take a lifetime to make neighborhoods safe again for little children to walk alone to the corner store. It may take a century to restore a forest destroyed by a wildfire. It may take generations to set a people free.

The point is that leaders must spend time thinking about the future and become better able to project themselves ahead in time. The percentage of time you spend on performing a task is related to how proficient you are at it, and that goes as much for envisioning the future as it does for managing your money. You have to spend more of today thinking more about tomorrow if your future is going to be an improvement over the present.

Feel Your Passion

There's another reason why the two of us didn't see the potential of the Internet back in the 1990s, and that's because we didn't care all that much about it. We didn't feel any passion for the technology. Our passion was for something else. We had, and have, a passion for liberating the leader in everyone, and to us the Internet was

> *Passion and attention go hand in hand.*

simply a convenient and cool tool for doing just that. Passion and attention go hand in hand. People don't see the possibilities when they don't feel the passion.

In the final analysis, what you envision for the future is really all about expressing your passion. It's all about what gets you up in the morning and won't let you sleep at night. It's all about something that you find so important that you're willing to put in the time, suffer the inevitable setbacks, and make the necessary sacrifices. Once you've reflected on the past, attended to the present, and prospected in the future you've got to step back and ask yourself, What *is* my burning passion?

One of University of Cincinnati president Nancy L. Zimpher's great passions is urban education. She is not content to watch the status quo—the achievement gaps, low test scores and high drop-out rates—continue without trying to achieve a better future. Couple that passion with a deep belief in the power of shared vision and you have a leader who consistently and persistently keeps the focus on the future, no matter what the audience or setting.

"Vision trumps everything," Nancy says. "Organizations are most effective when a well-articulated and ambitious vision of the future exists." That's exactly what UC's trustees wanted to hear when they were looking for a new university president; they wanted UC to have a clear and compelling image of what its next level of greatness would be. So when Nancy arrived to take the president's job in October 2003 she immersed herself in meetings, phone calls, lunches, dinners, and other activities to get in touch with UC stakeholders to hear their ideas about what the university's future might look like. Then she initiated an imaginative process of consultation that continued through the following April. "We astounded even ourselves," she says. "Our process proved to be unprecedented. We seemed to tap into a hunger to speak, to move this institution forward into a new level of greatness." Through eight town hall meetings involving 240 people, more than ninety input sessions with some 2,400 people participating, and a Web site that garnered thousands of hits, the full range of campus constituents—from donors, students, faculty, union leaders, and administrators to business partners, educational partners, alumni, and civic leaders—worked with Nancy to map out their vision of the university's future, which was unveiled at her inauguration in May 2004 as "UC/21: Defining the New Urban Research University."

That wasn't all. As soon as she arrived on campus at UC, Nancy approached her colleagues in other higher education institutions in the area—Xavier University's Father Michael Graham and Northern Kentucky University's James Votruba—to open a conversation on how they could work together to make a greater impact on the region. As first small steps, they began to collaborate on teacher recognition and helping victims of the December 2004 tsunami and Hurricanes Katrina and Rita. Eventually, by keeping the conversation focused on the education pipeline for the region, Nancy helped guide the formation of an unprecedented regional partnership aimed at getting students into and graduating from college. "I started my career as a teacher, and I have always held a very strong belief that education is the key to success. It's so important, not just for the individual student, but for our community and for our quality of life. And in the twenty-first century, a college education matters more than ever." Launched on August 16, 2006, after years of relationship-building, that partnership, called Strive, involves the public school districts in Cincinnati; Covington, Kentucky; and Newport, Kentucky, along with the region's Catholic urban schools on both sides of the Ohio River, all higher education institutions in the area, and business, civic, and nonprofit partners. The partnership is for the first time providing an age 0–21 approach to meeting students' needs by strategically coordinating social support and educational resources in the region.

Leaders want to do something significant, to accomplish something that no one else has yet achieved. What that something is—your sense of meaning and purpose—has to come from within. No one can impose a self-motivating vision on you. That's why, just as we said about values, you must first clarify your own visions of the future before you can expect to enlist others in a shared vision.

Researchers in human motivation have long talked about two kinds of motivation—extrinsic and intrinsic.[9] People do things either because of external controls—the possibility of a tangible reward if they succeed or punishment if they don't—or because of an internal desire. People do something because they feel forced, or because they want to. People do something to please others, or because it pleases them. Which condition is more likely to produce extraordinary results?

On this, the research is very clear. External motivation is more likely to create conditions of compliance or defiance; self-motivation produces far superior results. There's even an added bonus. People who are self-motivated will keep working toward a result even if there's no reward. But people who are externally controlled are likely to stop trying once the rewards or punishments are removed. In this case, as psychologist and motivational expert Edward Deci has so aptly put it, "Stop the pay, and stop the play."[10]

Your personal passion for something is the best indicator of what you find most worthwhile. It's the clue to what you find intrinsically rewarding. For example, David Kretz, engineering program manager at Lam Research Corporation, realized that "finding something you truly believe in" is the key to articulating a vision in the first place. Once you're in touch with this inner feeling, he says, then you can look and think "beyond the constraints of your current position and viewpoint into the future. This is how you connect your various tasks and team projects to how they help convert that feeling, and vision, into a reality."

We all have concerns, desires, questions, propositions, arguments, hopes, and dreams—core issues that can help us organize our aspirations and actions. We have a few things that are much more important to us than others. Whatever it is, you need to be able to name it for yourself so that you can talk about it with others.

Exemplary leaders have a passion for something other than their own fame and fortune. They care about making a difference in the world. If you don't care deeply for and about something and someone, then how can you expect others to feel any sense of conviction? How can you expect others to get jazzed, if you're not energized and excited? How can you expect others to suffer through the long hours, hard work, absences from home, and personal sacrifices if you're not similarly committed? Passion is the precursor to compassion!

FIND A COMMON PURPOSE

At some point during all this talk over the years about the importance of being future-oriented, leaders got the sense that they were the ones that had to be the visionaries. Often with the encouragement of a lot of leadership developers, including us, leaders came to assume that if others expected them to be forward-looking, then they had to go off alone into the wilderness, climb to the top of some mountain, sit in lotus position, wait for a revelation, and then go out and announce to the world what they foresee. Leaders have assumed that it's their vision that matters, and if it's their vision then *they* have to create it.

Wrong! This is *not* what constituents expect. Yes, leaders are expected to be forward-looking, but they aren't expected to impose their vision of the future on others. What people really want to hear is not simply the *leader's* vision. They want to hear about *their own* aspirations. They want to hear how their dreams will come true and their hopes will be fulfilled. They want to see themselves in the picture of the future that the leader is painting. The very best leaders understand that their key task is inspiring a *shared* vision, not selling their own idiosyncratic view of the world.

Noted author and futurist Joel Barker uses a historical analogy to provide insight into how leaders can engage others in their quest to discover what lies ahead. "Before a good wagon master rolled the wagons, he sent out scouts to see what was over the horizon," Joel explains. "Rapid exploration by scouts provided crucial information that allowed the wagon master to make quicker decisions with higher confidence and move the wagons forward at a faster pace. . . . Twenty-first-century leaders need their own scouts. But instead of searching the geography of place, your scouts need to search the geography of time. The most important frontier for you is the next five to ten years."[11]

> You can't mobilize people to willingly travel to places they don't want to go.

Your constituents are your scouts. You need to get everyone involved in asking, What's next? Where is this assignment right now taking us *in the future*? You need to talk out loud about the implications of the things you're now doing—the second- and third-order consequences. You need to sit around the campfire and together answer the question, What is the legacy we want to leave?

You can't mobilize people to willingly travel to places they don't want to go. No matter how grand the dream of an individual visionary, if others don't see in it the possibility of realizing their own hopes and desires, they won't follow willingly. Leaders must show others how they, too, will be served by the long-term vision of the future, how their specific needs can be satisfied.

Listen Deeply to Others

One talent leaders need to strengthen is the ability to hear what is important to others. By knowing their constituents, by listening to them, and by taking their advice, leaders are able to give voice to constituents' feelings. They're able to stand before others and say with assurance, "Here's what I heard you say that you want for yourselves. Here's how your own needs and interests will be served by enlisting in a common cause." In a sense, leaders hold up a mirror and reflect back to their constituents what they say they most desire. For many, this may be easier said than done.

By his own admission, listening didn't come very naturally to Jim Schwappach. As a U.S. Naval Academy graduate and former submarine officer, he was more used to simply leading by example than getting others to envision the future. Moreover, he believed that "since management was in the position of authority they were the rightful sources of vision and strategic direction." Now working in the private sector as a marketing manager, Jim has come to realize that "enlisting subordinates and other colleagues in defining the vision for the team pays off because the ideas that form the vision will be familiar to them and as a result it will be easier to get the buy-in that is essential for translating a single person's view to the rest of the team." Still, he couldn't accomplish this unilaterally.

> I began to actively and deeply listen to people. I started a collaborative, open environment so as to promote the free exchange of ideas. In turn, people began opening up with one another and actively talking about substantive improvements that they feel could be made to the organization as a whole.

I started meeting individually with each of them, asking questions as to what they thought were the key issues and best alternatives, and incorporating their feedback into our decisions. I asked people what they were proud of, what brought them to work every day, what management was doing well, and where they were blowing it. More importantly, once I asked the questions, I stopped and focused directly on the person answering. I found at first that some people were startled by the attention. After a few tries though, the level of response and the value of those responses in contributing to defining a vision for our team grew immeasurably. I also began spending more time going out and visiting my employees' and colleagues' workspaces, and this increase in interaction allowed me to benefit from their varied perspectives and further enabled us to craft a vision that we can call our own.

Leaders know very well that the seeds of any vision arise not from crystal-ball gazing in upper levels of the organization's stratosphere but from images passed on from people on the front line about what the clients or customers really want or from manufacturing's mumblings about poor product quality. The best leaders, like Jim, are great listeners. They listen carefully to what other people have to say, and how they feel. They have to ask good (and often tough) questions, be open to ideas other than their own, and even lose arguments in favor of the common good.[12]

Leaders find the common thread that weaves the fabric of human needs into a colorful tapestry. They develop a deep understanding of collective yearnings; they seek out the brewing consensus among those they would lead. They listen carefully for quiet whisperings and attend to subtle cues. They get a sense of what people want, what they value, and what they dream about. Sensitivity to others is no trivial skill; rather, it is a truly precious human ability. But it isn't complex: it requires receptiveness to other people and a willingness to listen. As Jim discovered, it means getting out of the office and spending time with people out in the field or on the factory floor or in the showroom or warehouse or back room. It means being delicately aware of the attitudes and feelings of others and the nuances of their communication.

Determine What's Meaningful to Others

When you listen deeply you can find out what gives work its meaning to others. The most important reason people give for staying with an organization is that they like the work they are doing, that they find it challenging, meaningful, and purposeful.[13] Indeed, when you listen with sensitivity to the aspirations of others you can discover that there are common values that link everyone together:[14]

- A chance to be tested, to make it on one's own
- A chance to take part in a social experiment
- A chance to do something well
- A chance to do something good
- A chance to change the way things are

Aren't these the essence of what most leadership challenges and opportunities are all about?

What people want has not changed very dramatically through the years. Even though job security is increasingly tenuous, regardless of industry or location, workers rank "interesting work" well above "high income." And quality of leadership ("working for a leader with vision and values") is more motivating than dollars. The most frequently mentioned measure of success in work life? Would it surprise you to learn that "personal satisfaction for doing a good job" is cited between three and four times as often as "getting ahead" or "making a good living"?[15]

These findings suggest that there's more to work than is commonly assumed. There's rich opportunity for leaders to appeal to more than just the material rewards. Great leaders, like great companies and countries, create meaning and not just money. For example, Mei Chih-Chen, controller at Ravix Group, is passionate about the quality of everything she does, even when it comes to something as mundane, but absolutely critical to her company's success, as financial reports. When taking over responsibility for the annual audit, she spoke with her staff not so much about the nuts-and-bolts of their tasks but on the larger purpose for getting their work done properly and efficiently. She carefully explained the bigger picture behind why their schedule is so critical, how many others are counting on her group's performance (and accuracy) so that they can do their jobs well, and what it means to produce at an extraordinary level. Mei took the time to show them specific examples of the difference between simply completing their tasks and doing great work, and appealed directly to their pride and sense of self-worth. From the explicit link to their interests and values, the audit staff gained a richer appreciation of their common purpose. "To my amazement," she told us, "the staff started to prepare schedules, make entries, perform analyses, and the like, ahead of time and without any reminders on my part. They understood that what they were doing was not number-crunching but work that really matters."

There is this deep desire within each of us to make a difference. We want to know that we've done something on this earth, that there's a purpose to our existence. Work can provide that purpose, and increasingly work is where men and women seek it. Work has become a place where people pursue meaning and identity.[16] Like Mei, the best organizational leaders are able to bring out and make use of this human longing by communicating the meaning and significance of the organization's work so that people understand their own important role in creating it. When leaders clearly communicate a shared vision of an organization, they ennoble those who work on its behalf. They elevate the human spirit.

Make It a Cause for Commitment

People commit to causes, not to plans. How else do you explain why people volunteer to rebuild communities ravaged by a tsunami, ride a bike from San Francisco to Los Angeles to raise money to fight AIDS, or rescue people from the rubble of a collapsed building after an earthquake? How else do you explain why people toil 24/7 to create the next big thing when the probability of failure is 60–70 percent? People are not committing to the plan in any of these cases. There may not even be a plan to commit to. They are committing to something much bigger, something much more compelling than goals and milestones on a piece of paper. That's not to say that plans aren't important to executing on grand dreams. They absolutely are. It's just to say that the plan isn't the thing that people are committing to. The most successful strategies are visions.[17] As McGill University professor Henry Mintzberg has observed, "Calculated strategies have no value in and of themselves. . . . Strategies take on value only as committed people infuse them with energy."[18]

> *People commit to causes, not to plans.*

The kind of leadership that gets people to infuse their energy into strategies is called transformational leadership. According to Pulitzer Prize–winning author and historian James MacGregor Burns, transformational leadership occurs when, in their interactions, people "raise one another to higher levels of motivation and morality. Their purposes, which might have started out as separate but related, as in the case of transactional leadership, become fused. . . . But transforming leadership ultimately becomes moral in that it raises the level of human conduct and ethical aspiration of both the leader and the led, and thus it has a transforming effect on both."[19]

When people are part of something that raises them to higher levels of motivation and morality they develop a belonging to something very special. This sense of belonging is particularly key in tumultuous times. When Jack Shiefer was an AT&T branch manager he learned just how important it was to raise levels of motivation as he and his team set forth to grow their business in the midst of some of the most challenging times in the telecommunications industry.

As Jack tells it, "We knew we had a problem as a team because we weren't a team. But none of us knew what to do to become one. We were too close to it." They began their quest to become a world-class sales organization with a leadership team offsite workshop based on The Five Practices of Exemplary Leadership framework. A decade later, Jack still acknowledges and confirms that the team was initially acquiescent, but not totally committed. Then, as the discussion moved to the idea of a shared vision, "you could feel the energy change in the room from a very casual attitude to—all of a sudden—becoming electric." The difference came when the members of the group "became committed to a journey to find out what to do to become more effective as leaders and help our associates grow."

At first, "the horizon that we were looking at was maybe a month to three months." They quickly saw that they needed a vision that would work, no matter what change was occurring, something that would stand the test of time. To get there, they shared with each other the heartfelt desires they each had for their sales center and for the kind of leaders they wanted to become. From that initial groundbreaking, the vision of a world-class sales organization, grounded in quality and reflecting a renewed commitment to their customers, their families, and each other, was born.

Theirs was much more than a one-time exercise to craft a slick-sounding statement; it was the creation of a new culture of success built on superior results and "values-based leadership." Has their vision work been helpful? In an industry in which pricing has dropped through the floor, annual associate turnover has averaged 30 percent, and massive, gut-wrenching business-unit-wide reorganizations have occurred almost every year, Jack's team has continued to put up astonishing results. Jack feels so strongly about the sales center's vision and their continuing attention to it that he says, "You have nothing to lose and everything to gain by accepting the possibility that a shared vision and a commitment to it will allow your professional life and your personal life to be richer than they are today." With the zealousness of a converted skeptic (and a businessman interested in delivering results as cost-effectively as possible), he says, "Inspiring a shared vision is the most efficient way to produce outstanding results."

Be Forward-Looking in Times of Rapid Change

In this digital age when the business world is changing at warp speed, people often ask, "How can I have a vision of what's going to happen five or ten years from now, when I don't even know what's going to happen next week?"

Venture capitalist Geoff Yang has taken risks on many new technology companies that are expected to move at a rapid pace. What types of innovators is he willing to back? "Men and women with great vision," he says. "They are able to recognize patterns when others see chaos in the marketplace. That's how they spot unexploited niche opportunities. And they are passionate about their ideas, which are revolutionary ways to change the way people live their lives or the way businesses operate. When they come to me they have conviction." [20]

Look at it this way. Imagine you're driving along the Pacific Coast Highway heading south from San Francisco on a bright, sunny day. The hills are on your left; the ocean, on your right. On some curves, the cliffs plunge several hundred feet to the water. You can see for miles and miles. You're cruising along at the speed limit, tunes blaring, top down, wind in your hair, and not a care in the world. Suddenly, without warning, you come around a bend in the road and there's a blanket of fog as thick as you've ever seen it. What do you do?

We've asked this question many, many times, and we get the same answers:

- I slow way down.
- I turn my lights on.
- I grab the steering wheel with both hands.
- I tense up.
- I sit up straight or lean forward.
- I turn the music off so I can hear better.

Then you go around the next curve in the road, the fog lifts, and it's clear again. What do you do? Relax, speed up, turn the lights off, put the music back on, and enjoy the scenery.

This analogy illustrates the importance of clarity of vision, especially when you're going fast. Are you able to go faster when it's foggy or when it's clear? How fast can you drive in the fog without risking your own or other people's lives? How comfortable are you riding in a car with someone else who drives fast in the fog? The answers are obvious, aren't they? We're better able to go fast when our vision is clear. We're better able to anticipate the switchbacks and bumps in the road when we can see ahead. There are always going to be times when the sun hides behind the clouds or the fog makes it difficult to maneuver, but when it comes to traveling at Internet speed it's definitely preferable to be able to see farther ahead.

The point is simply this: to become a leader you must be able to envision the future. The speed of change doesn't alter this fundamental truth about leadership. People only want to follow those who can see beyond today's problems and visualize a brighter tomorrow.

REFLECTION AND ACTION: ENVISIONING THE FUTURE

The most important role of visions in organizational life is to give focus to human energy. To enable everyone concerned with an enterprise to see more clearly what's ahead of them, leaders must have and convey an exciting and ennobling vision of the future. The path to clarity of visions begins with reflecting on the past, moves to attending to the present, and then goes prospecting into the future. But in the end, it's all about passion, about what people care about most deeply. Leaders can't effectively and authentically lead others to places they personally don't want to go.

While they have to be clear about their own visions before they can expect others to follow them, leaders must keep in mind that it's not one person's vision that people will willingly follow. If the vision is to be attractive to more than an insignificant few, it must appeal to all who have a stake in it. Only *shared* visions have the magnetic power to sustain commitment over time. Whether you're leading a small department of ten, a large organization of ten thousand, or a community of a hundred thousand, a shared vision sets the agenda and gives direction and purpose to the enterprise. It begins and ends with listening. Listening to the voices of all your constituents. Listening for their hopes, dreams, and aspirations. And because a common vision spans years and keeps everyone focused on the future, it has to be more than a job; it has to be a cause, something meaningful, something that makes a difference in people's lives.

In the action steps that follow, we offer some practical guidance in enhancing your own capacity to Envision the Future and to be open to the possibilities.

Determine the "Something" You Want to Do

Are you in your job to do something, or are you in your job for something to do? If your answer is "to do something," take out a sheet of paper and at the top write, "What I want to accomplish." Now make a list of all the things that you want to achieve on the job. For each item, ask yourself, "Why do I want this?" Keep on asking why until you run out of reasons. By doing this exercise, you're likely to discover those few higher-order values that are the idealized ends for which you strive.

Here are some additional questions that you can use as catalysts in clarifying your vision:

- How would I like to change the world for myself and our organization?
- How do I want to be remembered?
- If I could invent the future, what future would I invent for myself and my organization?
- What mission in life absolutely obsesses me?
- What's my dream about my work?
- What's my most distinctive skill or talent?
- What's my burning passion?
- What work do I find absorbing, involving, and enthralling?

- What will happen in ten years if I remain absorbed, involved, and enthralled in that work?
- What does my ideal organization look like?
- What's my personal agenda? What do I want to prove?

Take all the information you've just gathered and write your ideal and unique image of the future for yourself and for your organization.

Picture What You Will Do Next

Imagination, some have asserted, is more important than intelligence, and this is even more true for leaders dealing with rapidly changing times. But often the mundane day-to-day realities of dealing with problems bogs us down, and thinking about how to get beyond today's difficulties gets over-looked or forgotten. So try thinking more about what you're going to do *after* the current problem, task, assignment, project, or program has been completed. "What's next?" should be a question you frequently ask yourself.

Here's a useful way to calibrate how distant your time horizon should be. Answer this question: "When is the scheduled completion date for the longest-term project for which I am accountable?" Got that date? Okay, now ask yourself, "What will we be doing after that's over?" Have you given any thought to that question? You should. Whether that project ends one year, five years, or ten years down the road, your job as a leader is to think beyond that end date. If you're not thinking about what's happening after the completion of your longest-term project, then you're thinking only as long-term as everyone else. In other words, you're redundant! The leader's job is to think about the next project, and the one after that, and the one after that.

Great football coaches, for example, aren't thinking about the current play being called on the field—that's the execution left up to the players, and they'll be either successful or not. What the coach is thinking about is the play *after* this one, considering all the possibilities before even knowing the outcome of the play currently being executed. Similarly, Grand Master bridge or chess players (or even poker players) aren't simply thinking about their next play but are considering possible permutations that could emerge in the play after that one. The same is true in all sports and games. That's what you should be doing—thinking about what you and your team will be undertaking after what you're currently working on has been completed. As a leader you need to be thinking a few "moves" ahead of your team and picturing the possibilities.

Survey Your Constituents About Their Aspirations

The first consideration in learning about your constituents' aspirations is to be sure you're thinking broadly enough about who makes up your constituent group. Make a list of all the individuals or groups of individuals you want to enlist in your vision of the future. Your organizational managers and any direct reports obviously are on the list. In all probability, you'll also want your peers, customers, and suppliers to buy into your dream. Perhaps you'll want the support of the citizens of your local community, state, or even nation. You may even have a global vision. Don't limit your list to only present constituents. As your organization grows and develops, it will want to attract new people to it. The point is this: identify those who have a stake today and will have a stake tomorrow in the outcomes of what you envision.

Once you've identified your constituents, conduct what the marketing folks call "focus groups" with your key constituencies. Ask them to tell you about what they like and don't like about your product, services, programs, policies, leadership practices, and so on. But don't stop there. Ask them things such as the following:

- If you could create your ideal company, what would it look like?
- What are the qualities that would make this organization a great place to work?
- Describe the kind of organization that'd make you say, "I can't wait to go to work there (or shop there, or invest there)".
- As you look ahead five or ten years, tell us about the kind of organization, community, or world you would like to see.

- What are your hopes and dreams for you and your family?
- What keeps you awake at night?
- What drives you to do the very best you know how?

There are hundreds of questions like these. The idea is to probe and then listen to the voices of your constituents talking about their hopes, dreams, and aspirations. You want to know what motivates and drives them. In the process, it's important that your constituents know you value their opinions, and that you are listening carefully to their thoughts. What's more, in focus group or forum settings you benefit from the way people bounce ideas off one another. You also get a chance to test whether one person or group's needs are idiosyncratic or commonly held. Everyone learns in this process about what it takes to work together to achieve common objectives.

COMMITMENT NUMBER 3

Envision the Future

Essentials of Envisioning the Future

- Imagine the possibilities
- Find a common purpose

Taking Action

- Determine the "something" you want to do
- Picture what you will do next
- Survey your constituents about their aspirations

ENLIST OTHERS

*"You have to paint a powerfully compelling picture of the future
for people to want to align with the vision."*
Vicky Ngo-Roberti, VMware, Inc.

"What really drives performance," Keith Sonberg told us, "is not metrics. It's passion plus pride equals performance. I call it the three P's. The leader's job is to create an environment where people are passionate about what they're doing and take pride in what they're doing. The end result will always be performance." For Keith, director of site operations for Roche in Palo Alto, California, and his team, the three P's are all about sustainability, a vision of a company that delivers a triple bottom line. "We want to be environmentally sound, economically viable, and socially just," Keith explained.

This new vision of sustainability began in 2002 when Keith was delivering his annual "state-of the-union" speech to the seventy-five employees in site operations. That year he asked everyone—the mechanics, engineers, security people, folks from shipping and receiving, and the service groups—to reflect on a question Keith felt passionate about. "What's the legacy that you're leaving behind?" he asked. "When you're no longer here, no longer at Roche, or no longer on this earth, what is it that people will remember you for? What would you like them to remember you for?"

This is not exactly the kind of thing you expect to hear at an operations review, but that year Keith wanted to infuse renewed energy into the organization and more fully engage people. "With that in mind," he asked, "how are you going to approach your job and your life so that you are creating a legacy you can be proud of?"

For Keith, the answer was clear. "There's no greater legacy," he said, "than a positive environmental legacy. There was a great opportunity for people to really feel a passion for creating this legacy." So he met with his management team and they talked about a new vision for the organization, one that would engage everyone and inspire great pride and passion every day they came to work—and went home from work. "It was my vision of a legacy, and I wanted to make sure it was a compelling vision. . . . I absolutely felt that this was something that would benefit everyone, that would have an impact on people, and that at the end of the day would change people."

So Keith told his team, "Sustainability is about more than just daily operations that are environmentally friendly. This is something bigger. This is our responsibility, and that responsibility is something that we can't turn our backs on. We've got all these fantastic skills that we've developed over the years to make our business great. Now we have to take those same skills and focus them on sustainability in a way that really makes an impact. That's our responsibility." Then Keith popped the question. "Do you accept that responsibility?"

Indeed they did. "Once we talked about it," Keith told us, "it was a challenge that they could embrace and get behind as well." Then they took it a step further. "We wanted to be completely transformed," Keith said. "We wanted to do something that you go home and talk about." Beyond the vision and mission statements, Keith and his team developed a program with seven categories of projects—including energy conservation, natural resources conservation, recycling, green engineering and construction, and employee and community growth and development. They started to document everything, including developing manuals so they could share their successes with others. They wanted to become a model for what an organization could do to create sustainability.

When you listen to Keith you can't help but get caught up in his enthusiasm and excitement. He inspires you to accept your own responsibility for the future of the planet, and he enables you to see how that makes for good business. And for Keith, like all the leaders who enlist others in a common vision, it all comes down to something fairly simple and straightforward. "Have a passion for making a difference in people's lives," he said, "and at the end of the day that's what it's all about."

In the personal-best cases that we collected, people frequently talked about the need to get everyone on board with a vision and to enlist others in a dream. People talked about how they had to communicate and build support for the direction in which the organization was headed. These leaders knew that in order to get extraordinary things done everyone had to fervently believe in and commit to a common purpose.

We've also learned from our research that constituents expect their leaders to be *inspiring*. A shared vision of the future is necessary, but insufficient, to achieve extraordinary results. We all need vast reserves of energy and excitement to sustain our commitment to a distant dream, and leaders are expected to be a major source of that energy. We're not going to follow someone who's only mildly enthusiastic about something. They have to be *wildly* enthusiastic for us to give it our all.

Whether they're trying to mobilize a crowd in the grandstand or one person in the office, to Enlist Others leaders must improve their capacities to act on these two essentials:

- **Appeal to common ideals**
- **Animate the vision**

Successfully engaging in these two essentials can produce very powerful results. In our research we found that when leaders effectively communicate a vision—whether it's to one person, a small group, or a large organization—constituents report significantly higher levels of job satisfaction, motivation, commitment, loyalty, team spirit, productivity, and profitability. Clearly there's a big payoff to bringing the vision to life.

APPEAL TO COMMON IDEALS

In every personal-best case leaders talked about ideals. They expressed a desire to make dramatic changes in the business-as-usual environment. They reached for something grand, something majestic, something magnificent, something that had never been done before.

Visions are about ideals—hopes, dreams, and aspirations. They're about our strong desire to achieve something great. They're ambitious. They're expressions of optimism. Can you imagine a leader enlisting others in a cause by saying, "I'd like you to join me in doing the ordinary better"? Not likely. Visions necessarily stretch us to imagine exciting possibilities, breakthrough technologies, or revolutionary social change.

Ideals reveal our higher-order value preferences. They represent our ultimate economic, technological, political, social, and aesthetic priorities. The ideals of world peace, freedom, justice, a comfortable life, happiness, and self-respect are among the ultimate strivings of our existence—the ones that we

> *Visions are ideals.*

seek to attain over the long term. They're statements of the idealized purpose that we hope all our practical actions will enable us to attain.

By focusing on the ideal we gain a sense of meaning and purpose from what we undertake. When leaders communicate visions they should be talking to people about how they are going to make a difference in the world, how they are going to have an impact.

Connect to What's Meaningful to Others

In Chapter Five we talked about how it's essential for leaders to understand what's meaningful to others. In communicating a shared vision, leaders have to bring these ideals into the conversation. Remember, exemplary leaders don't impose their visions of the future on people—as if one could in this day and age—they liberate the vision that's already in their constituents. They awaken dreams, breathe life into them, and arouse the belief that we can achieve something grand.

When leaders talk about visions of the future, it's not all about the numbers, about revenue earned, growth rates, or returns to shareholders. Those things are certainly extremely important concerns for leaders and constituents, but they don't get people enthused and energized over the long haul. What truly pulls people forward, especially in the more difficult times, is the exciting possibility that what they are doing can make a profound difference to the future of their families, friends, colleagues, customers, and communities. They want to know that what they do matters.

When Preethi Chandrasekhar was put in charge of a newly developed technical support center for a VOIP company, she understood that others would be looking to her for direction and for setting standards. However, she quickly realized that in order to make the vision exciting and relevant to her team, she needed to make it meaningful. So she started out by having informational sessions in which she and the team members talked about the "big picture" and why their work matters: What difference do we make for this company and for our customers? How will our working together make a difference?

She proceeded to ask the team to continue thinking about a vision and a set of objectives. She conducted a follow-up brainstorming session in which everyone shared their ideas and suggestions on what they needed to do to reduce call volume, improve customer wait times, and reduce the time reps spent on the telephone. Preethi recalled, "I could see the team was motivated, and each individual took it upon themselves to provide thoughtful insights on how we could improve the call center." But it was always important, she told us, "to keep focusing on the big picture, while still concentrating on the details that would enable us to realize these aspirations."

While Preethi searched for a unique way to communicate to her team the meaning and significance of their work, what she discovered was that she could do something each and every day to keep people focused and excited about their vision. "All of us have the power within ourselves to accomplish whatever we desire," she told us, and, more important, she found ways each and every day to repeat this statement to the members of the call center in the context of achieving their shared vision. She made sure that each team member could repeat the vision, not just by rote but from the heart, and she showed how their individual and collective efforts could make a positive difference. "We put pride back in the workplace," Preethi observed. "We would be the envy of the company when it came to enjoying our work, basking in one another's accomplishments, and making our customers' lives not just easier but more productive. After all, what's better than being the geniuses who can answer other people's questions?"

In time, Preethi's message became a march. Everyone could connect with these ideas and aspirations. Each member of the team could easily see how they would answer a friend's question, "So, why do you work there?" Preethi lifted them up from the humdrum mechanics associated with the call center— or any workplace for that matter—and reminded them about the nobility of what they accomplish.

Leaders help people see that what they are doing is bigger than themselves and bigger, even, than the business. It's something noble. It's something that lifts their moral and motivational levels. When people go to bed at night they can sleep a little easier knowing that others are able to live a better life because of what they did that day.

Take Pride in Being Unique

Exemplary leaders also communicate what makes us—our work group or organization—and our product or service singular and unequaled. Compelling visions set us apart from everyone else. Visions must differentiate us from others if we're to attract and retain employees, volunteers, customers, clients, donors, or investors.[1] There's no advantage in working for, buying from, or investing in an organization that does exactly the same thing as the one across the street or down the hall. Saying, "Welcome to our company. We're just like everyone else," doesn't exactly make the spine tingle with excitement. When people understand how we're truly distinctive and how we stand out in the crowd they're a lot more eager to voluntarily sign up and invest their energies.

Compelling visions set us apart from everyone else.

Uniqueness fosters pride. It boosts the self-respect and self-esteem of everyone associated with the organization. The prouder all of us are of the places we shop, the products or services we buy, the school we (or our children) attend, the community in which we live, or the place we work, the more loyal we're likely to be.

Answer this question: Why should your customers or clients want to buy your service or product, attend your school, enroll in your program, or listen to your sermon?

The late Edward Goeppner, former managing partner of the Podesta Baldocchi flower shop, one of the oldest businesses in San Francisco and one of the oldest, continuously operating floral-design businesses in the United States, offered a simple yet eloquent response to the question of "Why should people want to buy from you?" He said, "We don't sell flowers, we sell beauty." Customers of a florist do exchange money for a dozen roses, but what they're really buying is something more than that; they want to beautify their homes, or express their love for others, or brighten the day. It doesn't take vision to sell a flower on a street corner, but it does take vision to sell beauty.

Uniqueness also makes it possible for smaller units within large organizations, or neighborhoods within large cities, to have their own visions while still encompassed by the collective vision. While every unit within a corporation, public agency, religious institution, school, or volunteer association must be aligned with the overall organizational vision, it can express its distinctive purpose within the larger whole. Every function and every department can differentiate itself by finding its most distinctive qualities. Each can be proud of its ideal and unique image of its future as it works toward the common future of the larger organization.

These days, though, with the latest and greatest available in a nanosecond at the touch of a key, it's become increasingly difficult to differentiate yourself from others. Log on to any Internet search engine, type in a key word, and up come thousands, sometimes tens of thousands, of sites and offerings. And it's not just the speed and volume of information that creates problems. It's a sea of sameness out there. Towns around the world are looking the same. Whether you're in the United Kingdom or the United States, Germany or Greece, you're likely to find establishments like Levi's, Starbucks, Citibank, and Wal-Mart. Everything begins to look and sound alike, and eventually it gets awfully boring. Businesses, new and old, must work harder and harder to differentiate themselves (and their products) from others around them. Business consolidations, the Internet, the information overload, the 24/7/365 always-on, everyone's-connected world means leaders must be even more attentive to ways in which they can be the beacon that cuts through the dense fog and steers people in the right direction.

Align Your Dream with the People's Dream

In learning how to appeal to people's ideals, move their souls, and uplift their spirits—and your own—there is no better place to look than to a master of this art: the Reverend Dr. Martin Luther King Jr. He certainly did offer people a brilliant beacon of light that cut through the fog of his troubled times to offer guidance to a more promising future. His "I Have a Dream" speech tops the list of the best American public addresses of the twentieth century.[2]

On August 28, 1963, on the steps of the Lincoln Memorial in Washington, D.C., before a throng of 250,000, Martin Luther King Jr. proclaimed his dream to the world. As he spoke, and as thousands clapped and shouted, a nation was moved. Imagine that you're a communication researcher studying how leaders enlist others in a dream. Imagine that you're there in the audience on that August day, listening to King. Imagine that you're there to better understand how King is so capable of moving people. As you read this text, pay attention not just to the content but imagine how he expressed these words and phrases. Think about the rhythm, the cadence, and the pauses. Place yourself on the steps of the Lincoln Memorial and attempt to get a feel for how the audience reacted as they listened to these words:

I say to you today, my friends, so even though we face the difficulties of today and tomorrow, I still have a dream. It is a dream deeply rooted in the American dream.

I have a dream that one day this nation will rise up and live out the true meaning of its creed: "We hold these truths to be self-evident: that all men are created equal."

I have a dream that one day on the red hills of Georgia the sons of former slaves and the sons of former slave owners will be able to sit down together at the table of brotherhood.

I have a dream that one day even the state of Mississippi, a state sweltering with the heat of injustice, sweltering with the heat of oppression, will be transformed into an oasis of freedom and justice.

I have a dream that my four little children will one day live in a nation where they will not be judged by the color of their skin but by the content of their character.

I have a dream today.

I have a dream that one day, down in Alabama, with its vicious racists, with its governor having his lips dripping with the words of interposition and nullification, one day right there in Alabama, little black boys and black girls will be able to join hands with little white boys and white girls as sisters and brothers.

I have a dream today.

I have a dream that one day every valley shall be exalted, every hill and mountain shall be made low, the rough places will be made plain, and the crooked places will be made straight, and the glory of the Lord shall be revealed, and all flesh shall see it together.

This is our hope. This is the faith that I go back to the South with. With this faith we will be able to transform the jangling discords of our nation into a beautiful symphony of brotherhood. With this faith we will be able to work together, to pray together, to struggle together, to go to jail together, to stand up for freedom together, knowing that we will be free one day.

This will be the day, this will be the day when all of God's children will be able to sing with a new meaning, "My country, 'tis of thee, sweet land of liberty, of thee I sing. Land where my fathers died, land of the pilgrim's pride, from every mountainside, let freedom ring."

And if America is to be a great nation this must become true. So let freedom ring from the prodigious hilltops of New Hampshire. Let freedom ring from the mighty mountains of New York. Let freedom ring from the heightening Alleghenies of Pennsylvania!

Let freedom ring from the snowcapped Rockies of Colorado!

Let freedom ring from the curvaceous slopes of California!

But not only that; let freedom ring from Stone Mountain of Georgia!

Let freedom ring from Lookout Mountain of Tennessee!

Let freedom ring from every hill and molehill of Mississippi. From every mountainside, let freedom ring.

And when this happens, and when we allow freedom to ring, when we let it ring from every village and every hamlet, from every state and every city, we will be able to speed up that day when all of God's children, black men and white men, Jews and Gentiles, Protestants and Catholics, will be able to join hands and sing in the words of the old Negro spiritual, "Free at last! Free at last! Thank God Almighty, we are free at last!"[3]

What do you observe? What do you hear? What do you notice about this speech? How was he able to move so many, what makes it so powerful, and why has this speech survived the test of time? Here are some of the observations that participants in our workshops and classes have made in reflecting on King's speech:

"He appealed to common bonds."

"He talked about traditional values of family, church, country."

"It was vivid. He used a lot of images and word pictures. You could see the examples."

"People could relate to the examples. They were familiar."

"His references were credible. It's hard to argue against the Constitution and the Bible."

"He mentioned children—something we can all relate to."

"He knew his audience."

"He made geographical references to places the people in the audience could relate to."

"He included everybody: different parts of the country, all ages, both sexes, major religions."

"He used a lot of repetition: for example, 'I have a dream,' 'Let freedom ring.'"

"He said the same thing in different ways."

"He began with a statement of the difficulties and then stated his dream."

"He was positive and hopeful."

"Although positive, he also said people might have to suffer in order to get there. He didn't promise it would be easy."

"There was a cadence and a rhythm to his voice."

"He shifted from 'I' to 'we' halfway through."

"He spoke with emotion and passion. It was deeply felt."

Dr. King's "I Have a Dream" speech illustrates how the ability to exert an enlivening influence is rooted in fundamental values, cultural traditions, personal conviction, and a capacity to use words to create positive images of the future. To enlist others, leaders need to bring the vision to life. Leaders have to animate the vision and make manifest the purpose so that others can see it, hear it, taste it, touch it, feel it. In making the intangible vision tangible, leaders ignite constituents' flames of passion.

To enlist others, leaders need to bring the vision to life.

And there is something else you can learn when you actually listen to King's speech.[4] What you'll hear is an audience that was participating. The people in the crowd that day were clapping and shouting back, "Yes," and "Oh, yes," and "Um-hmm," and "Hear, hear." They were fully engaged. It wasn't a one-way street. King was in a conversation with them about their lives and about their dreams. They could see the dream he was envisioning and they were affirming it. They were telling him with their shouts and nods and claps and responses, "You have heard me, and you are talking to me about what I long for. You are saying what I am feeling." Their shouts and claps prove that Dr. King's dream was not his dream alone. It was the people's vision. It was a shared vision.

ANIMATE THE VISION

Leaders have to arouse others to join in a cause and to want to move decisively and boldly forward. Part of arousing others is appealing to their ideals. Another part, as we see in Dr. King's "I Have a Dream" speech, is animating the vision, breathing life into it. To enlist others you have to help them *see* and *feel* how their own interests and aspirations are aligned with the vision.

You have to paint a compelling picture of the future, one that enables constituents to experience viscerally what it would be like to actually live and work in an exciting and uplifting future. That's the only way they'll become internally motivated to commit their individual energies to its realization.

"But I'm not like Dr. King," you say. "I can't possibly do what he did. Besides, he was a preacher, and I'm a businessperson. His constituents were on a protest march, and mine are here to get a job done." Most people initially respond this way. Most people don't see themselves as personally uplifting, and certainly don't get much encouragement for behaving this way in most organizations. Despite the potency of clearly communicated and compelling visions, the people we studied feel more uncomfortable with inspiring a shared vision than with any of the other leadership practices. And, more specifically, their discomfort comes less from envisioning the exciting possibilities of the future and more from having to express their emotions. That's not easy for working adults to do; it becomes a lot tougher as people get older to express naked enthusiasm for the work that they're doing and the ends they're striving to achieve. But we all underestimate ourselves. We sell ourselves short. We're too quick to discount our capacity to communicate with passion and enthusiasm.

People's perception of themselves as uninspiring is in sharp contrast to their performance when they talk about their personal-best leadership experiences or when they talk about their ideal futures. When relating hopes, dreams, and successes, people are almost always emotionally expressive. Expressiveness comes naturally when talking about deep desires for the something that could be better in the future than it is today. People lean forward in their chairs, they move their arms about, their eyes light up, their voices sing with emotion, and smiles appear on their faces. They're enthusiastic, articulate, optimistic, and uplifting. In short, they are inspiring!

This contradiction is most intriguing. Why is it that people seem to see no connection between the animated, enthusiastic behavior they use in describing their personal bests and their ability to be inspiring? This is because most people have attributed something mystical to the process of being inspirational. They seem to see it as supernatural, as a grace or charm that comes from the gods. This assumption inhibits people far more than any lack of natural talent for being inspirational. It's not necessary to be a famous, charismatic person to inspire a shared vision. It is necessary to believe, however—and to develop the skills to transmit that belief. A deeply felt belief, along with commitment and enthusiasm for it—genuinely displayed—brings the vision to life for all of us.

If you're going to lead, you have to recognize that your enthusiasm and expressiveness are among your strongest allies in your efforts to generate commitment in your constituents. By using symbolic language, creating word images of the future, practicing a positive communication style, tapping into verbal and nonverbal expressiveness, and speaking from the heart, you breathe life (the literal definition of the word *inspire*) into a vision.

Use Symbolic Language

Leaders make full use of the power of symbolic language to communicate a shared identity and give life to visions. They use metaphors and other figures of speech; they give examples, tell stories, and relate anecdotes; they draw word pictures; and they offer quotations and recite slogans. They enable constituents to picture the future, to hear it, to sense it, to recognize it.

Ricardo Semler is the chief executive of the Brazil-based company Semco, but he uses the CEO title in a very unusual way. "I'm a catalyst," he writes. "By definition a catalyst, usually an enzyme, initiates a reaction. The way I handle the role is by broaching weird ideas and asking dumb questions. Strictly speaking, I'm a highly evolved CEO, as in 'Chief Enzyme Officer.'"[5] Now Semler is not literally an "enzyme," but figuratively he is. This simple metaphor says more about how Semler sees his job than any lengthy job description could. And Semler is full of them. In a clear and clever contrast to the notion of work being 24/7 or a seven-day work week, he says, "I've got a much better idea, though, one that I've been testing now for many years: the seven-day weekend." In reference to how Semco develops people, he says, "Planting seeds is more effective than pulling weeds." And in discussing his approach to business planning, he comments, "Money doesn't grow on decision trees."[6]

"Leaders can use metaphors explicitly and deliberately to influence others, give shape to the world, and even manipulate listeners," write Thomas Oberlechner and Viktor Mayer-Schönberger of the John F. Kennedy School of Government at Harvard University.[7] There are war metaphors, game and sports metaphors, art metaphors, machine metaphors, and religious or spiritual metaphors. "Paying attention to metaphors and to their implications helps us recognize such influences more quickly and react to them in more informed and reflective ways."[8] When Amy Cole, then director of sales training and services at Intraware, was just assembling her team, she spoke about "painting a picture" and about "getting everyone on the bus." "I used the metaphor that we are a team traveling in a bus," she explained, "and it is important that we all travel in the same direction." All leaders need to be more conscious about the powerful effect that these tools of language can have in shaping the way people envision their work—and in shaping the ethics of a firm.

Andrew Coven, when taking over leadership of a technology design team for Adobe Systems, used another variation of symbolic language. He reframed the existing work of his team in terms of "telling a story"—this was a novel, engaging, and unique way of training third-party developers, who were used to just straight reference documentation.

> We created a fictional company that became our example third-party developer company in our documentation. The company was called "Code-Hawgs" (a play on words, to hog all the code). CodeHawgs was a systems integrator that was creating plug-ins to integrate our product with their own database and workflow management system. We even created a mascot (the CodeHawg), which then appeared everywhere—like shirts, flyers, walls, etc.—to remind folks what we were about.

"CodeHawg" was just one way that Andrew painted a word picture that portrayed the meaning behind their vision. Andrew went so far as to invent new words and phrases (such as "training-centric"), and then he would listen carefully to see who had read various documents by noting who was using these new catchphrases.

Leaders such as Andrew appreciate the way using symbolic language not only sparks people's imaginations but makes them feel part of a very special team. They learn to master the richness of figurative speech so that they can paint the word pictures that best portray the meaning of their visions.

Make Images of the Future

Visions are images in the mind, impressions and representations. They become real as leaders express those images in concrete terms to their constituents. Just as architects make drawings and engineers build models, leaders find ways of giving expression to our collective hopes for the future.

When talking about the future we all talk in terms of foresight, focus, forecasts, future scenarios, points of view, and perspectives. The thing that each of these words has in common is that they are visual references. The word *vision* itself has at its root the verb "to see." Statements of vision, then, should not be statements at all. They should be pictures—word pictures. They're more image than words. For a vision to be shared it needs to be *seen* in the mind's eye.

> For a vision to be shared it needs to be seen *in the* mind's eye.

In our workshops and classes we often illustrate the power of images with this simple exercise. We ask people to shout out the first thing that comes to mind when they hear the words, *Paris, France.* The replies that pop out—the Eiffel Tower, the Louvre, the Arc de Triomphe, the Seine, Notre Dame, good food, wine, romance—are all images of real places and real sensations. No one calls out the square kilometers, population, or gross domestic product of

Paris. Why? Human memory is stored in images and sensory impressions, not in numbers.

So what does this mean for leaders? It means that to enlist others and inspire a shared vision, you must be able to draw upon that very natural mental process of creating images. When you speak about the future, you need to paint word pictures so that others get a mental image of what things will be like when you are at the end of your journey. Images are windows on the world of tomorrow. When talking about going places you've never been—whether to the top of an unclimbed mountain or to the pinnacle of an entirely new industry—you have to be able to imagine what they'll look like. You have to picture the possibilities. Those who are more auditory by nature talk about it as a "calling." While Martin Luther King's underlying vision (and message) was about freedom, he called upon us to see by imagining a situation in which "little black boys and black girls will be able to join hands with little white boys and white girls as sisters and brothers."

The ability to enable others to see into the future is not some supernatural power. Every one of us possesses it. We do it every time we return from a vacation and show the photos to our friends. If you doubt your own ability, try this exercise. Sit down with a few close friends and tell them about one of your favorite vacations. Describe the people you saw and met, the sights and sounds of the places you went, the smells and tastes of the food you ate. Show them the photos or videos if you have them. Observe their reactions—and your own. What's that experience like? We've done this activity many times, and people always report feeling energized and passionate. Those hearing about a place for the first time usually say something like, "After listening to you, I'd like to go there someday myself."

Although some people may have a more creative imagination than others, all of us have the capacity to get other people to see places they've never been to before. The first challenge is to vividly imagine the destination in your mind's eye, and the second part is to describe it so colorfully that others will see it and want to visit it themselves.

Practice Positive Communication

To foster team spirit, breed optimism, promote resilience, and renew faith and confidence, leaders must learn to look at the bright side. They must keep hope alive. They must strengthen their constituents' belief that life's struggle will produce a more promising future. Such faith results from an intimate and supportive relationship, a relationship based on mutual participation in the process of renewal.

Constituents look for leaders who demonstrate an enthusiastic and genuine belief in the capacity of others, who strengthen people's will, who supply the means to achieve, and who express optimism for the future. Constituents want leaders who remain passionate despite obstacles and setbacks. In today's uncertain times, leaders with a positive, confident, can-do approach to life and business are desperately needed.

We all want leaders with enthusiasm, with a bounce in their step, with a positive attitude. We want to believe that we'll be part of an invigorating journey. We follow people with a can-do attitude, not those who give sixty-seven reasons why something can't be done. Researchers working with neural networks have found that when people feel rebuffed or left out, the brain activates a site for registering physical pain.[9] People actually remember downbeat comments far more often, in greater detail and with more intensity, than they do encouraging words. When negative remarks become a preoccupation, an employee's brain loses mental efficiency. In light of the impact their words have on other people's brains it is even more critical for leaders to be positive.

Consider the positive attitude and communication style that Joan Carter exhibited when she took over as general manager and executive chef of the Faculty Club at Santa Clara University. Before Joan's arrival, both membership and sales had been seriously declining for several years, the restaurant's remaining customers were unhappy, its balance sheet was "scary," and the staff was divided into factions.

Joan took all this in, and what she saw was a dusty diamond. "I saw a beautiful and historic building full of mission-era flavor and character that should be, could be, would be *the* place on campus." In her mind's eye, she saw the club bustling. She saw professors and university staff chatting on the lovely enclosed patio and enjoying high-quality, appealing yet inexpensive meals. She envisioned the club assisting alumni in planning wonderful, personal, and professionally catered wedding receptions and anniversary celebrations. Joan could see a happy staff whose primary concern was customer satisfaction, a kitchen that produced a product far superior to "banquet food," and a catering staff that did whatever it took to make an event exceptional. She wasn't quite sure how the club had deteriorated to the extent it had, but that really didn't matter. She decided to ignore the quick fix and set out to teach everyone how unique and wonderful the club could be.

Over the next two years, as she talked with customers and worked with her staff, she instilled a vision of the club as a restaurant that celebrated good food and good company. As food and service quality began to improve, smiles became more prevalent among customers and staff and sales began to rise: 20 percent the first year and 30 percent the next. When a top financial manager of the university asked how she had managed to turn the finances around so quickly and dramatically, Joan responded, "You can't turn around numbers. The balance sheet is just a reflection of what's happening here, every day, in the restaurant. I just helped the staff realize what we're really all about. It was always here," she said, "only perhaps a little dusty, a little ignored, and a little unloved. I just helped them see it."

Express Your Emotions

In explaining why particular leaders have a magnetic effect, people often describe them as charismatic. But *charisma* has become such an overused and misused term that it's almost useless as a descriptor of leaders. "In the popular media," notes leadership scholar Bernard Bass, "charisma has come to mean anything ranging from chutzpah to Pied Piperism, from celebrity to superman status. It has become an overworked cliché for a strong, attractive, and inspiring personality."[10]

Social scientists have attempted to investigate this elusive quality in terms of observable behavior.[11] What they've found is that people who are perceived to be charismatic are simply more animated than others. They smile more, speak faster, pronounce words more clearly, and move their heads and bodies more often. What we call charisma, then, can better be understood as energy and expressiveness. The old saying that "Enthusiasm is infectious" is certainly true for leaders.

"You, as leader, are responsible for the energy level—the level of authentic excitement—in your organization," write leadership developers Belle Linda Halpren and Kathy Lubar.[12] "Emotion drives expressiveness," they tell us, and leaders must communicate their emotions using all means of expression—verbal and nonverbal—if they are to generate the intense enthusiasm that's required to mobilize people to struggle for shared aspirations.

There's another thing that emotion drives. It makes things more memorable. And since leaders want their messages to be remembered, they need to add more emotion to their words and their behavior. James L. McGaugh, professor of neurobiology at the University of California, Irvine, and a leading expert on creation of memory, has reported that "emotionally significant events create stronger, longer-lasting memories."[13] No doubt you've experienced this yourself when something emotionally significant has happened to you—a serious trauma, such as an accident, or a joyful surprise, such as winning a contest. But the events don't have to be real to be memorable. They can simply be stories. For example, in one experiment researchers showed subjects in two groups a series of twelve slides. The slide presentation was accompanied by a story, one line for each slide. For one group in the study the narrative was quite boring, for the other the narrative was emotionally moving. Two weeks later the two groups returned and took a test of how well they remembered the details of each slide. (They didn't know when they watched the slides that they would be tested.) While neither group differed in their memory of the first few or last few slides, they did differ significantly in the recollection of the slides in the middle. "The subjects who had listened to the emotionally arousing narrative remembered details in those particular slides better" than the group that listened to the neutral story. "Stronger emotional arousal," says McGaugh, "is associated with better memory; emotional arousal appears to create strong memories."[14]

Emotion makes things more memorable.

It doesn't even have to be a complete narrative to make strong memories. It can be just the words themselves. In another laboratory experiment, researchers asked subjects to learn to associate pairs of words. "Some of the words in the pairs . . . were used because they elicited strong emotional responses, as indicated by changes in the subjects' galvanic skin response. . . . On a retention test a week later the subjects remembered the emotionally arousing words better than they remembered less arousing words."[15] Whether it's a story or a word, we're more likely to remember the key messages when they're attached to something that triggers an emotional response. The reasons for this have to do with our physiology. We're just wired to pay more attention to stuff that excites us or scares us. Keep all this in mind the next time you deliver a PowerPoint presentation. It's not just the content that will make it stick; it's also how well you tap into people's emotions.

The dramatic increase in the use of electronic technology also has an impact on the way people deliver messages. From podcasts to Webcasts, MySpace to YouTube, more and more people are turning to their digital devices for information. This trend only lends support to what researchers are discovering about memory. Entertainment is playing a bigger and bigger role in our lives. Leadership is a performing art, and this has become even truer as new technologies hit the market. It's no longer enough to write a good script—you've also got to put on a good show. And you've got to make it a show that people will remember.

Speak from the Heart

None of these suggestions will be of any value whatsoever if you don't believe in what you're saying. If the vision is someone else's, and you don't own it, it will be very difficult for you to enlist others in it. If you have trouble imagining yourself actually living the future described in the vision, you'll certainly not be able to convince others that they ought to enlist in making it a reality. If you're not excited about the possibilities, how can you expect others to be? *The prerequisite to enlisting others in a shared vision is genuineness.* The first place to look before talking to others about the vision of the future is in your heart.

When asked how she was able to lead the development team for the PCnet family of Advanced Micro Devices, breaking all barriers and launching this extremely successful family of products, Laila Razouk replied simply, "I believed. Believing is a very important part of the action. You have to have faith. If you don't have that, then you're lost even before you get started." It's easy to understand why people were eager to follow Laila: "If I believe in something badly enough, and if I have the conviction, then I start picturing and envisioning how it will look if we did this or if we did that. By sharing these thoughts with other people, the excitement grows and people become part of that picture. Without much effort—with energy, but not much effort—the magic starts to happen. People start to bounce ideas back and forth, they get involved, brainstorm, and share ideas. Then I know I don't have to worry about it."

How successful would the project have been if instead Laila had thought, "This project will never work. The person who thought this up doesn't understand the details. I'm doing this because I'm forced to, but I really think this project is a stupid idea!" For Laila, the net effect of speaking from the heart, as she explained, is that "by openly sharing what I saw, what I knew, and what I believed—not by dictating it, but by being willing to iterate and adjust things—I got other people involved."

There's no one more believable than a person with a deep passion for something. There's no one more fun to be around than someone who is openly excited about the magic that can happen. There's no one more determined than someone who believes fervently in an ideal. People want leaders who are upbeat, optimistic, and positive about the future. It's really the only way we can get people to want to struggle for shared aspirations.

REFLECTION AND ACTION: ENLISTING OTHERS

Leaders appeal to common ideals. They connect others to what is most meaningful in the shared vision. They lift people to higher levels of motivation and morality, and continuously reinforce that they can make a difference in the world. Exemplary leaders speak to what is unique and singular about the organization, making others feel proud to be a part of something extraordinary. And the best leaders understand that it's not their personal idiosyncratic view of the future that's important, it's the aspirations of all their constituents that matter most.

To be sustained over time, visions must be compelling and memorable. Leaders must breathe life into visions, they must animate them so that others can experience what it would be like to live and work in that ideal and unique future. They use a variety of modes of expression to make their abstract visions concrete. Through skillful use of metaphors, symbols, word pictures, positive language, and personal energy leaders generate enthusiasm and excitement for the common vision. But above all, leaders must be convinced of the value of the shared vision and share that genuine belief with others. They must believe in what they are saying. Authenticity is the true test of conviction, and constituents will only follow willingly if they sense that the vision is genuine.

Here are three action steps you can take to increase your ability to Enlist Others.

Record Your Shared Vision

You need to practice expressing your hopes, dreams, and aspirations fully. In Chapter Five we asked you to do a few things to envision the future. Now we'd like you to take all the information you've just gathered and write your *ideal and unique image of the future for yourself and for your organization*. We recommend that this statement be brief but not a one-liner. The one-liners come later. Martin Luther King Jr.'s "I Have a Dream" speech was five minutes and a few seconds in length, so we suggest you aim for something in the three- to five-minute range. Any longer, and people are likely to lose interest. Much shorter, and you won't be providing enough vivid detail for people to know where you really want to be ten or so years from now—what it truly feels like to really be there.

Using your notes from your responses to the questions about the "something" you want to do, expand your vision by answering these questions:

- What is your *ideal* work community? What do you personally aspire to create?
- What is *unique* about your hopes, dreams, and aspirations? How are they distinctive compared to all the other visions of the future?
- When you project this vision into the *future* ten to fifteen years, what does it look like? What innovations and trends will influence that future? What vision will carry us forward into the future?
- What *images* come to mind when thinking of the future? What does it look like, sound like, taste like, and feel like?
- How does this vision serve the *common good*? What are the shared aspirations among all the constituents? How does the vision fulfill others' ideal and unique images of their futures?

Don't censor yourself. This is about aspirations; it needs to be uplifting. Give voice to your dreams. Once you've written your vision, try drawing it, finding a picture that resembles it, or creating a symbol that represents it. Finally, create a short slogan of five to nine words that captures the essence of your vision. Something similar to Edward Goeppner's "We don't sell flowers, we sell beauty" is what we have in mind. A brief slogan is no substitute for a complete statement, but it does help others remember the essential message, and it can evoke images of a shared destiny.

After you've crafted your vision statement, revisit it periodically. Refine it and update it. The world changes, so be sure to adapt your statement and slogan to the changing times. Also keep in mind that while we're talking about your vision statement, we are definitely not suggesting that you impose your will on your constituents. Successful visions are shared. Much as we strongly encourage you to write and rehearse a consistent message to deliver to others, communicating a vision should be a conversation—not just a speech. What you articulate should provide others with the opportunity for dialogue.

Breathe Life into Your Vision

Remember earlier in this chapter when we related the images people had when they heard the words *Paris, France*? People recalled sights, feelings, tastes, and smells. When Martin Luther King Jr. spoke he used historical events, Biblical texts, patriotic songs, important documents, significant places, and patriotic symbols to give his speech a unique narrative quality. You have to be able to do the same thing. You have to make the future come alive in people's minds. You have to stir their hearts. Recall that study about the slides? It was the strong emotions that made each slide more memorable. You have to evoke strong emotions if you want people to remember where it is you want them to go.

Values such as quality, service, respect, freedom, creativity, and responsiveness don't exist in nature. They must be defined in concrete terms. Your job is to make these intangible values tangible by using the richness of language to transport people to a place they've never been. Use as many forms of expression as you can to transform the vision's intangibles into tangibles.

- If your vision speech were to have a sound track, what songs would be in it?
- What poem best expresses the shared vision of the future?

- What short stories express what you are trying to communicate?
- What memorable quotations enrich the delivery?
- What symbols best represent the shared vision?
- What metaphors and similes express the vision and achieve the effect you are seeking?
- What geographical locations come to mind when you think about the vision?

When it comes to making visions memorable you have to be evocative, even provocative. It's the figures of speech, not the figures on the balance sheet, that create that memory.

Expand Your Communication and Expressiveness Skills

In our research we found that expressing a vision is *the* most difficult of all the leadership skills. People find it easier to imagine an ideal and unique future than they do painting a compelling picture for others. When it comes to inspiring a shared vision, we all could use some help in articulating it.

A course in presentation skills will benefit you greatly. If you haven't taken one yet, sign up for the next available class. Join Toastmasters. More than likely there's a chapter in your town. Having to give a short speech once a week is great practice. Presentation skills workshops and meetings not only help you learn effective techniques for getting your ideas across, they also help you gain confidence in yourself. Whenever possible, volunteer to stand up in front of a group and speak, even if it's just to introduce someone or make an announcement. The more practice in public speaking you have, the more comfortable you will become.

Put on a DVD collection—or connect to a Web site—of famous speeches. Listen and watch. Notice what the speaker does to move the audience. Do the same thing when you are in the audience and someone is speaking. If the speaker doesn't connect, notice what he or she does that fails to arouse emotion and interest. And it's not too much of a stretch to suggest that you take an acting class. After all, the "Great Communicator," the late President Ronald Reagan, managed to use to great effect the skills he learned in the movies.

And be sure to put more energy and enthusiasm into your vision presentations. Let your emotions show. Smile. Use gestures and move your body. Speak clearly and quickly. Make eye contact. All of these signals are cues to others that you're personally excited about what you're saying. If you don't perceive yourself as an expressive person, begin to practice expressiveness by talking to a favorite friend about what most excites you in life. As you do this, pay attention to your verbal and nonverbal behavior. If possible, turn on a video camera so that you can watch yourself later. We bet that you'll discover that when you talk about things that excite you, you do a lot of the things we've just described.

And finally, practice, practice, practice. None of history's greatest speeches were delivered extemporaneously. They had been rehearsed and tested in other events and in other conversations. Be prepared to take your first draft (or latest draft, whatever its number) and continue to revise, hone, edit, and revise again until you think it expresses your ideas just right. Try it out in front of others, obtain feedback, and determine the words, phrases, and thoughts that most resonate (and which ones don't). You just never know when someone might ask you, "Tell me about your dreams for this organization." When that opportunity knocks you want to be ready to answer the door.

COMMITMENT NUMBER 4

Enlist Others

Essentials of Enlisting Others

- Appeal to common ideals
- Animate the vision

Taking Action

- Record your shared vision
- Breathe life into your vision
- Expand your communication and expressiveness skills

PART 4

CHALLENGE THE PROCESS

- SEARCH FOR OPPORTUNITIES

- EXPERIMENT AND TAKE RISKS

SEARCH FOR
OPPORTUNITIES

"I realized that my job as a leader was to make
change each and every day."
Robin Selden, Logitech

"I believe that transformation can happen in a heartbeat," Jacqueline Maartense told us. "And I believe that you can build a great company if the customer is the center of all you do." Jacqueline had the chance to boldly and quickly demonstrate her commitment to these ideals when she was appointed managing director of the United Kingdom division of Intuit, the personal and small-business financial software company. The U.K. division had never been profitable, and she was given one year to turn it around. Jacqueline felt she had to do something dramatically different, so she shut down the company for an all-day meeting on her very first day on the job!

The employees in the U.K. division were three weeks away from three product launches, and everyone had been working around the clock to meet the deadlines. Profitability of the entire year was dependent on the success of those launches. "I wasn't met with a warm fuzzy reception when I told everyone from the janitors to the engineering staff that they were to cancel all of their plans so they could attend a company meeting about building partnerships with customers," Jacqueline told us. When she arrived at the office straight from an overseas red-eye flight, she said, everyone was slumped in their chairs, their folded arms telegraphing their skepticism and resistance.

I asked the team to suspend judgment for one day. I invited them to be open to the possibility that we could turn the company profitable if we learned to listen to customers better than *everyone else on the planet.* I shared my belief that we will build products and programs right the first time, because collectively we will know what customers want. With that opening, I spent a half-day teaching people customer-contact techniques and how to gain insight from customer interactions.

By noon, I saw growing optimism, but there were still some grumpy people. That's when I handed out the customer phone list and challenged the team to make calls to find out how they could make a difference in our customers' lives.

Magic took place in that afternoon as they began to hear about what customers were experiencing and started to realize "Wow, I can do something about this," or "Wow, I didn't know you felt that way." In many cases, the reports back from customers were wonderful, and it was just an opportunity for employees to hear about how great the company was. That in itself was inspiring. . . .

Following the phone calls, the entire company broke into cross-functional groups to talk about what they had learned and what actions needed to be taken to change the system as well as to address specific customer problems. "By the end of the day," Jacqueline reported, "the place was on *fire*. After we regrouped to share our stories, the people who had been the most disgruntled were the ones who were now saying, 'Wow, I can't even imagine developing a product without doing this kind of thing on an ongoing basis.'"

The ideas generated that day about how to create customer delight became the fabric of their business plan, and the beginning of a new way of doing business. To ensure that the momentum continued, over the next several months Jacqueline made a point to listen in on calls and to get on the phone herself every week so that everyone could hear her calling customers. She spent lots of time with the customer service and technical support reps, continually asking them, "What did you learn about what we could do to make a difference in a customer's life today?" That question became a ritual in her interactions with employees, and she encouraged leaders of her organization to also ask it regularly.

As Jacqueline told us, "Sometimes you just have to go against the grain and do what you think is right because you believe so strongly in a philosophy and a long-term way of doing business." Within seven months, the U.K. operation became profitable for the first time in its history.

What Jacqueline did at Intuit is what all exemplary leaders do. When we analyzed the very first set of personal-best cases, we discovered that the situations people chose to discuss were about major change that had a significant impact on their organizations. The leaders in our study talked about times when they turned around losing operations, started up new plants, developed new products or services, installed untested procedures, renewed operations threatened with closing, or released the creative spirit trapped inside stifling bureaucratic systems. The personal-best leadership cases continue to be about radical departures from the past, about doing things that have never been done before, and about going to places not yet discovered.

The work of leaders is change. And all change requires that leaders actively seek ways to make things better, to grow, innovate, and improve. To Search for Opportunities to get extraordinary things done, leaders make use of two essentials:

- **Seize the initiative**
- **Exercise outsight**

Sometimes leaders have to shake things up. Other times they just have to grab hold of the adversity that surrounds them. Whether change comes from outside challenges or inside challenges, leaders make things happen. And to make *new* things happen they rely on *outsight* to actively seek innovative ideas from outside the boundaries of familiar experience.

SEIZE THE INITIATIVE

When people think about their personal bests they automatically think about some kind of challenge. Why? The fact is that when times are stable and secure, people are not severely tested. They may perform well, get promoted, even achieve fame and fortune. But certainty and routine breed complacency. In contrast, personal and business hardships have a way of making people come face to face with who they really are and what they're capable of becoming.

Thus the study of leadership is the study of how men and women guide others through adversity, uncertainty, hardship, disruption, transformation, transition, recovery, new beginnings, and other significant challenges. It's the study of people who triumph against overwhelming odds, who take initiative when there is inertia, who confront the established order, who mobilize people and institutions in the face of strong resistance. It's also the study of how men and women, in times of constancy and complacency, actively seek to disturb the status quo and awaken others to new possibilities. Leadership, challenge, and seizing the initiative are inextricably linked. Humdrum situations simply aren't associated with award-winning performance.

Evident in the tone of almost all the personal-best stories is that leaders are people who seize the initiative with enthusiasm, determination, and a desire to make something happen. They embrace the challenge presented by the shifts in their industries or the new demands of the marketplace and commit themselves to creating exciting new possibilities that make a meaningful difference.

Change Requires Leadership

What's significant about the emphasis on change in our leadership cases is that we don't ask people to tell us about *change,* we ask them to tell us about their personal-best leadership experiences. They can discuss any leadership experience they choose—past or present, unofficial or official; in any functional area; in any community, voluntary, religious, health care, educational, public-sector, or private-sector organization. In electing to talk about times of change, our respondents underscore the fact that leadership demands altering the business-as-usual environment.

Rosabeth Moss Kanter, a distinguished Harvard Business School professor, investigated the human resource practices and organizational designs of innovation-producing organizations, seeking to learn what fostered and what hindered innovation in corporations. Our study and Rosabeth's were done independently of each other, in different regions and periods in time, and with different purposes. We were studying leadership; Rosabeth was studying innovation. Yet we arrived at similar conclusions in analyzing our respective cases: *leadership is inextricably connected with the process of innovation,* of bringing new ideas, methods, or solutions into use. To Rosabeth, innovation means change, and "change requires leadership . . . a 'prime mover' to push for implementation of strategic decisions."[1] Like hers, our cases are evidence of that.

Arvind Deogirikar knows firsthand what it takes to build from the ground level up. Arvind was the regional marketing director in Moscow for Sun CIS (Commonwealth of Independent States) when he was charged with putting together the Russian Hockey All Star Tour. The Tour was initiated during the NHL player strike by Scott McNealy, then Sun Microsystems' CEO (himself an ardent hockey player and fan), and sponsored by Sun to address the challenges the CIS operation faced. Having entered this marketplace late—both IBM and HP had well-established operations in place—Sun had found it difficult to either attract and retain top talent or secure premier organizations to work with them as channel partners. Arvind saw the Russian Hockey All Star Tour as a golden opportunity. "It would open many doors and pave the way for success in establishing a successful organization," he told us. "This was an opportunity to change the way Sun was perceived by customers and partners alike in that region and beyond."

With his background in managing complex technical development projects and working with teams from different parts of the world, Arvind was confident that he'd be able to assemble and lead a team to execute this project. Arvind also understood that he'd be working with the Russian bureaucracy, a pursuit that was, in his words, "an art and not a science . . . There is no structure," he explained, "and nearly anyone along a chain of command can simply say 'Nyet' and everything stops right then and there."

Arvind seized the opportunity to make a difference and created a series of partnerships that pulled off something that had never been done before. He changed the way that people interacted with one another, for example, by creating teams composed of members from multiple organizations. Each team was given clear instructions as to the expectations, timelines, and communication channels. They were encouraged to select a team leader and a backup person. And by fostering a "we are all in it together in the same boat" spirit, Arvind empowered each team to come up with methods for making the Tour successful.

Team leaders were assigned and then encouraged to share their results with other team members. Regular meetings and conference calls with all the stakeholders—both local and remote—kept the team organized and allowed me to integrate and coordinate effectively. Each team was provided with tools and information they needed to succeed and worked collaboratively throughout the process. Everything had to happen on time and be orchestrated correctly to make sure all the pieces of the puzzle fell in place at the right time. We also had our corporate HQ and regional HQ team tied into these subgroups. For two months I had daily conference calls with these HQ team managers to ensure that things were on track, and I kept the team up-to-date on the situation on a daily basis.

We were also quite innovative in coming up with our own local solutions to critical problems. For example, we brought together our internal team from the Moscow office along with staff and managers from the channel partners. We had a kick-off meeting where we clearly identified the opportunities and challenges associated with this project. We laid out a draft plan of action for everyone's comment. We formed four teams to study and come back in a couple of days with concrete recommendations. That allowed them to voice their opinions and feel part of the team right from the beginning, especially the channel partners. This kind of management style was new to Russians; they were used to top-down approaches. My approach was to integrate them into a team right up front and tell them in no uncertain terms that we are all in it together. I was very open and honest in clearly letting all know what the success or failure of this event meant to Sun CIS employees and partners.

Once he got going, it seemed that no opportunity to challenge the status quo was too large or too small for Arvind. A good example is the cold morning when Arvind presented a plan to paint Moscow's decaying fleet of trams and buses. At first, people thought he was kidding—on reflection, they figured he must be crazy. But when the painting was completed—envision trams running all over the city with huge purple Sun logos all over them—the company's reputation went from "Sun who?" to "Sun, the great computer company." As a result of all of these undertakings, sales went from essentially nothing to over $30 million in less than three years. What's more, these innovations created considerable good will in the local community, which in turn helped in recruiting top-notch channel partners and gaining the confidence of key customer accounts.

It's quite clear that leaders must be innovators to navigate their organizations into and through the global economy. And the need to be innovative is by no means limited to a single company or country, time or place. Innovation pays off big time. The real result of the work of all the leaders with whom we talked was that the organization was substantively improved. There was a significant difference that could be seen, felt, and measured. It wasn't just that a new system, structure, or process was installed but that it was being used and making a positive difference for everyone.

Leaders Make Something Happen

Leaders, like Arvind, are fundamentally restless. They don't like the status quo. They want to make something happen. They want to change the business-as-usual environment.

Notre Dame professor J. Michael Crant found, for example, that M.B.A. students who rated high on proactivity were considered by their peers to be more transformational leaders, and were more engaged in extracurricular and civic activities targeted toward bringing about positive change.[2] Similarly, managers who rated themselves high in proactivity were assessed in turn by their immediate managers as more transformational and charismatic leaders.[3] And it's not just that proactive individuals make better leaders; Crant also found that real estate agents who scored high on proactivity were likely to make significantly more sales and receive higher commissions than those who tended to score low on proactivity.[4] Similar results about the connection between performance and proactivity have been found among entrepreneurs, administrative staff, and even college students searching for jobs. Proactivity consistently produces better results than reactivity or inactivity.[5] And in a recent study we found that proactive managers scored high on the leadership practice of challenging the process, and that this inclination was independent of both gender and national culture.[6] It seems everyone performs better when they take charge of change.

Why? One reason is that proactive people tend to work harder at what they do. They persist in achieving their goals, while others tend to give up, especially when faced with strong objections or great adversity.

Everyone performs better when they take charge of change.

Just look at Jean Campbell's actions when her computer-based medical billing company was literally knocked down to its very foundations by an earthquake. Even this, the most serious crisis in her company's history, did not seem insurmountable to her. Jean didn't wait for anyone or anything to begin taking initiative and formulating ways to keep clients apprised of the company's status. Her primary concerns were to keep the revenues flowing for her clients and to be fully operational within two weeks. She knew that her employees would need money and didn't want anyone to go without a paycheck any longer than absolutely necessary. Yet as she inspected their facility—its ceiling collapsed on the floor, its twenty-eight-foot-high south wall pulled ten inches off the concrete base, its desks overturned, its files scattered, and its ceiling pipes leaking—she saw that she had a "no-business business." Faced with such destruction, others might have thought her goal of being fully operational within two weeks utterly impossible. Not Jean.

Working closely with IBM Business Recovery Services, Jean organized, planned, listened, reassured, and motivated the employees and contractors to restore essential services within forty-eight hours and full services in less than ten business days. Jean and her team seized the initiative and energized a partnership of employees, suppliers, and customers so powerful that it overcame the forces of devastation unleashed by nature. She used her initiative and encouraged others to do the same; in so doing, she accomplished the extraordinary amid incredible chaos and change.

Encourage Initiative in Others

Stephen Ravizza went from learning how to seize initiative himself to helping others do the same. Stephen, ECAD engineer at Straec Technologies, told us that the driving force behind his willingness to "stick my neck out" and continually practice being a leader came from the way he had *redefined* success:

> In the past, my definition had been too rigid; it was all or nothing. Instead of focusing on each and every thing that went wrong, I began concentrating on what worked and considered those successes. For example, I submitted a proposal for five changes in our design methodology that I thought would enhance performance. Only one of the suggestions was implemented, and the other four were rejected. In the past I would have considered this an utter failure. By my new way of thinking, I was pleased with myself for taking the initiative. I considered my proposal a success because at least one of my suggestions was good enough to be implemented. That's one more than we would have had if I'd never stuck my neck out to propose them.

Stephen found that "building myself up with the positives, as opposed to tearing myself down, made me more confident and willing to take on new challenges. My successes made me confident." He started looking for opportunities to apply this insight. When a senior engineer responded with "it won't work" to a manager's question about a project's feasibility, everyone jumped on this melody and sounded ready to accept defeat. Stephen asked the group to take another tack: "What *is* working?"

Posing this question, he explained to us, stimulated new discussion. People slowly turned their cynicism into a positive outlook, concentrating their discussion on the positive elements of the project. Stephen then asked, "Suppose we could magically remove this particular obstacle—how will this help us?" Focusing on possibilities and not being hampered by limitations of conventional thinking gave birth to a number of new ideas for how to revive the project. People responded with new levels of creativity and imagination, and decided that they could make the project successful.

Leaders, as Stephen illustrates, seize the initiative themselves and encourage initiative in others. They want people to speak up, to offer suggestions for improvement, and to be straightforward about their constructive criticism. Yet when it comes to situations that involve high uncertainty, high risk, and high challenge, many people feel reluctant to act, afraid they might make matters worse. There are a number of ways that leaders can create conditions so that their constituents will be ready and willing to seize the initiative in tumultuous as well as tranquil times.

First, people who speak out and challenge the status quo believe in their ability to do something about the situations they face.[7] People who are high in self-efficacy—who consider themselves capable of taking action in a specific situation—are more likely to act than those who are not. The most important way leaders create this can-do attitude is by providing opportunities for people to gain mastery on a task one step at a time. Training is crucial to building self-efficacy and to encouraging initiative. During periods of rapid change it may seem as though there's no time to stop for training, but this short-term thinking is sure to doom the organization. The best leaders know that the investment in training will pay off in the long term. People can't deliver on what they don't know how to do, and short of firing everyone who doesn't come with all the skills intact—a virtual impossibility—you have to upgrade capabilities continuously.

Training is one form of preparation; another effective way to prepare is mental simulation.[8] As Stephen Ravizza showed with his questions to the group dealing with the moribund project, being able to imagine how things will be done before they need to be done is a powerful heuristic strategy for making people confident that they can act when the situation requires. It's much the same as practice fire drills, except you run them in your head. Playing a scenario through in your mind until you can picture it frame by frame is a terrific way to encourage and support initiative.

In addition, leaders find ways for people to stretch themselves. They regularly set the bar *incrementally* higher, understanding the importance of setting it at a level at which people feel they can succeed. Raise it too high, and people will fail; if they fail too often, they'll quit trying. Raise the bar a bit at a time, and eventually more and more people master the situation and build the self-confidence to continue moving the bar upward. Leaders balance this human need to grow and develop with a similar need to be successful.

Leaders find ways for people to stretch themselves.

Providing positive role models of peers who are successful at meeting the new challenges also fosters initiative. Seeing one of their own succeed in doing something new and different is an effective way to encourage others to do it, too. Leaders also recognize that simply saying "I know you can do it; I know you can do it" actually works. When people hear those words they are more likely to try harder than if they hear nothing, or, worse yet, hear those deflating words, "I'm not sure we're going to make it, but . . ."

Challenge with Purpose

Arlene Blum knows firsthand the importance of challenging the status quo and taking matters into her own hands. Arlene, who earned a doctorate in biophysical chemistry, has spent most of her adult life climbing mountains—literally and figuratively. She's had more than three hundred successful ascents. Her most significant challenge—and the one for which she is best known—was not the highest mountain she's ever climbed. It was the challenge of leading the first all-woman team up Annapurna I, the tenth-highest mountain in the world.[9]

"The question everyone asks mountain climbers is 'Why?' And when they learn about the lengthy and difficult preparation involved, they ask it even more insistently," says Arlene. "For us, the answer was much more than 'because it is there.' We all had experienced the exhilaration, the joy, and the warm camaraderie of the heights, and now we were on our way to an ultimate objective for a climber—the world's tenth-highest peak. But as women, we faced a challenge even greater than the mountain. We had to believe in ourselves enough to make the attempt in spite of social convention and two hundred years of climbing history in which women were usually relegated to the sidelines."[10] Arlene talks about how women had been told for years that they were not strong enough to carry heavy loads, that they didn't have the leadership experience and emotional stability necessary to climb the highest mountains.

"Our expedition would give ten women the chance to attempt one of the world's highest and most challenging peaks, as well as the experience necessary to plan future Himalayan climbs. If we succeeded, we would be the first Americans to climb Annapurna and the first American women to reach eight thousand meters (approximately 26,200 feet)."[11] At 3:29 P.M. UTC on October 15, 1978, they succeeded.

In talking about what separates those who make a successful ascent from those who don't, Arlene says, "The real dividing line is passion. As long as you believe what you're doing is meaningful, you can cut through fear and exhaustion and take the next step."[12]

Leadership isn't about challenge for challenge's sake. It's not about shaking things up just to keep people on their toes. It's about challenge for meaning's sake. It's about challenge with passion. It's about living life on purpose. What gets leaders—and all of us, really—through the tough times, the scary times, the times when you don't think you can even get up in the morning or take another step, is a sense of meaning and purpose. The motivation to deal with the challenges and uncertainties of life and work comes from the inside, and not from something that others hold out in front of you as some kind of carrot.[13]

The evidence from our research, and from studies by many others, is that if people are going to do their best, they must be internally motivated.[14] The tasks or projects in which they're engaged must be intrinsically engaging. When it comes to excellence, it's definitely not "What gets rewarded gets done," it's *"What is rewarding gets done."* You can never pay people enough to care—to care about their products, services, communities, families, or even the bottom line. After all, why do people push their own limits to get extraordinary things done? And for that matter, why do people do many things for nothing? Why do they volunteer to put out fires, raise money for worthy causes, or help children in need? Why do they risk their careers to start a new business or risk their security to change the social condition? Why do they risk their lives to save others or defend liberty? How do people find satisfaction in efforts that don't pay a lot of money, options, perks, or prestige? Extrinsic rewards certainly can't explain these actions. True leaders tap into people's hearts and minds, not merely their hands and wallets.

True leaders tap into people's hearts and minds, not merely their hands and wallets.

Why concern yourself with intrinsic rewards? After all, people in the workplace aren't volunteers; they are getting paid. However, it's precisely because people are getting paid, because people are eligible for bonuses and other awards, that a leader ought to be concerned. If work comes to be seen solely as a source of money and never as a source of fulfillment, organizations will totally ignore other human needs at work—needs involving such intangibles as learning, self-worth, pride, competence, and serving others. Employers will come to see people's enjoyment of their tasks as totally irrelevant, and they will structure work in a strictly utilitarian fashion. The results will be—and already have been—disastrous. Just take a look at the cost of recruitment and the cost of retention in some of the celebrated New Economy companies. Have big stock option plans or huge signing bonuses really done much to make them successful? There's very convincing evidence that reliance on extrinsic motivators can actually lower performance and create a culture of divisiveness and selfishness, precisely because it diminishes our inner sense of purpose.[15]

EXERCISE OUTSIGHT

You only have to read the cover story of weekly newsmagazines to know how dramatic the changes are that influence people's lives at home and at work. The old norms are being replaced by still uncertain ground rules. Recent research on the sources of innovation clearly indicates that the most disruptive and destructive innovations can wreak havoc on even the very best companies.[16]

The only effective response from leaders is to be ahead of the innovation curve. For sure, they can never afford to be behind it. So where do these new ideas for products, processes, and services come from? Research tells us that innovations come from just about anywhere,[17] and according to a global study of CEOs, two of the three most significant sources of innovative ideas are outside the organization.[18] Sometimes ideas come from customers, sometimes from the lead users, sometimes from suppliers, sometimes from business partners, and sometimes from the R&D labs. That may not be a very satisfactory answer, but it's the only legitimate one. Well then, if innovation can come from anywhere, what practical lessons can be drawn from this unpredictable phenomenon? Perhaps none is more important than this: leaders must always be actively looking for the fuzziest signs and intently listening to the weakest signals to anticipate that there's something new about to emerge over the horizon. This means honing their "outsight"—the capacity to perceive external things—and helping their constituents develop that ability as well.

If leaders are going to detect demands for change, they must stay sensitive to external realities, especially in this networked, global world. They must go out and talk to their constituents, be they citizens, customers, employees, stockholders, students, suppliers, vendors, business partners, managers, or just interested parties. They must listen—in person, on the phone, via e-mail, via Web sites—and stay in touch.

As CEO of Bay Area Credit Services, Michael Priest learned firsthand that leaders must look outward for fresh ideas. "Sometimes you just can't predict where the change will come from," he says, "but you have to have your eyes wide open if you have any hope of even catching a glimpse of it." In forecasting growth for his nearly $4 million collection agency, he realized that his biggest client, a large grocery retailer, generated about one-quarter of the agency's revenue and that the growth predicted for that client's business was not very likely. Therefore, his company's growth prospects were limited if it stayed with this client and with its current business model. To solve the problem, in essence caused by the major client's situation, Michael realized that they would need to change the company from a collection agency into a much larger one of a general call center operation. And to do so meant canceling the company's contract with its largest customer because this was the only way to free up the resources necessary for the change. The transformation was not without its risk, but in the two years following the agency's realignment as a call center, revenue has jumped nearly five-fold.

Kathleen Wilson Holtzer, while working with Ketchum, a full-service public relations agency, underscored Michael's point when she told us that she's always been surprised by where successful ideas come from, even in the course of everyday responsibilities. One example came when she was working on promotional campaigns for Kikkoman Soy Sauce:

I inherited a high-budget program that involved local celebrity chefs providing cooking demonstrations using the product inside grocery stores. The demonstration provided free samples as well. These promotional campaigns (hitting a targeted group at the point of purchase) were the traditional approach. But after completing a few of them I realized that we always had lots of samples left over. The costs for the food giveaways (samples) were negligible when compared with all of the other expenses involved in conducting the events. So, after one of these events, we simply distributed the remaining leftover samples throughout the greater shopping area where the store was located. And it turned out that this store had the highest coupon redemption rate of any of the other events.

This experience gave birth to the idea of moving our events to much larger, more trafficked areas than a single store location. This idea paid off big-time, with increased redemption rates and huge overall sales bumps bigger than the store events. You just never know where the inspiration will come from.

> *Innovation requires more listening and communication than does routine work.*

Innovation requires more listening and communication than does routine work. Leaders guiding a change must establish more relationships, connect with more sources of information, and get out and walk around more frequently. Successful innovations don't spring from the fifty-second floor of the headquarters building or the back offices of City Hall. It's only by staying in touch with the world around them that leaders can ever expect to change the business-as-usual environment.

Promote External and Internal Communication

Leaders can expect demand for change to come from both inside and outside the organization. But organizational leaders are likely to cut themselves off from critical information sources over time, often precisely because they're so busy trying to build an organization that'll be operationally efficient and sustain itself. And when the pressures for profit and efficiency are greatest, they may even mistakenly act to eliminate or severely limit the very things that provide the new ideas they need to weather the storms of uncertainty—by cutting the budgets for travel and training, for example. Unless external communication is actively encouraged, people interact with outsiders less and less frequently and new ideas are cut off.

Noam Shendar, while with MIPS Technologies, was charged with creating a marketing requirements document that reflected the views—and was deemed credible, he said—by all the company's departments. This meant, quite literally, that he had to bring together people from "all parts of the company" and actively engage them in constructive debate. "Face-to-face meetings are essential," he told us, "even in this era of electronic communication. Phone calls and e-mail are poor substitutes for ensuring that everyone puts a face—and a function—with a name . . . we didn't allow any bystanders," Noam explained, and because of this "everyone was committed to rolling up their sleeves and greatly contributed to the process from start to finish."

Research by professors Ralph Katz and Tom Allen of the MIT Sloan School of Management supports Noam's experience. As part of their study of research and development teams, they examined the relationship between the length of time that people had been working together in a particular project area—what they called "group longevity"—and the level of communication of project groups at various stages of their lives. Three areas of interpersonal oral communication were examined for each team: intra-project communication, organizational communication, and professional communication. Each team's technical performance was also measured by department managers and laboratory directors.[19]

The higher-performing groups had significantly more communication with people outside their labs, whether with organizational units such as marketing and manufacturing or with outside professional associations. Intriguingly, however, groups that had been together the longest reported lower levels of communications in all three areas and "were significantly more isolated from external sources of new ideas and technological advances and from information within other organizational divisions, especially marketing and manufacturing."[20] It seems the long-lived teams cut themselves off from the kind of information they needed the most to come up with new ideas, and thus reduced their performance. They'd been together so long, it appears, that they felt they didn't need to talk to outsiders. They were content just to talk to each other. It's easy to understand how some workgroups and organizations become myopic and unimaginative. The people themselves aren't dull or slow-witted; they've just become too familiar with their routines and too isolated from outside influences.

There simply aren't enough good new ideas floating around inside, however, to fill the innovation pipeline. You have to listen to the world outside. You've got to tap into the rich field of ideas that exist outside your own borders. Procter & Gamble's Larry Huston, vice president for innovation and knowledge, and Nabil Sakkab, senior vice president for corporate research and development, talk about the shift in thinking this way:

> We needed to move the company's attitude from resistance to innovations "not invented here" to enthusiasm for those "proudly found elsewhere." And we needed to change how we defined, and perceived, our R&D organization—from 7,500 people to 7,500 plus 1.5 million outside, with a permeable boundary between them. It's against this backdrop that we created the *connect and develop* innovation model.[21]

Huston and Sakkab go on to relate how this new model has worked for P&G. "Today more than 35% of our new products in market have elements that originated from the outside, up from 15% in 2000. And 45% of the initiatives in our product development portfolio have key elements that were discovered externally."[22] This is quite a shift for a company that had previously developed almost all of its new products internally or had acquired other companies in order to buy the new offerings. Huston and Sakkab believe theirs is not an isolated case: "We believe that the connect and develop will become the dominant innovation model in the twenty-first century."[23] We suggest that you heed their advice and begin connecting to others with great ideas and developing those much needed innovations.

Let Ideas Flow Freely from the Outside In

On a visit to Northern California, we stumbled across some extremely important advice for leaders. When exploring the Mendocino coast we picked up a pamphlet describing a particular stretch of shoreline. Printed boldly across the top of the first page was this warning: *"Never turn your back on the ocean.*" And why shouldn't you turn your back on the ocean to look inland to catch a view of the town? Because a rogue wave may come along when your back is turned and sweep you out to sea, as it has many an unsuspecting beachcomber. This warning holds lifesaving advice for travelers and for leaders alike. When you take your eyes off the external realities, turning inward to admire the possibilities within your own organization, you may be swept away by the swirling waters of change.

You must continuously scan the external realities. To be sure, innovation requires insight—the ability to apprehend the inner nature of things—but it also requires even keener outsight. When you keep the doors to the outside world open, ideas and information can flow freely into the organization. That's the only way you can become knowledgeable about what goes on around you. Outsight is the sibling of insight, and without it innovation could not happen. Insight without outsight is like seeing clearly with blinders on; you just can't get a complete picture.

Jacqueline Maartense, whom we met at the beginning of this chapter, told us how Intuit has become the only company in the world that has repeatedly and consistently beaten Microsoft in its software category (Quicken has outsold Microsoft's flagship personal finance brand by over 5 to 1). How do they beat Microsoft year after year when they're outgunned in terms of budget and resources? The answer is a penchant for seeking ideas from outside sources. Jacqueline calls it "customer-driven innovation."

"Customer-driven innovation was the key source of Intuit's competitive advantage," she says. "It was so deeply ingrained in our operations that it became part of our very fabric—it was the way we did business—it wasn't a research project or a task to be completed. It was a philosophy that permeated the organization from top-to-bottom." Jacqueline points to Scott Cook, cofounder, former CEO, and now chairman of the executive committee, as the embodiment of that philosophy.

Scott insisted that every employee in the company—from him to the janitor—spend time in "customer contact activities." There was call listening for a minimum of eight hours per employee after a product launch. And, "follow-me-home" programs where we would have our development staff visit buyers' homes to watch them use our software after purchase. I used to stand in the shopping aisles of CompUSA asking for research volunteers when people bought our software. During airline flights Scott would engage other travelers in conversation about our products and bring me back the Post-It notes with ideas. The list goes on and on.

If you want the innovative and competitive edge of an Intuit, then you need to destroy confining barriers and adopt an inquisitive attitude toward others' opinions and insights. Keep your eyes and ears open for new ideas. Remain receptive and expose yourself to broader views. Remove the protective covering in which organizations often seal themselves. Be willing to hear, consider, and accept ideas from sources outside the company.

Take Chef Allen's, an award-winning restaurant in North Miami Beach specializing in "Palm Tree Cuisine." Chef Allen uses a seemingly endless supply of unconventional techniques to keep pace with the emerging trends in his marketplace. One time, for example, he ran a "Chow Now" program. Allen gave servers and cooks $50 each to dine at any restaurant with cuisine similar to that of Chef Allen's. Employees returned with short written and oral reports on what they learned.

One cook reported that he had sampled a competitor's fare and was dismayed to find elegant food being served on cold plates, ruining the meal. Nearly all staffers participated. "They like to laugh at the little mistakes and believe they wouldn't make them," said Allen. And there's no doubt they paid more attention to warming plates up—and the hundreds of other details that make a restaurant truly elegant and successful.[24]

Leaders who are dedicated to getting extraordinary things done are open to receiving ideas from anyone and anywhere. They are adept at using their outsight to constantly survey the landscape of technology, politics, economics, demographics, art, religion, and society in search of new ideas. Because they never turn their backs on what is happening outside the boundaries of their organizations, exemplary leaders are not caught by surprise when the waves of change roll in. They are prepared to search for opportunities to address the constant shifts in the organization's environment. And because they are proactive they don't just ride the waves of change, they make the waves that others ride.

Challenges Often Find You

Although leaders personally seize the initiative, encourage others to do the same, and actively look everywhere for great ideas, that doesn't mean that you can't get extraordinary things done if you're leading a project that's been assigned to you. It doesn't mean you have to wait to start your own business to change the business-as-usual environment. Consider what we found when we asked people to tell us who initiated the projects that they selected as their personal bests. We assumed that the majority of people would name themselves, but, surprisingly, that's not what we found. Someone other than the leader—usually the person's immediate manager—initiated more than half the cases. Yet if leaders seize the initiative, how can we call people leaders when they're assigned the jobs and tasks they undertake? Doesn't this finding fly in the face of all that we've said about how leaders behave?

As we see it, the fact that over half the cases were not self-initiated should be a relief to the leaders who thought they had to initiate all the change, and it should be encouragement to everyone in the organization that responsibility for innovation and improvement is everyone's business. If the only times people reported doing their best were when they got to be the founder, CEO, county supervisor, police chief, agency director, or other head honcho, the majority of leadership opportunities would evaporate—as would most social and organizational changes. The reality is that much of what people do is assigned; few of us get to start everything from scratch. That's just a fact of organizational life.

Stuff happens in organizations and in people's lives. Sometimes they choose it; sometimes it chooses them. People who become leaders don't always seek the challenges they face. Challenges also seek leaders. It's not so important whether you find the challenges or they find you. What's important are the choices you make. What's important is the purpose you find for challenging the way things are. The question is: When opportunity knocks are you prepared to open the door?

To prepare yourself to welcome the next challenge that comes to your door, think hard about what motivates you. What gets you going in the morning, eager to embrace whatever might be in store? What inspires you to do your best, day in and day out? When you find the answers to these questions, when you discover what gives your work and life meaning and purpose, you'll become a generous host to the next change that comes to visit.

REFLECTION AND ACTION: SEARCHING FOR OPPORTUNITIES

In this chapter, we've emphasized how closely associated leadership is with change and innovation. Whether entrepreneurs, managers, community activists, educators, volunteers, or individual contributors, whether young or old, at the top, middle, or bottom of the organizational pyramid, when people describe their personal-best leadership experiences, they talk about the challenge of change. When we look at leaders, we see that they're associated with transformations, large and small. Leaders don't have to change history, but they do have to change "business as usual."

The pace of change has accelerated, and opportunities may come and go in a nanosecond. Exemplary leaders, therefore, are proactive: they actively seek and create new opportunities. They're always on the lookout for anything that lulls a group into a false sense of security; they constantly invite and create new initiatives. Leaders, by definition, are out in front of change, not behind it trying to catch up.

The quest for change is an adventure. It tests your wills and your skills. It's tough, but it's also stimulating. It brings forth talents that have been dormant.

It introduces you to yourself. For leaders to get the best from themselves and others, they must understand what gives meaning and purpose to work and what makes it intrinsically motivating. External rewards aren't sufficient when you struggle for shared aspirations.

Innovation and leadership are nearly synonymous. Leaders are innovators; innovators are leaders. The focus of a leader's attention is less on the routine operations and much more on the untested and untried. Leaders are always asking "What's new? What's next? What's better?" And when searching for opportunities to grow and improve, the most innovative ideas are most often not your own, and not in your own organizations. They're elsewhere, and the best leaders look all around them for the places in which breakthrough ideas are hiding. Exemplary leadership requires outsight, not just insight. That's where the future is.

Here are three steps that you can take toward that future. They are things you can begin to do today to Search for Opportunities to challenge the status quo and move along the path of getting extraordinary things done.

Treat Every Job as an Adventure

Even if you've been in your job for years, treat today as if it were your first day. Ask yourself, "If I were just starting this job, what would I do?" Begin doing those things now.

Approach every new assignment as a start-over. Stay alert to ways to constantly improve the organization. There's no magic to making a previously poor-performing unit a high-performing one. All you have to do is unlock the talent and resources for excellence. Often the critical difference is a leader who sees untapped energy and skill in the existing group and who assumes that excellence can be achieved. It's that old pioneering spirit reawakened.

Think of your leadership assignment as an exciting adventure through unexplored wilderness. Think of your constituents and colleagues as pioneers and discover new territory together. Identify those projects that you've always wanted to undertake but never have. Ask your team members to do the same. Pick one major project per quarter. Implement one smaller improvement every three weeks. Figure out how to do all of this within the budget you now have (or using the money you'll save or earn when your project succeeds). If you still need more money, go out and raise it from your supporters, as other adventurers do.

Be an adventurer, an explorer. Where in your organization have you not been? Where in the communities that you serve have you not been? Make a plan to explore those places. As kids we called it a field trip. Take a field trip to a factory, a warehouse, a distribution center, or a retail store. If you're in a school district, go sit in on the class that was once your favorite subject. How's it different today? If you're in city government, go to a department that really intrigues you. If you're in a professional services organization, go on a site visit with someone in a different practice. Field trips are more fun with other people. Take your team. Go on a bus or in a van so you can talk on the way there and the way back. Go!

Question the Status Quo

Some standard practices, policies, and procedures are critical to productivity and quality assurance. However, many are simply matters of tradition. To divide them out, make a list of all the practices in your organization that are "the way we've always done it around here." For each one, ask yourself, "How useful is this in helping us become the best we can be? How useful is this for stimulating creativity and innovation?" If your answer is "absolutely essential," then keep it. If not, find a way to change it.

Then, review all the policies and procedures. For each one, ask yourself the same questions and assign it "keep" or "change" status. Vow to eliminate every useless rule and every needless routine within the next month, the next quarter, the next year—whatever time frame is feasible. Wander around the plant, the store, the branch, the halls, or the office. Look for things that don't seem right. Ask questions. Probe.

A new assignment is a perfect opportunity to use your naive understanding of the operation to your advantage. Everyone tolerates your dumb questions. By constantly asking, "Why do we do this, and why do we do that?" you'll uncover some needed improvements. Don't stop at what you can find on your own. Ask employees what really bugs them about the organization. Ask what gets in the way of doing the best job possible. Promise to look into everything they bring up and get back to them with answers in ten days. Commit yourself to removing three frequently mentioned organizational roadblocks that stand in the way of getting extraordinary things done.

Questioning the status quo is not only for leaders. Effective leaders create a climate in which others feel comfortable doing the same. If your organization is going to be the best it can be, everyone has to feel comfortable in speaking up and taking the initiative.

Send Everyone Shopping for Ideas

Be on the lookout for new ideas, wherever you are. If you're serious about promoting innovation and getting others to listen to people outside the unit, make gathering new ideas a personal priority. Encourage others to open their eyes and ears to the world outside the boundaries of the organization. Choose among the abundant processes for collecting suggestions and make them fun for employees and customers. There are focus groups, advisory boards, suggestion boxes, breakfast meetings, brainstorming sessions, customer evaluation forms, mystery shoppers, mystery guests, visits to competitors, and scores more. The World Wide Web is a gold mine for this kind of thing. Chat rooms are great chances to swap ideas with those outside your field—anonymously, if you'd like. You can get a number of free online newsletters that are dedicated to innovation and include contributions from far and wide. At least once a day do a Web search for something related to what you do—and visit the site even if it's totally unrelated to your business. We're not in the restaurant business, but Chef Allen gave us a great idea. Just as he did, give your team members some cash and send people shopping for new ideas at competitors' stores or at totally unrelated businesses.

Make idea gathering part of your daily, weekly, and monthly schedule. Call three customers or clients who haven't used your services in a while and ask them why. Call three customers or clients who have made recent purchases and ask them why. Sure, we know about e-mail—the human voice is better for this sort of thing. Work the counter and ask people what they like and don't like about your organization. Shop at a competitor's store. Better yet, anonymously shop for your own product and see what the salespeople in the store say about it. Call your organization and see how the phones are answered and how questions are handled.

Make sure that you devote at least 25 percent of every weekly staff meeting to listening to outside ideas for improving processes and technologies and developing new products and services. Don't let staff meetings be simply status reports on routine, daily, inside stuff. Invite customers, suppliers, people from other departments, and other outsiders to your meetings to offer their suggestions on how your unit can improve.

Keep your antenna up, no matter where you are. You can never tell where or when you might find new ideas.

COMMITMENT NUMBER 5

Search for Opportunities

Essentials of Searching for Opportunities

- Seize the initiative
- Exercise outsight

Taking Action

- Treat every job as an adventure
- Question the status quo
- Send everyone shopping for ideas

EXPERIMENT AND TAKE RISKS

"Leaders are not afraid to take risks and step outside their comfort zones."
Chris Hintz, Cisco Systems

When Patricia Maryland came on board as president of Sinai-Grace Hospital in Detroit, Michigan, she found a hospital in distress. Sinai-Grace was the one hospital remaining after a series of mergers, and all the "burning and slashing" had left the staff feeling angry and distrustful. In addition, the hospital was still losing money. It was a hospital looking not only for new leadership but also a new identity.[1]

One of the first things Patricia noticed was that employees mostly related to the way things had been done in the past. No one was speaking about the need to do things differently, and that was very troubling to her. As Patricia explained, "Given the major challenges we face in this field, you have to think outside the box when analyzing your situation and implementing change."

Patricia began by talking with and listening to her staff, searching for things they could begin to work on that would create momentum for improvement. An obvious challenge was the long waits patients experienced in the emergency room. "When I arrived at Sinai-Grace, people in Emergency had to wait an average of eight hours to be seen and admitted to a hospital bed," Patricia said. "This was clearly unacceptable."

Another challenge was the way the hospital was perceived by the community. "It was a dirty hospital," Patricia related. "People who lived within a block of us were going to other hospitals. It was clear that the physical environment was a significant part of our image problem."

Then there was the way patients saw the staff—and how the staff saw themselves. Staff would argue and talk inappropriately with patients. Attendance was poor and morale was low. The staff didn't wear uniforms—they were pretty much wearing street clothes—which Patricia felt was very unprofessional.

These kinds of issues demanded immediate action, and because they had existed for so long, they required experimenting with some fundamentally new approaches. They turned out to be things that could be quickly addressed, enabling Patricia to win a few early victories in her efforts to improve the quality of care, patient satisfaction, and staff morale.

To address the unacceptable ER wait times, Patricia challenged the long-standing tradition of how the department was organized. "One of the changes we wanted to make was to create a separate area for chest pain patients so they would be triaged immediately. Then our urgent care population was moved to another area called Express Care." In Express Care they built exam rooms with walls, improving privacy and confidentiality. These simple changes reduced wait time by more than 75 percent.

Building on this success was a $100,000 foundation grant to upgrade hospital décor. Fresh paint, new carpets, and new furniture can do wonders.

Patricia got the doctors to donate artwork, and the place started to look like a contemporary medical center. "I really felt it was important to create an environment that was warm and embracing, allowing incoming patients to feel some level of trust and comfort," Patricia explained.

Patricia improved the staff's "décor" by challenging the practice of informal dress. "If you place your employees in uniforms," she said, "that sets a tone of professionalism, because if you look good, people get the first impression that you are very organized and care about what you're doing."

Patricia also challenged staff to take a look at the way they related to patients: "Imagine this patient were your mother or your father. How would you work with them? How would you talk to them? How would you feel if someone was cold, unfriendly, and treated you like an object rather than a human being?"

These first few changes at Sinai-Grace Hospital started an outstanding turnaround. Patricia got increasing buy-in from the staff because these early visible successes demonstrated that things could be different. Customer service scores went up tremendously—from mostly ones and twos on a five-point scale to mostly fours and fives. Morale went up, and a new vitality and enthusiasm emerged at Sinai-Grace. Today, the hospital is doing quite well financially. Most important, said Patricia, "The community has confidence in Sinai-Grace, and they are feeling more comfortable about using the hospital for their health care."

Patricia Maryland moved on to seek more ways to shake up the status quo when she accepted the position of president at St. Vincent Hospitals and Health Services in Indianapolis, one of Indiana's largest hospitals and the flagship of the Ascension Health system, the nation's largest network of Catholic hospitals. There she continues to challenge herself and others to "think outside the box," just as she did at Sinai-Grace. "We've decided, as an organization, that we will look for opportunities for improvement," she says, "and we will challenge the way we do things if we feel we have not been effective in the past."

To pursue your passions and fulfill your dreams, as Patricia Maryland points out, you have to do the unorthodox. Every single personal best we have heard and read speaks to the need to take risks with bold ideas. It's clear why this is the case. Nothing new and nothing great is achieved by doing things the way you've always done them. You have to test unproven strategies. You have to break out of the norms that box you in. You have to do the things you think you cannot. You have to venture beyond the limitations you normally place on yourselves. Getting extraordinary things done in organizations demands a willingness to experiment and take risks with innovative ideas.

Boldness is not necessarily about go-for-broke, giant-leap projects. More often than not it's about starting small and gaining momentum. Fresh paint, new carpets, professional uniforms, and a new Express Care service are just as important as grander schemes. In fact, these small, visible steps are more likely to win early victories than are big-bang efforts, and they gain early supporters.

Of course, when you experiment, not everything works out as intended. There are mistakes and false starts. They are part of the process of innovation. What's critical, therefore, is that leaders promote learning from these experiences.

To create a climate in which the norm is to Experiment and Take Risks, it's essential for leaders to

- **Generate small wins**
- **Learn from experience**

These essentials can help leaders transform challenge into an exploration, uncertainty into a sense of adventure, fear into resolve, and risk into reward. They are the keys to making progress that becomes unstoppable.

GENERATE SMALL WINS

If we're talking about challenging the process, you should just pull out all the stops and go for it, right? Wrong. There's an old African proverb that advises, "Never test the depth of the water with both feet." Wise counsel whenever you're trying something brand new. Leaders should dream big, but start small. Dream big about crossing that enormous cosmos to find some new world, but start small with a few short journeys to test your theories and your abilities.

Consider what Gary Jamieson told us about a project involving the introduction of a new source-control system across several sites and countries, while he was with Scientific Atlanta (now part of Cisco Systems):

> At the start of the project there was this general belief that it could never be completed. It was important to prove to the team early in the project that it could be achieved. In order to do so, I structured the project so that key early milestones had significant and distinct deliverables that could be seen as clear achievements under difficult circumstances. Making these early milestones gave the team members confidence in their ability to deliver. I then ensured that intermediate milestones were announced as small achievements within the larger project, and demonstrated the benefits of achieving the milestone. This helped to build not only excitement but momentum.

Why not start big? Because, as leaders like Gary understand, if you think of problems too broadly or too expansively they appear overwhelming. They suffocate people's capacity to even conceive of what might be done, let alone begin doing something immediately. Imagine solving the global warming problem, the international terrorism problem, or the homelessness problem. Or imagine solving the problems of rising fuel costs, lack of affordable housing, shrinking pension funds, or rising college tuition. What can *you* do about these big issues?

Leaders face this dilemma all the time. They want people to reach for big heights, but not become fearful of falling. They want them to be challenged, but not overwhelmed. They want them to be curious, but not lost. They like to see people excited, but not stressed. Framing the challenge as something too big can actually have the effect of dampening motivation to do something about it. Making a dent, let alone a difference, in the major problems people face can seem to require such overwhelming force that it's a challenge to even set out on the journey.

The most effective change processes are incremental, not one giant leap.

So how do you get people to want to move in a new direction, break old mind-sets, or change existing behavior patterns in order to tackle big problems and attempt extraordinary performance? The answer: step-by-step through the generation of small wins. The most effective change processes are incremental, not one giant leap. Each step forward creates a psychological "win" that propels people to continue in that direction. A "win" generates excitement, energy, and commitment.

Progress Step-by-Step

Leaders know they have to break down big problems into small, doable actions. They also know that you have to try a lot of little things when initiating something new before you get it right. Not every innovation works, and the best way to ensure success is to experiment with a lot of ideas, not just one or two big ones. Successful leaders help others to see how breaking the journey down into measurable milestones can move them forward. Which is exactly what Venkat Dokiparthi experienced at a large enterprise software company when he was asked to lead a technical development team in India.

We needed to do a task to improve a certain part of the product, and I asked the team to come up with a proposal for how to go about it. After several weeks with no response, they finally told me that it was "beyond their scope." Then I realized that I needed to break down the task and make it simple for them to feel successful.

So I divided the task into a ten-week program and asked them to try the first week's assignment. The task for that week was now so clear to them, and so much within their capabilities, that they actually implemented it within three days. So I encouraged them to start on the following week's assignment. They showed considerable progress and in fact completed the entire implementation process in six weeks! Initiating incremental steps and encouraging small wins has really been the key for success of this task.

A small wins approach fits especially well with the nature of work in the information society. The pace is fast and fragmented. Today's manager typically spends an average of three minutes of uninterrupted time on any single event and around twelve minutes on a "work sphere" before switching to something else.[2] That means a manager could be switching from project to project forty or more times a day. It's enough to make any leader dizzy. This kind of work pattern requires leaders to act on their dreams in brief bursts. The beauty of a small win is that it's compact, it's simple, and it can catch the attention of people who have only a few minutes to listen to an idea or read a proposal.

We can learn something about taking it step-by-step from how successful coaches help young players become successful. Incremental progress was exactly what Institute for Women's Leadership founder Rayona Sharpnack had in mind when she was coaching her eight-year-old daughter's softball team. Rayona certainly knew the game: she was the first player-manager in the 1980s of the most profitable franchise of the International Women's Professional Softball League. Before that, she set a Junior Olympic record by throwing a softball 189 feet. On one of the first days of practice for her daughter's team, she had everyone try to do some batting. As she explains,

I take a really soft, spongy ball, and I toss it to the first girl. She's standing maybe 10 feet away, I'm throwing baby tosses, and she screams and hides her head. So I say, "Hey, no problem, Suzy. Go to the back of the line. That's fine. Betsy, you step up." Next girl in line, she does the same thing—buries her head and screams. So I'm realizing that this is going to be a really long practice if we don't do something different.

I go out to my car where I have my handy whiteboard markers in my briefcase. I take the bag of practice balls and draw four smiley faces—red, black, blue, and green—on each ball. When you look at a ball, all you see is one smiley face. I go back out and call the girls back over: "Okay. We're going to play a different game this time," I say. "This time, your job is to name the color of the smiley face. That's all you have to do."

So little Suzy stands up, and I toss a ball by her. She watches it all the way and goes, "Red." Next girl, Betsy, gets up there. Betsy goes, "Green." They're all just chirping with excitement because they can identify the color of the smiley face, so I say, "Okay. Now I want you to do the same thing, only this time I want you to hold the bat on your shoulder when the ball goes by." Same level of success. Excitement builds. The third time through, I ask them to touch the smiley face with the bat.

We beat our opponents 27 to 1 in the first game.[3]

Rayona took something that was initially frightening and gradually overcame the team's fear and the lack of skill. She coached the girls in increments on how to focus on the task and then to execute. If we could all approach new and challenging tasks this way, we could enjoy the same success as Rayona's team.

Try a Lot of Little Things

When Philip Diehl was appointed director of the U.S. Mint, he didn't spend his early days at this multibillion dollar organization making big promises and bold declarations; he chose the small wins path. "I didn't rush the changes at the Mint," says Diehl. "I started small, with a few initiatives here and there. Then as the envelope was pushed or as roadblocks appeared, problems were tackled as they cropped up, and progress continued. Big changes have been made over the past six years, but they've been made incrementally. You do big things by doing lots of small things."[4]

Consider the Mint's 50 State Quarters Program, one of the most successful consumer-product launches ever. It's a long-term project that is designed to rejuvenate the public's interest in coins and in coin collecting. The program honors each state with its own special quarter. The public gets involved, through the governor's office in each state, in the design process. Every ten weeks for ten years a new state quarter gets put into circulation, released in the order in which each state joined the Union. One step, or quarter, at a time.[5]

> *You do big things by doing a lot of small things.*

The U.S. Mint continues its small wins approach to growth and improvement with the almost monthly introduction of limited edition and commemorative coins, from the Bison Nickel and Buffalo Quarter to the "Granite Lady" honoring the San Francisco Old Mint. It's incremental innovations like these that keep the collector coming back. Diehl's point that "You do big things by doing a lot of small things" ought to be the mantra of leaders engaged in transforming change. We heard it over and over in the personal-best cases we collected.

Take the turnaround at the car dealerships within the Whites Group in London, which chairman Lindsay Levin told us could be credited to an organizational culture that supported experimentation and incremental improvement. Volunteers were recruited to get started on doing anything that they thought would make the customer experience more delightful. Many of the early projects addressed in-house headaches—such as redoing the kitchen and cleaning up the workshop—and not necessarily things that would have an immediate impact on customers. With these small wins, the teams escalated up the learning curve and rapidly moved on to projects that would directly benefit the customer.

Parking, for instance, had been a problem for customers and staff alike. A team at Camberley completely reorganized the parking lot and managed to create twenty new spaces. Flowerbeds had to be moved, concrete dividers had to be torn up, and the whole area repainted. It may sound simple, but it was a major achievement, not least because it was a problem that had been talked about for years and no one had done anything about it. This experience became a model showing people what could be done, as well as rein-forcement that learning was taking place. This success so uplifted people's spirits that the "Camberley parking lot" became a showcase for how teams could make a difference in their own locations.

Models like the Camberley parking lot are limited experiments in accomplishing change. They're laboratories for trying, failing, and learning. They're also great visual aids for teaching people about what success looks like. They're tangible showcases for change. By showcasing some "little thing" you've experimented with you give people a tangible sense of what success looks like. You also boost morale and confidence. People see that it's possible to do something about what might otherwise be perceived as an intractable problem.

Whatever you call your experiments—model sites, pilot studies, demonstration projects, laboratory tests, field experiments, market trials—all are methods about trying lots of little things in the service of something much bigger. These are the tactics that continually generate lots of possibilities for small wins. And all those possibilities can add up to big results.

Small Wins Produce Results

Small wins produce results for a simple reason: it's hard to argue against success. The fact that small wins work isn't news to scholars of technological innovation. An extensive study involving five DuPont plants documented that minor technical changes (for example, introduction of forklift trucks)—rather than major changes (for example, introduction of new chemical processing technologies)—accounted for over two-thirds of the reductions in production costs over a thirty-year period.[6] The minor technical changes were small improvements, made by people familiar with current operations. Less time, skill, effort, and expense were required to produce them than to implement the major changes. Much of the improvement was really part of the process of learning by doing.

The scientific community has always understood that major breakthroughs are likely to be the result of the work of hundreds of researchers, as countless contributions finally begin to add up to a solution. Taking the sum total, all the "little" improvements in technology, regardless of the industry, likely have contributed to a greater increase in organizational productivity than all the great inventors and their inventions.[7] Indeed, researchers have found that rapid prototyping, and plenty of it, results in getting higher-quality products to the marketplace more quickly.[8]

Small wins produce results because they form the basis for a consistent pattern of winning that attracts people who want to be allied with a successful venture. Small wins build people's confidence and reinforce their natural desire to feel successful. Because additional resources tend to flow to winners, this means that slightly larger wins can be attempted next. A series of small wins therefore provides a foundation of stable building blocks. Each win preserves gains and makes it harder to return to preexisting conditions; each win also provides information that facilitates learning and adaptation.

Small wins produce results because they actively make people feel like winners and make it easier for others to want to go along with their requests. If people can see that a leader is asking them to do something that they're quite capable of doing, they feel some assurance that they can be successful at the task. If people aren't overwhelmed by a task, their energy goes into getting the job done, instead of wondering "how will we ever solve that problem?" They then have heightened interest in continuing with the journey.

Small wins produce results because they build personal and group commitment to a course of action. Think about the way professional fundraisers operate: they begin by asking for a small or indeterminate contribution. They know that it's easier to go back and request more in the future from those who've made an initial contribution than to return to someone who's already said no. By working at finding all the little ways that people can succeed at doing things differently, effective leaders make people want to be involved and stay involved because they can see that what they are doing is making a difference. Small victories attract constituents, create momentum, and get people to remain on the path.

We appreciated the lessons Kathryn Winters recounted to us about a time when one of her experiments working with the communications department at NVIDIA Corporation didn't pan out as intended. Her review of what she would do differently the next time around is a blueprint for how exemplary leaders set up small wins to produce extraordinary results:

> In the future I plan to set up experiments, start small, listen and talk with people about how they think the process should be accomplished, give people choices, and make it easy for them to say "yes." We'll build upon each success and make certain that people are recognized for moving forward.

Stanford University's Debra Meyerson refers to people who engage in this sort of action as "tempered radicals"—cautious catalysts whose small victories, won over time, lay the groundwork for something grander.[9]

LEARN FROM EXPERIENCE

People never do anything perfectly the first time they try it—not in sports, not in games, not in school, and most certainly not in work organizations. When they engage in something new and different people make a lot of mistakes. That's what experimentation is all about, and, as research scientists know very well, there's a lot of trial and error involved in testing new concepts, new methods, and new practices.

Consider the times when you tried to play a new game or a new sport. Maybe it was skiing, snowboarding, tennis, bridge, golf, hockey, or poker. Did you get it perfect the very first day? Not likely. For example, do you imagine that you could navigate a skateboard or snowboard all day long the first time you get on it? Are you very likely to win a game of chess the very first time you play or record a par the first time you play golf?

Over and over again, people in our studies tell us how important mistakes and failure have been to their success. Without mistakes we'd be unable to know what we can and cannot do (at least at this moment). Without those experiences, respondents said, they would have been unable to achieve their aspirations. It may seem ironic, but many echo the thought that the overall quality of work improves when people have a chance to fail. Studies of the innovation process make the point: "Success does not breed success. It breeds failure. It is failure which breeds success."[10]

Just consider what James E. West, research professor at Johns Hopkins University, who has secured nearly fifty domestic and more than two hundred foreign patents, has to say about the topic: "I think I've had more failures than successes, but I don't see the failures as mistakes because I always learned something from those experiences. I see them as having not achieved the initial goal, nothing more than that."[11] To be sure, failure can be costly. For the individual who leads a failed project, it can mean a stalled career or even a lost job. For an adventurous leader, it can mean the loss of personal assets. For mountain climbers and other physical adventurers, it can mean injury or death. The point is that there is no success without the possibility of failure.[12]

The overall quality of work improves when people have a chance to fail.

We don't advocate for a moment that failure ought to be the *objective* of any endeavor. The objective is *learning*. Learning happens when people feel comfortable in talking about both successes and failures. It happens when people can openly talk about what went right and what went wrong. Leaders don't look for someone to blame when the inevitable mistakes are made in the name of innovation. They ask, "What can be learned from the experience?"

This is precisely the attitude of the FAA (United States Federal Aviation Administration)—they want pilots to learn from one another's mistakes in an effort to keep accident rates low. *Inc.* magazine's contributing editor David Freedman, author of several books on business and technology, is himself a licensed pilot. He explains,

I once managed to land a small plane on the wrong strip at a small airport. I could have gotten in plenty big trouble for it, so you might have thought my best move would have been to keep my mouth shut and hope the FAA wouldn't find out. But I couldn't wait to report my screwup to the government. I wish I could say it was because I'm such a conscientious fellow. But the truth is, I fessed up fast because the U.S. government *rewards* pilots for quickly owning up to their mistakes, agreeing to waive punitive action if they report themselves. In fact, most pilots carry the self-reporting form with them in their flight case, just in case.

Nearly three thousand of these self-reported confessions are filed monthly, gathered by NASA (the U.S. National Aeronautics and Space Administration), and selectively published in a monthly newsletter (*Callback*) that is avidly read. "You can't stamp out mistakes at your company, no matter how good a manager you are or how brilliantly you hone your processes," Freedman tells us. One thing you can do, he says, is "create an environment in which each mistake becomes a collective learning experience."[13]

Create a Climate for Learning

Promoting learning requires a spirit of inquiry and openness, patience, and building in a tolerance for error and a framework for forgiveness. "Learning requires tolerating people who make mistakes," says Universant's cofounder and chairman Joe Hage, "and it requires tolerating some inefficiencies and failures. Learning requires letting people try things they've never done before, things that they probably won't be all that good at the first time around." It means accepting the necessary trade-off between proficiency and learning.

Similarly, when projects or programs don't pan out as intended at Xilinx, a leader in the programmable logic device market, the conclusion is always that the project or concept failed, not the individuals or the group involved. Otherwise, there would be little support for innovation and experimentation. They never focus on "who screwed up" but always focus on "what was the problem, and how can we solve it or learn from it?" Chris Taylor, the company's senior director of communications, explained: "We're not about finger-pointing. Everyone is going to make mistakes; the issue is what you do with this experience, how you grow and learn from it." She described how one ("failed") product was canned, and, in fact, the project team itself determined that it wasn't worth pursuing, even after years of intensive development. They could make that recommendation because they knew they themselves wouldn't be blamed. This same group subsequently came up with the most significant new product ever for the company—out of this so-called failure. Leaders at companies like Xilinx appreciate that learning always comes with a cost, but that the price is worth it.

Because people know that they won't do well the first time they try something, learning new things can be a bit scary. They might embarrass themselves in front of peers. They might look stupid in front of their manager. Learning is more likely to happen in a climate in which people feel safe in making themselves vulnerable, safe in taking the risk of failure.

It may seem paradoxical, but the safer people feel the more risks they'll take and the more mistakes they'll be willing to make. For example, we'd all agree that jumping out of an airplane with a parachute on our backs is very risky. Jumping out of an airplane *without* a parachute on our backs is foolhardy. The parachute and the training to use it make that dangerous activity safe enough for some people to be willing to take the risk.

Feeling safe is not just about parachutes. Safety is also about a climate that encourages people to offer ideas, even crazy ideas. Too often, though, people like to cling to the familiar and put down new ideas by saying things such as "It's not in the budget," "It'll never work," or "We've never done that before." When confronted with change, some tend to respond like firefighters hosing down a fire—they douse ideas before they can flare up—and thereby extinguish enthusiasm, spirit, and new possibilities.[14]

When Maureen Fries was administrator of the Los Olivos Women's Medical Group, a staff member suggested at a department meeting that anyone heard "firehosing" should have to put 25 cents into a "no negativism" fund. Everyone agreed, and the policy went into effect immediately.

As time went by, Maureen says, staff members were obviously thinking more carefully about what they were saying to one another in order not to be—or sound—negative. People policed one another on a daily basis. Cries of "That's worth a quarter!" and "Another quarter for the kitty!" could be heard all over the department. Collection jars sprang up everywhere. Morale improved noticeably, as did the number of innovative ideas. The jars were a physical reminder of the importance of keeping a positive attitude about learning.

Leaders Are Active Learners

Curious about the relationship between leadership and learning, we conducted a series of empirical studies to find out if managers could be differentiated by the range and depth of learning tactics they employ when facing a new or unfamiliar experience.

First we looked at how engaged these managers were in four different approaches to learning: "taking action" (preferring to learn by trial and error), "thinking" (reading articles or books or going online to gain knowledge and background), "feeling" (confronting themselves on what they are worrying about), and "accessing others" (bouncing hopes and fears off someone they trust). We then correlated these with leadership practices. We found that managers who were more rather than less engaged in each of these learning tactics were also more engaged in The Five Practices of Exemplary Leadership.[15] Others have shown that people more engaged in these various learning tactics were more likely to have started something from scratch, played a significant role in an acquisition, turned around an organizational unit, negotiated a major contract, and the like.[16] In other words, the more you're engaged in learning the more successful you are at leading—and at just about anything. One reason that leaders take learning seriously is that they're humble about their own abilities.[17]

Despite what may objectively be extraordinary achievements, many leaders are loath to attribute these to some extraordinary competency on their part. They recognize that they don't know it all and can't do everything, and they realize they still have a lot to learn. Think about the people in your organization who are the most likely to voluntarily sign up and participate in leadership-development programs. Chances are they're the ones who are already quite capable based on their track record. They're going to those programs to get even better.

Another reason that leaders are serious learners is that they're apt to adopt a "scientific method" perspective to their analysis of problems, challenges, and opportunities. The scientific method has long emphasized the virtues of disproving a hypothesis and then testing new ones as the path to understanding. Rather than trying to prove that something is true, researchers try to prove themselves wrong (that is, disconfirming the hypothesis). Only by rejecting or ruling out rival hypotheses can they be more confident that some phenomenon is what they believe it to be. Mistakes are a necessary part of the learning process.

The only way that people can learn is by doing things they've never done before.

For this reason, scientists, designers, and inventors generally focus on potential flaws, which makes failure, and the lessons that come with it, quite revealing and informative.[18] Leaders, while accepting the observation that most innovations are "failures in the middle," simply recognize that if we're not making mistakes then we're only doing what we already know how to do.

There's no simple test for determining the best tactic for learning. But it's clear that leaders approach each new and unfamiliar experience with a willingness to learn, an appreciation for the importance of learning, and a recognition that learning necessarily involves making some mistakes. The only way that people can learn is by doing things they've never done before. This entails resiliency and becoming psychologically hardy.

View Change as Challenge

Even though we urge every leader to experiment, take risks, and learn from the accompanying mistakes, we know that many learning experiences can be very stressful and painful. Falling down when skiing can result in injury. Failing to achieve the expected results from an innovation can set you back. And despite the overwhelmingly positive emotions associated with personal-best cases, we can't overlook the fact that they were filled with stress. Although 95 percent of the cases were described as exciting, about 20 percent of leaders also called the experiences frustrating, and approximately 15 percent said that their experiences aroused fear or anxiety.

But instead of being debilitated by the stress of a difficult experience, leaders said they were challenged and energized by it. Stress always accompanies the pursuit of excellence, but when you're doing your best it never overtakes you. Disruptive change demands significant commitment and sacrifice, but the positive feelings associated with forward progress generate momentum that enables you to ride out the storm. It's this kind of attitude that leaders must develop in their constituents when challenging the process to improve and grow.

Making mistakes is part of the price people pay for innovation and for learning. Even if you could compute risk to the fifth decimal place, every innovation would still expose you to some peril. There's just no way you can make it perfectly safe to make a change. Knowing this, leaders have to approach adversity with a belief that they and others can bounce back from failure. They have to believe that they and their constituents can recover from mistakes, and that they can learn and move on. They have to be hardy and resilient.

But it turns out that the ability to grow and thrive under stressful, risk-abundant situations is highly dependent on how you view change. The stress of doing something new doesn't affect everyone in the same way. Many people associate stress with illness. They've been led to believe that if they experience seriously stressful events, they'll become ill. If we all adopted this point of view, we might as well sit back in our overstuffed easy chairs, surf through the television channels, and never venture into the world. But the reports of illness resulting from stress are misleading. Stress—even at its most strenuous—doesn't necessarily contribute to severe illness. After all, many people have experienced life-threatening, even torturous, circumstances and remained healthy. Indeed, some stress even energizes people. The personal bests shared with us by the leaders in our study are clear examples of difficult, stressful projects that generated enthusiasm and enjoyment. It isn't stress that makes you ill but how you perceive and respond to stressful events.

Intrigued by people who'd experienced a high degree of stress yet had a relatively low degree of illness, psychologists have hypothesized that such individuals must have a distinctive attitude toward stress, which they call "psychological hardiness."[19] Studies of psychological hardiness began with a twelve-year longitudinal study of executives at Illinois Bell Telephone as that organization experienced the firestorm of changes produced by the federal antitrust case against the Bell system and the resulting breakup of the company. Some executives were undermined by the mounting stresses of this upheaval; they had high stress scores along with high rates of illness. Yet another group of executives with equally high stress scores thrived and were below average on incidence of illness.

As the researchers had predicted, there was a clear attitudinal difference between the high-stress and high-illness group and the high-stress but low-illness group. Psychologically hardy executives made these assumptions about themselves in their interaction with the world:

- They felt a strong sense of control, believing that they could beneficially influence the direction and outcome of what was going on around them through their own efforts. Lapsing into powerlessness, feeling like a victim of circumstances, and passivity seemed like a waste of time to them.
- They were strong in commitment, believing that they could find something in whatever they were doing that seemed interesting, important, or worth-

while. They were curious about what was going on around them, and this led them to find interactions with people and situations stimulating and meaningful. They were unlikely to engage in denial or feel disengaged, bored, and empty.

- They felt strong about the need for challenge, believing that personal improvement and fulfillment come through the continual process of learning from both negative and positive experiences. They felt that it was not only unrealistic but also stultifying to simply expect, or even wish for, easy comfort and security.

We found this same kind of psychological hardiness in the personal-best cases we collected. The leaders we studied experienced the change in which they were engaged, whether they initiated it or not, as a challenge out of which something extraordinary would come. They were fully engaged, curious, and committed to making something happen. They believed that they had the power to influence the destiny of their own and their teams' lives. What's more, they made the people on their teams feel the same way.

Take a look at Sandra Stach, media manager for Safeway, and the way she and her team have been fortified by taking on new challenges. As one example, Sandra told us how media buys for display advertising in her company, as is true for most companies, were not centralized. "For some inexplicable reason, these buys were personal," she explained. Sandra challenged the conventional thinking about the validity of this buying process and quickly found like-minded supporters within her team. "Once I was enthusiastic about determining and justifying the right media buy," she said, "it was easy to generate enthusiasm with my team members by questioning the buy at every turn. Soon I found my team asking questions on their own."

Sandra and her team viewed change as challenge, believed strongly that asking questions about the status quo led to better results, and felt they could effect a difference. Their psychological hardiness, Sandra reported, has "improved the team's performance," and she characterized them as having a "continuous sense of ongoing learning."

Each project has given them the opportunity to demonstrate their knowledge, creativity, and passion for a shared cause. Though some of the team's suggestions have been unrealistic or impossible to execute, I have tried to direct discussions to encourage innovations but discourage renegade-ism. In doing so, I have been able to obtain very innovative ideas that can be applied to other areas. I have tried to push each team member to work beyond his or her limit and to support each idea as valid and applicable.

Over the last few months, we have experimented with various ideas, and some have proven unsuccessful. Each time we have failed, I have asked the team to recap the failure with what they perceive the reason to be. Many team members have been discouraged when a measurement technique fails, for example, but we've found that there is significant improvement once it is analyzed and everyone understands why it failed. These very team members have been the ones to propose the next experiment. Enthusiasm seems to build even higher with each new challenge.

Apparently it isn't just innovation and challenge that play important roles in your personal progress; it's also the way you view the challenges that come your way. If you see them as learning opportunities, you're much more likely to succeed than if you see them simply as check marks on a report card. Thus your view of events contributes to your ability to cope with change and stress: with a positive view, you can transform stressful events into manageable or desirable situations rather than regressing, or ignoring or avoiding issues and situations.

Foster Hardiness

How do you develop psychological hardiness? Hardiness, it turns out, can be learned and cultivated at any time in life.[20] Leaders can help their constituents cope more effectively by creating a climate that develops hardiness by building the following:

- A sense of control through choosing tasks that are challenging but within the person's skill level
- Commitment with the offer of more rewards than punishments
- An attitude of challenge by encouraging people to see change as full of possibilities

In our advice on promoting hardiness, there are two important implications for leaders. First, people can't lead if they aren't psychologically hardy. No one will follow someone who avoids stressful events and won't take decisive action. Second, even if leaders are personally very hardy, they can't enlist and retain others if they don't create an atmosphere that promotes psychological hardiness. People won't remain long with a cause that distresses them. They need to believe that they can overcome adversity if they're to accept the challenge of change. Leaders must create the conditions that make all of that possible.

> *People won't remain long with a cause that distresses them.*

Fortune magazine senior writer Adam Lashinsky, in writing about Google, says, "Spend just a few minutes on Google's sprawling campus and you'll feel it right away: This is a company thriving on the edge of chaos. . . . It's a place where failure coexists with triumph and ideas bubble up from lightly supervised engineers."[21] All engineers, in fact, are required to spend 20 percent of their time pursuing their own ideas. The company's goal, says Shona Brown, senior vice president for business operations, is "to determine precisely the amount of management it needs—and then use a little bit less."[22]

This is an organization that doesn't just foster psychological hardiness, it promotes it. How did founder and CEO Larry Page respond to Sheryl Sandberg's admission of an error she'd made that cost Google several million dollars? "I'm so glad you made this mistake," he said, "because I want to run a company where we are moving too quickly and doing too much, not being too cautious and doing too little. If we don't have any of these mistakes, we're just not taking enough risk."[23]

The personal-best examples involved change and stressful events in the lives of leaders; they involved significant personal and organizational change. And nearly all of these cases were described in terms consistent with the conditions for psychological hardiness. Participants experienced commitment rather than alienation, control rather than powerlessness, and challenge rather than threat.

Although our cases represent a sample of only the best of times, it's instructive to know that people associate doing their best with feelings of meaningfulness, mastery, and stimulation, that people are biased in the direction of hardiness when thinking about their best. It's equally helpful to know that people don't produce excellence when feeling ignored, insignificant, and threatened.

Furthermore, feelings of commitment, control, and challenge provide internal cues for recognizing when you're excelling and when you're only getting through the day. They tell leaders what signs to look for when assessing the capacity of their constituents to get extraordinary things done and give them guidelines to use when creating an environment for success.

This sense of being committed and in control during times of great challenge is very similar to what other researchers have referred to as "optimal performance." These are the times when people feel that they are performing effortlessly despite the difficulty of the experience, a state that athletes often refer to as "flow." People perform at their best when they are confident that their skills match the level of challenge of the experience, even though the challenge might be a bit of a stretch. The relationship of challenge and skill to optimal performance is illustrated graphically in Figure 8.1.

When the forces of challenge never test their skills and abilities are not in balance, people feel apathy and boredom. When the challenges overwhelm their capabilities, they feel worry or anxiety. Neither of these conditions pro-

FIGURE **8.1** OPTIMAL PERFORMANCE, CHALLENGE, AND SKILL.

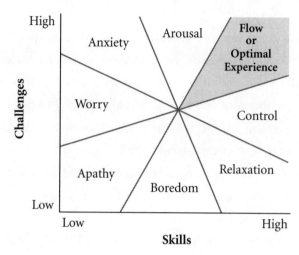

Source: M. Csikszentmihalyi, Finding Flow: The Psychology of Engagement with Everyday Life, New York: Basic Books, 1997, p. 31. Reprinted by permission of Basic Books, a member of Perseus Book Group.

duces optimal performance. It's only when the challenges are moderate to high and the skills are at the same level—or are moderately stretched—that people can attain a sense of effortless and optimal performance.

The vast majority of us can feel in charge of change at least some of the time. As the personal-best cases demonstrate, people have an intuitive sense of what makes them strong and what makes them weak. The challenge is to apply these lessons to daily life at work. Leaders have a responsibility to create an environment that breeds hardiness on a regular, not an occasional, basis.

REFLECTION AND ACTION: EXPERIMENTING AND TAKING RISKS

A major task for all leaders is to identify and remove self-imposed constraints and organizational conventions that block innovation and creativity. Yet innovation is always risky—and leaders recognize failure as a necessary fact of the innovative life. Instead of punishing it, they encourage it; instead of trying to fix blame for mistakes, they learn from them; instead of adding rules, they encourage flexibility.

Leaders are experimenters: they experiment with new approaches to all problems. They venture outside the constraints of normal routine and experiment with creative and risky solutions. They create climates in which organizational members can also accept the challenge of change.

Leaders guide and channel the often-frenetic human motion of change toward some end. When things seem to be falling apart, leaders show their constituents the exciting new world they can create from the pieces. Out of the uncertainty and chaos of change, leaders rise up to show how accepting the present challenge will actually help shape a better tomorrow. This is critical to commitment levels, since people need to believe that they're dedicating themselves to the creation of a noble and meaningful future that is worthy of their best efforts.

By having and fostering an attitude of psychological hardiness, leaders can turn the potential turmoil and stress of innovation and change into an adventure. By creating opportunities for small wins, leaders make it possible for people to get started on new adventures. In establishing step-by-step ways to learn from both success and failure, leaders create the climate and the conditions for turning their constituents into leaders themselves.

Here are three actions you could start doing today to encourage yourself and your constituents to Experiment and Take Risks.

Conduct Postmortems

No matter what your position or location, learning from mistakes—yours and others'—is key. The U.S. Army is known for conducting "After Action Reviews" that enable participants to analyze, discuss, and learn from both the successes and failures of a variety of military initiatives. Similarly, hospitals use "Morbidity and Mortality" conferences (in which physicians convene to discuss significant mistakes or unexpected deaths) as a forum for identifying, discussing, and learning from failures. Indeed, we sometimes suggest that participants in our training programs write a case on their personal-worst leadership experience. Although it's tempting to let painful memories fade, the lessons from failure are too precious to go unrecorded.

At the completion of a project (or at periodic intervals while in progress) take the team through a review retreat. Build the agenda around four questions:

- What did we do well? Or, what are we doing well at the moment?
- What did we do poorly? Or, what are we doing poorly?
- What did we learn from this project? Or, what are we learning from this project?
- How can we do better the next time? Or, how can we be doing better than we are currently?

Make sure that everyone contributes. Record all the ideas so that everyone can see, and then type up the notes and make them available to all. Take immediate action as needed when you return, and begin the next project with a review of any lessons learned.

Conduct Pre-Mortems

Another idea is to anticipate how to fix problems before they happen. Have your team conduct a "pre-mortem" to discover the possibly hidden flaws and minefields in any new project. It works like this: when your team gathers to kick off a new project, conclude that meeting by pretending to gaze into a crystal ball and say, "Look six months into the future. The news is not good. Despite our hopes, the project has failed. How did this happen?" Give your team members three minutes to run a mental simulation, and ask them to write down why they think their work derailed. All sorts of reasons will emerge. For example, "There were too many distractions," "The project was overly ambitious," or "We pushed the project too much toward our own self-interests, without considering those of our partners."

At this beginning stage people in the group are usually quite candid, and that's because the context of this conversation is very different from a real-life retrospective critique. The entire focus is on trying to understand why the project might fail. By looking six months into the future, people feel secure enough to say what they really think. Each comment is recorded, so that everyone knows the potential speed bumps before they go forward. Pre-mortems are much like planning for small wins, only in a backwards mode.[24]

A similar technique is the "worst-case scenario." Ask yourself and your team to imagine what it could be like if things don't quite go the way you expect them to. For example:

- People throughout the organization don't seem to buy in.
- It's demanding far more of your time than you thought it would.
- The bottom line is suffering in the short term.
- You communicate but still people say they haven't been informed.
- You can see the improvements and you know that others can too, but you don't have the right measures and facts to illustrate this.
- Improvements have been made, but everyone's expectations have also gone up, so people still complain!

Any of these could happen to you and your team. What are you going to do to ensure that if they do happen, you can cope with them? Use a list like this one, stressing that it's a worst-case scenario, and get everyone's ideas upfront about how to avoid or minimize these risks and deal effectively with them as they (inevitably) arise.

Strengthen Resilience

Hardiness and resilience are mental, not physical, states. They have to do with how we view stress, disruption, and change in our lives. Throughout human history people have overcome severe hardships not because of physical prowess but because of "mental toughness." Here are a few things you can do to help yourself and others in developing the capacity to bounce back from failures and take charge of change.

First, step back and gain some perspective. How bad is the situation? What's the absolute worst thing that can happen as a result of the change? How bad is it, really? Don't allow yourself to dwell on the "ain't it awfuls." Instead find the opportunities in the change. What exciting possibilities might exist for you? Look for ways that you can transform the change into a challenge that will propel you forward.

Second, ask yourself what new skills and knowledge you will need. One of the wonderful things about change is that it affords you the chance to learn new things. Just think about how it felt to learn something like a new game or software. Immerse yourself in learning so that you can master the new and not become overwhelmed by it.

Third, set some goals and make a plan. People gain control over change when they have a clear direction in which they want to head, achievable milestones that they can anticipate, ways to measure their progress, and action steps they can take. Without your own personal plan, you yield control to the circumstances or get swept along by the plans others make for you. Stay focused on what you want to accomplish.

Fourth, get some help and support from others. In times of significant change, people need each other more than ever. The worst thing you can do is to isolate yourself. Form support groups, ask others to assist you in some very specific ways, get some coaching, and find a friend you can lean on. And don't forget that others need you. Offer them the same kind of encouragement that you need. Remember, you're not in it alone.

COMMITMENT NUMBER 6

Experiment and Take Risks

Essentials of Experimenting and Taking Risks

- Generate small wins
- Learn from experience

Taking Action

- Conduct postmortems
- Conduct pre-mortems
- Strengthen resilience

PART

ENABLE
OTHERS
TO ACT

- FOSTER COLLABORATION

- STRENGTHEN OTHERS

FOSTER
COLLABORATION

"To be successful, teams must adopt a www.com (we will win) mind-set,
and not an imm.com (I, me, myself) mind-set."
Lily Cheng, PACE Learning & Consultancy, Singapore

The first order of business for Jill Cleveland when she became finance manager at Apple, Inc., was, "to learn how to trust my employees. After being responsible only for myself for so long, it was very difficult to have to relinquish control. But I understood that in order for my employees, and thus myself, to be successful I needed to learn to develop a cohesive and collaborative team, beginning with trust as the framework." This is a key realization for all leaders.

Jill recognized that she needed not only to give her constituents the tools to succeed but also to trust them to get their work completed. She began by creating an environment in which people felt comfortable asking questions at any time: "I felt that if I provided a climate where everyone felt safe to make mistakes that they would be better prepared to learn from those mistakes. I wanted people to know that the only stupid question was the one not asked." Jill explained that she also realized "that leaders can't gain the respect of their team without instilling a sense of confidence within their employees and allowing them the freedom to come to their own conclusions."

Jill opened up lines of communication within her team by supporting face-to-face interactions. She set aside dedicated time to talk with each person—in addition to any daily interactions or telephone conversations—about mutual expectations and progress on key objectives. This provided an opportunity for people to raise questions or concerns and reinforced her commitment to her constituents and to their continued growth. Jill also made certain that her employees developed working relationships with others outside of their department. As she explained,

> I wanted to avoid becoming a bottleneck for information. In the past I remembered how extremely helpless I felt when asked to complete a task when I knew I was missing some important piece of information and I thought some previous managers had kept me in the dark in order to bolster their sense of self-importance. This type of situation definitely did not foster collaboration within a team and, in fact, only prompted distrust. I think the only way for our team to succeed is if we tap into every available source of information and attack problems and situations together.

This meant ensuring that people were given ownership of their projects and asked to determine the best course of action and do it. "The best way for me to give power to other people," Jill said, "is to allow creativity and freedom to explore new ideas and ways of thinking. I have to relinquish control and let my employees be responsible for their own jobs." Jill made sure she provided "the necessary training and support" before she let go, but felt that

> I had to let go of some responsibility and let my employees either succeed or fail at some particular task. They had to know that although I would always be there for support and guidance, they were ultimately responsible for the outcome and quality of work.

She also made certain to acknowledge people's areas of expertise, especially those outside of their immediate team, because "employees feel empowered when they feel important, especially in the eyes of others." She made it a point to recognize people for their work because "knowing that your work doesn't go unnoticed builds accountability as well as pride."

Jill appreciated that another crucial foundation for collaboration was having cooperative goals. So she made certain that employees knew, for example, "what they were doing, why they were doing it, and who they were doing it for. We had to see ourselves as part of a whole, not some individual cog in a wheel."

Leaders understand that to create a climate of collaboration they need to determine what the group needs in order to do their work and to build the team around common purpose and mutual respect. Just as Jill did, leaders put trust and team relationships on the agenda; they don't leave it to chance.

Leadership is not a solo act, it's a team effort. In the thousands of cases we've studied, we've yet to encounter a single example of extraordinary achievement that's occurred without the active involvement and support of many people. When talking about their personal bests, people spoke passionately about teamwork and cooperation as the interpersonal route to success, particularly when conditions were extremely challenging and urgent. Throughout the years, leaders from all professions, from all economic sectors, and from around the globe have continued to tell us, "You can't do it alone."

The ever-increasing turbulence in the marketplace demands even more collaboration, not less.[1] The emphasis on networks, business-to-business and peer-to-peer e-commerce, strategic acquisitions, and knowledge work, along with the surging number of global alliances and local partnerships, is testimony to the fact that in an ever more complex, wired world, the winning strategies will be based on the "we not I" philosophy. Collaboration is a social imperative—without it you can't get extraordinary things done in organizations.[2]

Indeed, world-class performance isn't possible unless there's a strong sense of shared creation and shared responsibility. To Foster Collaboration, leaders have to be skilled in two essentials. They must

- **Create a climate of trust**
- **Facilitate relationships**

Collaboration is a critical competency for achieving and sustaining high performance. In a world that's trying to do more with less, competitive strategies naturally lose to strategies that promote collaboration.[3] With multiple constituencies come diverse and frequently conflicting interests. As paradoxical as it might seem, leadership is more essential when collaboration is required.

CREATE A CLIMATE OF TRUST

At the heart of collaboration is trust. It's the central issue in human relationships within and outside organizations. Without trust you cannot lead. Without trust you cannot get extraordinary things done. Individuals who are unable to trust others fail to become leaders, precisely because they can't bear to be dependent on the words and work of others. Either they end up doing all the work themselves or they supervise work so closely that they become overcontrolling. Their obvious lack of trust in others results in others' lack of trust in them.

To build and sustain social connections, you have to be able to trust others and others have to trust you. Trust is not just what's in your mind; it's also what's in your heart.

Trusting Others Pays Off

Several major research studies support the trust-building actions taken by exemplary leaders.[4] For example, in a PricewaterhouseCoopers study on corporate innovation in companies listed on the *Financial Times* 100, trust was "the number one differentiator" between the top 20 percent of companies surveyed and the bottom

> *The more trusted people feel, the better they innovate.*

20 percent. The top performers' trust empowered individuals to turn strategic aims into reality.[5] The more trusted people feel, the better they innovate.

Psychologists have also found that people who are trusting are more likely to be happy and psychologically adjusted than are those who view the world with suspicion and disrespect.[6] We all like people who are trusting and seek them out as friends. We listen to people we trust and accept their influence. Thus the most effective leadership situations are those in which each member of the team trusts the others. "Trust is the most fundamental element of a winning team," says business trends thinker Geoffrey Colvin. "If people think their teammates are lying, withholding information, plotting to knife them, or just incompetent, nothing valuable will get done. The team doesn't create synergy. It creates 'dysynergy'—two plus two equals three, with luck."[7]

In one research experiment, for example, several groups of business executives in a role-playing exercise were given identical factual information about a difficult manufacturing-marketing policy decision and then asked as a group to solve a problem related to that information. Half of the groups were briefed to expect trusting behavior ("You have learned from your past experiences that you can trust the other members of top management and can openly express feelings and differences with them"); the other half, to expect untrusting behavior.

After thirty minutes of discussion, each team member completed a brief questionnaire as did other executives who had been simply observing the exercise. The responses of team members and observers were quite consistent: the group members who'd been told that their role-playing peers and manager could be trusted reported their discussion and decisions to be significantly more positive than did the members of the low-trust group on every factor measured. The members of the high-trust group

- Were more open about feelings
- Experienced greater clarity about the group's basic problems and goals
- Searched more for alternative courses of action
- Reported greater levels of mutual influence on outcomes, satisfaction with the meeting, motivation to implement decisions, and closeness as a management team as a result of the meeting

In the group whose participants were told that their manager wasn't to be trusted, genuine attempts by the manager to be open and honest were ignored or distorted. Distrust was so strong that members viewed the manager's candor as a clever attempt to deceive them, and generally reacted by sabotaging the manager's efforts even further. Managers who experienced rejection of their attempts to be trusting and open responded in kind. Said one who played the manager role, "If I had my way I would have fired the entire group. What a bunch of turkeys. I was trying to be honest with them but they wouldn't cooperate. Everything I suggested they shot down; and they wouldn't give me any ideas on how to solve the problem."[8]

The responses of the other members were no less hostile. Said one, "Frankly, I was looking forward to your being fired. I was sick of working with you—and we had only been together for ten minutes."[9] Not surprisingly, more than two-thirds of the participants in the low-trust group said that they would give serious consideration to looking for another position. People don't want to stay very long in organizations devoid of trust.

It's crucial to keep in mind that this was a simulation; participants were executives from various organizations attending an executive development program. They behaved and responded as they did simply because they'd been told that they couldn't trust their role-playing manager. Their actions showed that trust or distrust *can come with a mere suggestion*—and in mere minutes.

After this simulation, participants were asked to think about what factors might have accounted for the differences between the outcomes and feelings reported by the various groups in the experiment. *Not one person perceived that trust had been the overriding variable.* "I never knew that a lack of trust was our problem (at work) until that exercise," reported one executive in the study. "I knew that things weren't going well, but I never really could quite understand why we couldn't work well together. After that experience, things fell into place."[10]

To put it quite simply, trust is the most significant predictor of individuals' satisfaction with their organizations.[11] When you create a climate of trust, you take away the controls and allow people to be free to innovate and contribute. Trusting leaders nurture openness, involvement, personal satisfaction, and high levels of commitment to excellence. They are willing to ante up first in the game of trust, they listen and learn from others, and they demonstrate their trust by sharing information and resources with others.

Be the First to Trust

If we could offer you only one bit of advice on how to start the process of creating a climate of trust it would be this: be the first to trust. Building trust is a process that begins when one party is willing to risk being the first to open up, being the first to show vulnerability, and being the first to let go of control. If you want the higher levels of performance that come with trust and collaboration, demonstrate your trust in others before asking for trust from them. Leaders go first, as the word leader implies.

Going first requires considerable self-confidence. If you show a willingness to trust others with information (both personal and professional), constituents will be more inclined to overcome any doubts they might have about sharing information. Trust is contagious. And distrust is equally contagious. If you exhibit distrust, others will hesitate to place their trust in you and in their colleagues. It's up to you to set the example.

Self-disclosure is one way that you go first. Letting others know what you stand for, what you value, what you want, what you hope for, and what you're willing (and not willing) to do means disclosing information about yourself. That can be risky. You can't be certain that other people will appreciate your candor, agree with your aspirations, want to enroll, or interpret your words and actions in the way you intend. But once you take the risk of being open, others are more likely to take a similar risk—and thereby take the next step necessary to build interpersonal trust.

> Trust is contagious.

When Peter Vermeulen was executive manager in Tianjin, China, for the Belgium-based INVE (a family holding of more than thirty companies that provides nutritional and health solutions in animal rearing), he was responsible for setting up a startup venture in China, and he admits he had a lot to learn. What's more, he wasn't afraid to let others know it, and that he needed their help and support. "I had to work very hard to educate myself in the fields of finance, sales negotiations, and production flow processes, to name a few areas," Peter explains. "I also relied on personal mentors and business consultants for help with outlining business strategies and strategies for building bridges between our Chinese business partners and the headquarters in Belgium." Peter made it a point to involve people in the decision-making process who would be directly or indirectly affected by various outcomes. "I shared lots of information that might otherwise have been reserved only for top management," he says. "The trust I placed in them, in turn, opened others up to sharing information with me. Everyone involved did a great job of keeping everyone else informed about what was going on."

Trust can't be forced, however. If someone is bent on misunderstanding people and refuses to perceive them as either well-intentioned or competent, there may be little you can do to change that perception. If you find yourself in a climate of fear and distrust created by someone else, recognize that it's natural for people to be reluctant to trust others. Give them time, but don't give up.

Be Open to Influence

Brian Coughlin was an outsider when he took on the challenge to work in Ireland as managing director of Brown Brothers Harriman Fund Administration Services. But, as he tells it, "I just jumped in. I wanted to know what all the aspects of the business were doing. I wanted to get to know the individuals involved, to understand who they were, what motivated them, and how we could work collectively to achieve things. I attempted to be open, honest, and consistent. I made a conscious effort to listen and learn from them—the local experts."

Brian knew that with a new group it was especially important to build trust early on. He also understood that he couldn't mandate changes, especially when he didn't yet know the people or the organization. Instead he had to listen and learn. His openness to being influenced by the "local experts" quickly earned Brian the respect of his new colleagues, and enabled all of them to significantly improve the quality of their services.

Knowing that trust is key, exemplary leaders make sure that they consider alternative viewpoints, and they make use of other people's expertise and abilities. Because they're more trusting of their groups, they're also more willing to let others exercise influence over group decisions. It's a reciprocal process—trust begets trust. By demonstrating openness to others' influence, you contribute to building the trust that enables your constituents to be more open to *your* influence.

In contrast, managers who create distrustful environments often take self-protective postures. They're directive and hold tight to the reins of power.

Those who work for such managers are likely to pass the distrust on by with-holding and distorting information.[12]

Brian sums up the success of his own openness to influence this way: "We had people from all levels of the organization talking to each other about ways of doing things differently and better. We had tremendous amounts of success identifying opportunities for improvement. We were able to mobilize people because they all had a sense of ownership and commitment." Isn't this exactly what all leaders want?

Sensitivity to people's needs and interests is another key ingredient in building trust. The simple act of listening to what other people have to say and appreciating their unique points of view demonstrates your respect for others and their ideas. And people listen more attentively to those who listen to them. For instance, in one management simulation, whenever the person assuming the role of chief executive officer was informed that the financial vice president was a "friend," the latter's influence was far more readily ac-cepted than when their relationship was merely professional—even though in all cases the "information" presented was adequate to solve the company's problem.[13] Friends and family are the most important sources of believable information about everything from health care to restaurants, and leaders who listen are more likely to become accepted as members of the family than those who don't.

Share Information and Resources

Maggie Hammid knows firsthand the importance of listening. She also knows how frustrating it can be to get people to share information. Maggie joined Lam Research Corporation as a senior program manager for Lam's Customer Report Card Program—the company's only vehicle for understanding the cus-tomers' perspective and what improvements were needed to build and sustain customer loyalty. The challenge Maggie faced was immense: she had about sixty people reporting indirectly (or in a dotted-line relationship) to her, in jobs scattered all over the world. None of them worked in Fremont, California, where she was based. In addition, she didn't know any of them—and she was 100 percent dependent on their support. "My job," Maggie says, "was to find out from the field reps what the customers felt were Lam's barriers to success and work with the reps to remove those barriers. In essence, I was to serve as the glue that connected the field reps to the Fremont factory, a practice that—as I soon discovered—had been fought by the field for a long time."

Among the many initiatives that Maggie undertook was a sustained campaign of information sharing. She gathered, analyzed, and shared all the data that had been collected in the preceding year—which, prior to her arrival, had never even been looked at. She shared the collective goals and objectives for the next year and told the reps that they were in control of their own destiny. Yet Maggie knew that information sharing had to be in all directions, not just from her to the reps. They had to exchange information with her and with each other. So she shared her desire to hear from every one of the reps, and she told them that she was there to support them. "But the problem I had," Maggie reports,

> was that initially some of the reps resisted sharing their knowledge with other reps, claiming that they were in competition with each other. I very quickly sent out an e-mail to all the reps and explained that there was absolutely no competition among any of us. If one of us failed, then we all failed. By helping each other gain customer loyalty with each customer, we were working for the good of the organization, and ultimately, ourselves, since we were each stockholders and had a stake in the company's success. We would sink or swim together. After that, they started experimenting on their own and sharing their knowledge with me and their peers. This freed me up a lot to focus on other aspects of the program.

Maggie modeled the value of collaboration by sharing information herself. She made very effective use of electronic communications in a situation in which very little communication had existed. But hers is not a case of just sending messages. It's one of leadership: she made good on her own promises to the group, and established the fact that sharing information was to everyone's benefit. It's these kinds of actions that can begin to create the climate of trust and collaboration so critical to success.

By consulting with others and getting them to share information, you make certain that people feel involved in making decisions that affect them. This is no guarantee that a particular final decision will be accepted, but it's certain to decrease resistance. By seeking diverse inputs, you also help to get people's cards out on the table; they provide a more open forum for competing viewpoints to be aired and discussed. Knowing how other people feel about issues enables you to incorporate aspects of all the relevant viewpoints into a project and demonstrate to others how their ideas have been heard and included.

FACILITATE RELATIONSHIPS

"I was new to Axon Instruments, and the first woman in a significant product-development leadership position," Siobhan Pickett explained,

> and when I started with this project it was already several months behind schedule. There were endless minor technical problems and production issues that caused repeated delays to the launch. Turning this situation around required, among many things, making sure that everyone saw how they were interconnected with one another, and that our success would not be the result of any one person or group's efforts, especially in the short-term, but because we were able to work together with an end goal in our collective sight. We prioritized deliverables to the group over other more individual responsibilities.

Although Siobhan conducted weekly meetings to keep herself and the team informed, they didn't wait for a meeting to discuss particular issues with any of the members. When problems arose, they identified those who would be best able to resolve them, then allowed and expected those people to explore solutions and bring forward their own recommendations. When problem solving, Siobhan said, "I kept the team focused on identifying the best solution and ways to prevent the problem from recurring in the future rather than placing blame."

Emphasizing the big picture, and the long term, is crucial in helping people deal with short-term setbacks. Leaders reframe any such incidents as learning experiences that will help the team meet more difficult challenges in the future. By emphasizing the ultimate goal, leaders strengthen team members' resolve.

One of the most significant ingredients to cooperation and collaboration is a sense of interdependence, a condition in which everyone knows that they cannot succeed unless everyone else succeeds, or at least that they can't succeed unless they coordinate their efforts. If there's no sense that "we're all in this together," that the success of one depends on the success of the other, then it's virtually impossible to create the conditions for positive teamwork.

To get extraordinary things done, people have to rely on each other. They need to have a sense of mutual dependence—a community of people in which each knows that they need the others to be successful. To create conditions in which people know they can count on each other a leader needs to develop cooperative goals and roles, support norms of reciprocity, structure projects to promote joint efforts, and support face-to-face interactions.

Develop Cooperative Goals and Roles

Whether it's hockey or health care, education or financial services, the public or private sector, for a team of people to have a positive experience together, they must have shared goals that provide a specific reason for being together. No one person can single-handedly teach a child, build a quality car, make a movie, create a world-class guest experience, connect a customer to the Internet, or treat a patient. No one can do these—or most other extraordinary things—alone. A focus on a collective purpose binds people into cooperative efforts.

As the engineering manager for the InfoMedia Business Unit, Parthus Technologies (Ireland), John Doyle needed to ensure that team members assumed

A focus on a collective purpose binds people into cooperative efforts.

ownership of their tasks and took responsibility for meeting their schedules, but, most important, to also make certain they knew that they were members of a team that had the same end goal in mind. John told us how he did it:

I made sure that each team member depended on the other and that success could only be achieved through cooperation and teamwork. Each individual was completely informed in terms of feedback from customers, and they were fully aware of the financial impact the program was going to make to Parthus. This helped to create a buzz about being part of the team. I also made certain that each team member realized how important their contribution was to the overall success of the program and the company. Finally, I focused the team on what we were doing that was special and differentiated us from other projects in the past. In the end, we were all striving toward the same common goal.

John, like other leaders we studied, realized that keeping individuals focused on a common goal promoted a stronger sense of teamwork than emphasizing individual objectives. For cooperation to succeed, roles must be designed so that every person's contributions are both additive and cumulative to the final outcome. Individuals must clearly understand that unless they each contribute whatever they can, the team fails. It's like putting together a jigsaw puzzle. Each person has a piece, and if even one piece is missing the puzzle is impossible to complete.

Support Norms of Reciprocity

In any effective long-term relationship, there must be a sense of reciprocity. If one partner always gives and the other always takes, the one who gives will feel taken advantage of and the one who takes will feel superior. In such a climate, cooperation is virtually impossible. To develop cooperative relationships, leaders must quickly establish norms of reciprocity within teams and among partners. John Doyle, at Parthus, ensured that each member of his team understood how they depended on one another for getting the job done. One of the ways he achieved this was by having individuals from each team periodically transfer to other team sites so they could experience firsthand what others in the project were working on and what challenges they were experiencing. This reinforced awareness that they were all in it together, and how no one could be successful unless everyone was successful.

Political scientist Robert Axelrod dramatically demonstrated the power of reciprocity in the best-known study of the "Prisoner's Dilemma" puzzle.[14] The dilemma is this: two parties (individuals or groups) are confronted with a series of situations in which they must decide whether or not to cooperate. They don't know in advance what the other party will do. There are two basic strategies—cooperate or compete—and four possible outcomes based on the choices players make: win-lose, lose-win, lose-lose, and win-win.

The maximum individual payoff comes when the first player selects a noncooperative strategy and the second player chooses to cooperate in good faith. In this "I win but you lose" approach, one party gains at the other's expense. Although this might seem to be the most successful strategy—at least for the first player—it rarely proves to be successful in the long run, largely because the second player won't continue to cooperate in the face of the first player's noncooperative strategy. If both parties choose not to cooperate and attempt to maximize individual payoffs, then both lose. If both parties choose to cooperate, both win, though the individual payoff for a cooperative move is less than for a competitive one (in the short run).

Axelrod invited scientists from around the world to submit their strategies for winning in a computer simulation of this test of win-win versus win-lose strategies. "Amazingly enough," says Axelrod, "the winner was the simplest of all strategies submitted: cooperate on the first move and then do whatever the other player did on the previous move. This strategy succeeded by eliciting cooperation from others, not by defeating them."[15] Simply put, people who reciprocate are more likely to be successful than those who try to maximize individual advantage.

The dilemmas that can be successfully solved by this strategy are by no means restricted to theoretical research. We all face similar predicaments in our everyday lives:

- Should I try to maximize my own personal gain?
- What price might I pay for this action?
- Should I give up a little for the sake of others?
- Will others take advantage of me if I'm cooperative?

Reciprocity turns out to be the most successful approach for such daily decisions, because it demonstrates both a willingness to be cooperative and an unwillingness to be taken advantage of. As a long-term strategy, reciprocity minimizes the risk of escalation: if people know that you'll respond in kind, why would they start trouble? And if people know that you'll reciprocate, they know that the best way to deal with you is to cooperate and become recipients of your cooperation.

Reciprocity leads to predictability and stability in relationships, which can keep relationships and negotiations from breaking down.[16] Why? Part of the reason is that the knowledge that people share goals and will reciprocate in their attainment makes working together less stressful. Improved relationships and decreased stress: fine objectives under any circumstances.

It's absolutely essential that every leader keep the norms of reciprocity and fairness in mind. As Harvard professor of public policy Robert Putnam tells us, "The norm of generalized reciprocity is so fundamental to civilized life that all prominent moral codes contain some equivalent of the Golden Rule."[17] And when we treat others as we'd like for them to treat us, it's likely they'll repay us many times over.

When Leon Perepelitsky, senior software engineer at Scientific Atlanta, a Cisco company, reflected back upon why their core teams interact and operate rather smoothly, he realized that the key factor was getting these various groups, distributed around the country, to appreciate that they could accomplish more by working together than they could by working all alone. As Leon explained,

> because the team members are experienced engineers they often can come up with the solution for the problem by themselves. However, what we found out over the years is that if we involved the entire group we would benefit more than twofold. First, the quality of the solution would be much higher, more long-term, and less error prone. Second, the entire group knows what the rest of the group is doing and can be on the lookout for ways to help—knowing that others are doing the same thing on their behalf. This reciprocity has created great team camaraderie, which has helped us in so many situations to make that last push to deliver a task or a project on time.

Once you help others to succeed, acknowledge their accomplishments, and help them shine, especially in front of others, they will never forget it. The "norm of reciprocity" comes into play, and they are more than willing to return the favor. Whether the rewards of cooperation are monetary or not, when people understand that they will be better off by cooperating, they're inclined to recognize the legitimacy of others' interests in an effort to promote their own welfare.

Structure Projects to Promote Joint Effort

The leader's job is to make sure that all parties understand each other's interests and how each can gain more from working together than from working alone or with only their own interests in mind. People are more likely to cooperate, whether in the corporation, community, or classroom, if the payoffs for interdependent efforts are greater than those associated with working independently. This more collectivist perspective is quite prominent in a number of cultures around the world, whereas people growing up in many Westernized countries that emphasize individualistic or competitive achievement have the perception that they'll do better if everyone were each rewarded solely based on their individual accomplishments. They're wrong. The fact is that cooperation pays bigger bonuses than individualistic or competitive achievement.

Leaders such as Siobhan Pickett and John Doyle, and others we studied, structured projects so that each person's tasks made a visible contribution to the end result. The motivation for working diligently on one's own job, keeping in mind the overall common objective, is reinforced because it is the end result that gets rewarded and not simply individual efforts. Most profit-sharing plans, for example, are based on meeting the company's goals and not simply those of separate independent units or departments. Certainly individuals within the group each have distinct roles, but on world-class teams everyone knows they can't achieve the group goals unless they all play well their individual parts. After all, if you could do it alone, why would you need a team? Soccer isn't a one-on-eleven sport; hockey isn't one-on-six; baseball isn't one-on-nine; basketball isn't one-on-five. They require team effort—as do all extraordinary organizational achievements.

After all, if you could do it alone, why would you need a team?

For cooperation to succeed, individuals need to understand that by working together they will be able to accomplish something that no one can accomplish on their own. Jim Vesterman learned an indelible lesson in the power of group effort when he joined the Marine Corps. "I considered myself a pretty good team player," he said, "yet everything I thought I knew about working with other people was about to change."[18] It started on his first day of boot camp at Parris Island when he and his fellow recruits learned to make their beds—an exercise called "two sheets and a blanket."

When the drill instructor begins counting, you've got three minutes to make the bed—hospital corners and the proverbial quarter bounce. When you're done, you're told to get back in a line. The goal is to have every bed in the platoon made. So I made my bed, then I stood on the line. I was pretty proud, because when three minutes were up, there weren't more than ten men who had finished. "Ahead of the pack," I thought. But the drill instructors weren't congratulating us. *Everyone's* bed had to be made. . . . *"We've got all day to get this right,"* the drill instructors were saying, looking at all the unfinished beds. *"Two sheets and a blanket!"*

I ripped off the sheets again, and again, and again. Finally one of the drill instructors looked me in the eye. "Your bunkmate isn't done. What are you doing?" I thought, "What *am* I doing?" Standing on line, thinking I'd accomplished something while my bunkmate struggled.

Together my bunkmate and I made our beds about twice as fast as we did alone. Still, not everyone was finishing. Finally we realized, "Okay, when we're done, we've got to go help the bed next to us, and the bed down from that," and so on. I went from thinking, "I'll hand my bunkmate a pillow, but I'm not going to make the bed for him" to making beds for anyone who needed help.[19]

Two sheets and a blanket was an epiphany for Jim: in the Marines, you can't survive without helping the guys next to you. Naomi Boyd learned a similar lesson in her very first leadership role, serving as the senior quality assurance analyst for Visa International. "I had to build a team," she told us, "provide them with proper training, ensure a test plan, create test cases and get them signed off, and make certain that this new software was up and running within one month—which actually required three months!" Naomi knew the group couldn't complete this assignment without the cooperation of everyone involved. She explained the situation to the team. To meet this deadline they decided they would have to work almost around the clock. So they made the decision to split the team up into two shifts (one working from 7 A.M. and finishing up around 4 P.M. and the other starting at 3 P.M. and ending at 2 A.M.).

Naomi encouraged them to think of other ways that they could work together rather than each on their own.

For example, we had separate stations that each member of the team could use to test the application. The team found that by working in pairs per station, they were able to test better. Because we all had the same common goal in mind—which had to be completed under uncomfortable circumstances and incredible time pressures—we were all willing to help each other as much as possible. None of us would be finished until all of us were finished. This realization kept us mutually focused from the start through the finish of this project.

Another way of facilitating cooperation through promoting joint efforts is to emphasize long-term payoffs—that is, to make certain that the long-term benefits of mutual cooperation are greater than the short-term benefits of working alone or competing with others. Naomi achieved this, even within a one-month time frame, by getting the people on her team to see that by working together they would get the project completed faster than by thinking about short-term victories resulting from doing their own thing, or complaining, blaming, or competing with others for scarce resources.

Support Face-to-Face Interactions

Group goals, reciprocity, and promoting joint effort are all essential for collaboration to occur, but what is also critical is positive face-to-face interaction.[20] And this need for face-to-face communication increases with the complexity of the issues.[21] Roberta Linsky, vice president of worldwide human resources for the Swiss-owned Logitech, asserts that "a group of individuals can only act as a team when they have met face-to-face four or five times." Stephanie Powell, eBusiness marketing manager at Plantronics, echoed this observation, claiming, "Until you see someone's face, they are not a real person to you." Stephanie approaches each interaction "as if it'll last a lifetime, and as if it will be important to everyone's mutual success in the future." It's the leader's job, as both Roberta and Stephanie point out, to provide frequent and lasting opportunities for team members to associate and intermingle across disciplines and between departments. As handy as virtual tools are for staying in touch, they are no substitute for positive face-to-face interactions.

As all of us become more and more dependent on virtual connections, we think that if we can reach across boundaries with the stroke of a key and the click of a mouse, we can more easily establish the foundation for better relationships. The hitch is, there's really no such thing as virtual trust.[22]

Virtual trust, like virtual reality, is one step removed from the real thing. We're social animals; it's in our nature to want to interact, and bits and bytes make for a very weak social foundation. That said, in today's global economy our work relationships depend more and more on electronic connections, and many work "places" are virtual in nature. How are we to combine and balance the benefits of technology with the social imperative of human contact? How can we reconcile the reality of our virtual organizations with our knowledge that building trust depends on getting to know one another intimately? The implication for leaders is that in addition to the e-mails, instant messages, teleconferences, and video conferences, they need to look to another technology—the airplane! There is no more effective way to build trust and promote teamwork than making it a practice to get people together regularly, face-to-face.

People who expect durable and frequent face-to-face interactions in the future are more likely to cooperate in the present. Knowing that you'll have to deal with someone tomorrow, next week, or next year ensures that you won't easily forget about how you've treated them, and how they've treated you. When durable interactions are frequent, the consequences of today's actions on tomorrow's dealings are that much more pronounced. In addition, frequent interactions between people promote positive feelings on the part of each for the other.[23] Again, as John Doyle found out, "People knew we were in this together; and we were in this for the long run. Encouraging people to transfer between team sites for a period of time ensured familiarity with the culture and practices of their peers. This resulted in an increased level of trust between the teams, confidence in one another and a solid foundation for success."

We recognize that in this global economic environment, in which speed is a competitive advantage and loyalty is no longer a strong virtue, the notion of durable interactions may seem quaint and anachronistic. But that doesn't make the reality disappear. Sure, it's more difficult. That's a fact of life in the Global Economy. Knowing that sustaining durable and face-to-face interactions is likely to make you more effective, you have to make it one of your leadership imperatives.

Every significant relationship should be treated as if it'll last a lifetime.

We know that people don't stay in one job forever, nor should they. Marriages do fall apart, and abusive ones should end. Companies do fail, sometimes because of bad management and sometimes because the marketplace isn't buying. No matter. The point is that fostering collaboration is so crucial to the success of teams, companies, and communities today that every significant relationship should be treated as if it'll last a lifetime—as if it will be important to all parties' mutual success in the future. Universities and many successful consulting and executive search firms trade on this attitude in their treatment of alumni and clients, every one of whom is viewed as a potential source of good will and good business. Begin with the assumption that in the future you'll be interacting with this person in some way, and both you and the whole society will be better served.

REFLECTION AND ACTION: FOSTERING COLLABORATION

"You can't do it alone" is the mantra of exemplary leaders—and for good reason. You simply can't get extraordinary things done by yourself. Collaboration is the master skill that enables teams, partnerships, and other alliances to function effectively. Collaboration can be sustained only when you create a climate of trust and facilitate effective long-term relationships among your constituents. To get extraordinary things done, you have to promote a sense of mutual dependence—feeling part of a group in which everyone knows they need the others to be successful. Without that sense of "we're all in this together" it's virtually impossible to keep effective teamwork going.

Trust is the lifeblood of collaborative teamwork. To create and sustain the conditions for long-lasting connections, you have to be able to trust others and others have to trust you. Without trust you cannot lead. Without trust you and your constituents cannot get extraordinary things done. So share information and resources freely with your constituents, show that you understand their needs and interests, open up to their influence, make wise use of their abilities and expertise, and—most of all—demonstrate your trust in others before asking for them to trust you.

Leaders embrace the challenge of facilitating relationships among all the people involved in any undertaking, ensuring that everyone recognizes their *inter*-dependence more than their independence. Cooperative goals and roles contribute to a sense of collective purpose, and the best incentive for others to work to achieve your shared goals is their knowing that you'll reciprocate, helping them in return. Help begets help just as trust begets trust. Supporting norms of reciprocity enables people to clearly understand why it is in their best interest to cooperate, as does structuring projects to reward joint efforts. Extraordinary leaders go to great lengths to get people interacting. They know there's no such thing as virtual trust, so they encourage face-to-face interactions as often as possible to reinforce the durability of relationships and enhance interpersonal team dynamics.

Here are three action steps that you can take to fulfill the leader's commitment to Foster Collaboration:

Show Trust to Build Trust

Building trust is a process that begins when one party is willing to risk being the first to ante up, being the first to show vulnerability, and being the first to let go of control. Since you're the leader, the first to trust has to be you. If you, as the leader, show a willingness to trust others, your constituents will be more inclined to leave behind their doubts and apprehensions. To promote trust throughout the organization, *be the first to*

- Disclose information about who you are and what you believe
- Admit mistakes
- Acknowledge the need for personal improvement
- Ask for feedback—positive and negative
- Listen attentively to what others are saying
- Invite interested parties to important meetings
- Share information that's useful to others
- Openly acknowledge the contributions of others
- Show that you're willing to change your mind when someone else comes up with a good idea
- Avoid talking negatively about others
- Say, "We can trust them," and mean it!

Of course there are risks. You might end up looking off-the-wall, weak, or incompetent. But the risks are well worth it in creating a trustworthy system.

Trustworthiness is in the eye of the beholder. This means that in order for your constituents to call you "trustworthy" they must believe that you have their best interests at heart. It means that you don't want to see them get hurt, be embarrassed, feel harassed, or suffer. You want them to succeed, to be healthy, happy, and prosperous. And because of this, people believe they can take the risks of putting themselves in a relationship with you, even if there are no rock-solid guarantees of positive outcomes.

Say We, *Ask Questions, Listen, and Take Advice*

Because no one ever accomplishes anything significant alone, your approach can never be "Here's what I plan for you to do"; instead, it's "Here's what *we*'ve agreed *we*'ll do together." This inclusive language reinforces the fact that goals are truly collaborative, not imposed. When talking about what is planned or what has been accomplished, it's essential that you talk in terms of *our* vision, *our* values, *our* goals, *our* plans, *our* actions, and *our* achievements. Your task as a leader is to help other people reach mutual goals, not your goals, and to get there with a sense that *we* did it together. None of this is to say that you don't have individual goals or individual tasks. It's just that as the leader your job is to make sure that everyone sees themselves as a part of the larger mission, and your language needs to reflect that sense of being part of the team.

So, conduct an I-We language audit. Ask someone to observe the meetings you hold, whether one-on-one or large-group, and count the number of times you say *I* and the number of times you say *We*. On balance, there ought to be more references worded in first-person plural than first-person singular. Do the same with your memos and e-mail.

You can also use this technique when interviewing candidates for roles in which leadership is required. Candidates who use *I* more than *We* will make poor leaders, and the organization will suffer from their attempts to push their own agenda on the group or claim credit for themselves.

Also audit your talking and listening behavior. If you want people to trust you, and if you want to build a climate of trust in your organization, the listening-to-talking ratio has to be in favor of listening. People need to feel that their voice matters and that their vote counts. The best way to get the conversation going so that you can listen is to ask a question or ask for advice. (Of course, people will stop giving you advice if you never take it, and they'll see your listening as a disingenuous technique.) If you truly listen to the advice people give you in response to your questions, extraordinary things can happen.

Whether it's in one-on-one discussions or town hall meetings, you've got to have a routine for asking questions, listening, and taking advice from others. Here are two assignments for you at the next two team meetings you have. At the first meeting, ask questions more than give information. Ask someone to monitor your actions and record your questioning-to-informing ratio. See how you did. The ratio should be at least 2:1.

At the second team meeting, practice listening. Remember that listening doesn't mean not speaking. It may mean asking questions for clarification or paraphrasing what someone else said. Your job is not to give advice and win arguments; it's to pay attention to what others want and need. Once again, have someone monitor you and make note of your listening-to-informing ratio. See how you did. If it's not at least 2:1, try again.

Get People Interacting

Here are just a few of the many ways in which you can create opportunities for people to interact with one another and in the process form more trusting, more collaborative relationships:

- Put a couple of chairs outside your cubicle or office. Encourage people who pass by to sit down for a conversation. Have some of your own informal one-on-ones out in the open.
- Be sure that the coffee, refrigerator, and other shared resources are in a central place where everyone walks by, not in some corner or basement hideaway.
- Hold ten-minute stand-up meetings at the start of every morning in an open area. Move the meeting around the workplace so that you tour the facility.
- If you don't yet hold regular group meetings at established times so people get used to coming together, start doing this. There's more to meetings than disseminating information and solving problems. They're also ways of building connections.
- Start your formal meetings with five or ten minutes of community building before you get down to business. Ask a question as simple as, "So what did everyone do over the holiday weekend? Stephanie or Bill, would you mind starting?"
- Make sure there's food in the middle of the table during meetings (rather than in the corners or on some end table).

- Hold small celebrations in very public places—like on the plant floor—instead of in distant, secluded conference rooms or off-site venues.
- Intentionally move your office—sorry, cubicle—to the furthest spot from the restroom so you have to walk by everyone's desk before you get there. Start using the restrooms on another floor.
- Rotate team meeting leadership so everyone gets a turn.

Some people may see these ideas as gimmicky and a waste of time and resources. Those who have used them disagree. The reality is that people can't all be in this together unless you get them interacting on both a personal and professional basis. People need these opportunities to socialize, exchange information, and solve problems informally.

COMMITMENT NUMBER 7
Foster Collaboration

Essentials of Fostering Collaboration

- Create a climate of trust
- Facilitate relationships

Taking Action

- Show trust to build trust
- Say *we,* ask questions, listen, and take advice
- Get people interacting

10

STRENGTHEN OTHERS

"Great leaders grow their constituents into leaders themselves."
Edmar Soriano, Tutoring Club of Fremont/Newark

When Sanjay Bali was assigned as officer-in-charge on an Indian navy tanker, his department was not up to standards—neither his nor those of the fleet. "It was clear to me," he explains, "that while the staff members were talented, they lacked the leadership that was necessary to bring them together as a team. My challenge was to instill confidence in them and help them recognize their abilities."

Although the Indian navy, like armed services around the globe, is largely hierarchically structured, within his unit Sanjay created an organization that was greatly influenced by individual personalities and aspirations, areas of competence, career paths, resources, and, of course, "military mandates." Sanjay felt strongly that it was important to recognize each individual's area of interest and skill in assigning him or her a task and responsibility:

> To understand what each person aspired to and enjoyed doing, I sat down and discussed these things with them individually. By doing this I was able to avoid assigning people to roles with which they were not comfortable. We used honest, disciplined, and respectful communications and fostered mutually beneficial relationships with people. They were willing to help out and cooperate with me and with one another because they were confident that we would do the same for them.

Sanjay asked group members to share their ideas and suggestions, and to "think outside of the box" because "the regimented life of the service kills one's creativity. My being open to their thoughts made them more willing to think of solutions and alternate courses of action instead of waiting to be told what to do." Sanjay made sure that making suggestions was always a positive experience—even if someone's idea wasn't implemented. "I appreciated the fact that they were putting forth the effort of coming up with ideas. How were they going to get stronger without practice?" This is an approach, Sanjay says, "that's not often seen in the Indian navy, but I believe it made the group members feel empowered."

Sanjay felt that mutual respect and accountability were key to the team's success. "I emphasized that no one in the group was smarter or better than anyone else," he explains, "and the key was to share knowledge and information rather than hoard it. We needed to recognize that every individual in the group brought value to the whole team. Rather than dwelling on areas in which they lacked skills, I pointed out the importance of them playing complementary roles . . . so that they, as well as the entire group, would benefit."

Although lack of experience was unavoidable, lack of knowledge or enthusiasm was not acceptable to Sanjay. If someone didn't have knowledge in an essential area, he or she was responsible for gaining that knowledge. To make this possible, Sanjay set up a buddy system in which a younger, less knowledgeable individual was paired up with someone who had more experience and expertise. This way, one person gained knowledge while the other reinforced knowledge by helping someone else learn. An additional benefit to this system was cross-training, so that more than one person was able to perform a particular task. Sanjay later expanded this idea at a peer instruction program in which individuals would share past experiences with the group, explaining situations that had arisen and how they were dealt with. They also did research within their areas of expertise, which they would then share with the group. Everyone had something to contribute.

By the end of his tour, the sailors in Sanjay's tanker were rated first among the more than forty fleet ships, even higher than the aircraft carrier, which had five times the number of people and had traditionally achieved the number one ranking. The tanker subsequently instituted an internal award in the name of Sanjay Bali to honor the best department on the ship.

Like Sanjay, exemplary leaders strengthen others. They enable others to take ownership of and responsibility for their group's success by enhancing their competence and their confidence in their abilities, by listening to their ideas and acting upon them, by involving them in important decisions, and by acknowledging and giving credit for their contributions.

Creating a climate in which people are fully engaged and feel in control of their own lives is at the heart of strengthening others. People must have the latitude to make decisions based on what they believe should be done. They must work in an environment that both develops their abilities to perform a task or complete an assignment and builds a sense of self-confidence. They must hold themselves personally accountable for results as well as feel ownership for their achievements.

We've distilled these observations into two leadership essentials that Strengthen Others:

- **Enhance self-determination**
- **Develop competence and confidence**

By using these essentials, leaders significantly increase people's belief in their own ability to make a difference. Leaders move from being *in control* to *giving over control* to others, becoming their coaches and teachers. Leaders help others learn new skills and develop existing talents, and they provide the institutional supports required for ongoing growth and change. In the final analysis, what leaders are doing is turning their constituents into leaders.

ENHANCE SELF-DETERMINATION

Leaders accept and act on the paradox of power: *you become more powerful when you give your own power away.* Long before empowerment was written into the popular vocabulary, exemplary leaders understood how important it was that their constituents felt strong, capable, and efficacious. Constituents who feel weak, incompetent, and insignificant consistently underperform, they want to flee the organization, and they're ripe for disenchantment, even revolution.

People who feel powerless, be they managers or individual contributors, tend to hoard whatever shreds of power they have. Powerless managers tend to adopt petty and dictatorial styles, for example. Powerlessness also creates organizational systems in which political skills are essential and "covering yourself" and "passing the buck" are the preferred modes of handling interdepartmental differences.[1]

To get a better sense of how it feels to be powerless as well as powerful, we often ask people to tell us about their own experiences of being in these situations. First, we ask them to identify actions or situational conditions that have made them feel powerless, weak, or insignificant, like a pawn in someone else's chess game. Here are some representative statements:

- I had no input into a hiring decision of someone who was to report directly to me. I didn't even get to speak to the candidate.

- People picked me apart while I was making a presentation, and the champion of the project didn't support me.
- I was told I couldn't ask questions because I lacked the appropriate educational or experience level.
- They treated us like mushrooms. They fed us horse manure and kept us in the dark.
- I worked extremely hard—long hours and late nights—on an urgent project, and then my manager took full credit for it.
- No one would answer my questions.

But when people have felt powerful—strong, efficacious, like the creators of their own experience—they report actions and conditions such as these:

- I was able to make a large financial decision on my own. I got to write a large check without being questioned.
- I was asked to take on a project for which I didn't have the experience. My manager said, "I'm confident you'll be successful."
- My president supported my idea without question.
- After having received a memo that said "Cut travel," I made my case about why it was necessary to travel for business reasons; and I was told to go ahead.
- I was five years old, and my dad said, "You'll make a great mechanic one day." He planted the seed.
- All the financial data were shared with me.

As we examine powerless and powerful times, we're struck by one clear and consistent message: *feeling powerful—literally feeling "able"—comes from a deep sense of being in control of your own life.* People everywhere share this fundamental need. When they feel able to determine their own destiny, when they believe they're able to mobilize the resources and support necessary to complete a task, then they persist in their efforts to achieve. But when they feel they're controlled by others, when they believe that they lack support or resources, they show no commitment to excel (although they may comply).

Any leadership practice that increases another's sense of self-determination, self-confidence, and personal effectiveness makes that person more powerful and greatly enhances the possibility of success.[2] For Arjun Lahiri, who was working as a business development manager for a Silicon Valley–based start-up company at the time, this meant enabling each and every member of his team to articulate the value of their technological solution in business terms for their customers. Arjun explained,

> *Feeling powerful comes from a deep sense of being in control of your own life.*

I encouraged them to express their ideas and concerns, no matter how ridiculous they might have seemed. This made them comfortable that they were being heard, paid attention to, and they experienced a sense of ownership for the project delivery. Within the team, I listened carefully to their suggestions and discussions patiently without jumping to conclusions. This gave them the opportunity to present their ideas in a safe environment which, in turn, allowed them to be more confident and articulate advocates. They knew that I trusted them, had confidence in their judgment, and that I was ready and prepared to back them up whenever necessary. Each one of them felt powerful and acted with the confidence that they could meet any challenge put before them.

Arjun's personal experience is supported by a quarter-century of research showing that the more people believe that they can influence the organization, the greater organizational effectiveness and member satisfaction there will be. A sense of personal power results in higher job fulfillment and performance throughout the organization.[3] Gallup surveys involving more than ten million employees, from over 110 countries in industries as varied as electrical utilities, retail stores, restaurants, hotels, hospitals, paper mills, government agencies, banks, and newspapers, as well as dozens of others, clearly show that the extent to which people feel powerful and engaged in their work is directly linked to positive business outcomes (sales growth, productivity, customer loyalty, and so forth).[4] Or consider the fact that business units with actively *dis*engaged workers experience 30 to 50 percent more turnover than those with engaged employees, and that these employees annually miss more than three times the number of days reported by their more engaged peers.[5]

Self-determination can be enhanced in a number of ways. The most significant actions a leader can take to ensure that people can decide for themselves are to provide more choices, design jobs that offer latitude, and foster personal accountability.

Provide Choices

"What made this experience so significant," explained John Zhang, who was just starting out his career at Dalin International Trading Corporation, "was that my manager listened carefully to me and then *asked me what I thought we should do.*" After presenting several alternatives, his manager asked John again what he thought should be done and said, "It's your decision." They talked some more about the alternatives, and John recommended a particular strategy. "He backed me up completely," John said of his manager, "and I subsequently did everything I could to ensure our success. There was no way I was going to let us not be successful." Choice builds commitment. Imagine what would have happened if John's manager had said, "It's *my* decision, and you have no choice in the matter but to do what I've decided." Would John have reported that he'd do everything he could to ensure success? Would you? We doubt it.

Many have written about how choice is required for organizations and their employees to provide exceptional customer service.[6] Responsive service and extra employee efforts emerge when people have the necessary leeway to meet customer needs and sufficient authority to serve customer wants. These ideas don't just apply to frontline service personnel. Consider a study of the Fortune 200. Over a period of two decades, 13 of the top 200 companies outperformed the other 187 organizations. Only a few factors separated the top 13 from the rest of the pack. One of the key factors was a much higher spending authority at the divisional level. For example, divisional managers in the most successful firms could spend up to $20 million on their own signature (ten times the amount at the other organizations).[7]

When Rajalakshmi (Raji) Santhanam was managing the Technical Publications Department in Bangalore, India, for ENCIRQ Corporation, her team had zero attrition over a three-year period. She told us that this group was "considered the most cohesive and tightly knit team" in the company. In explaining the reasons for this, Raji was keen to point out the importance of making certain that every member of the team had many opportunities to exercise choices about what they did. For example, apart from conducting the typical performance review with each individual, Raji introduced a "personal *blank-page* exercise where we would talk about what the person really wanted to do, and we generally included this in their jobs to help build them." Raji went on to explain that for each new assignment the team took on, they got together and determined collectively who should do what and why. The creation of these peer teams worked very well, she said, because "they had the latitude to decide what to do and they could go out and develop it in any way that they thought fit."

People simply cannot lead and can't make a difference unless they have a choice. If someone has no freedom of choice and can only act in ways prescribed by the organization, then how can they respond when the customer or another employee behaves in ways that are not in the script? They will have to ask the "boss" what to do—even if they think they know what needs to be done and feel they could do it! And a boss who doesn't know will have to ask his or her manager. And up the ladder it goes.

Design Jobs to Offer Latitude

If leaders want higher levels of performance and greater initiative from their constituents, they must be proactive in designing work that allows people discretion and choice. In another word, latitude. To feel like they're in control of their own work lives people need to be able to take nonroutine action, exercise independent judgment, and make decisions that affect how they do their work without having to check with someone else. It means being creative and flexible—liberated from a standard set of rules, procedures, or schedules. It means having more broadly defined jobs, offering more alternatives. Narrow job categories confine choices; broader categories permit increased flexibility and discretion. Those who hold broadly defined jobs have more options about how to accomplish the assigned objectives.

The shift to fewer job classifications in large organizations is a clear sign that breadth is essential to rapid response. Narrow job classifications limit our options, and narrower options mean people can't do very much to respond to customer needs. We've all heard this line: "It's not my job." In fact, the old notion of work as a collection of "jobs" is being replaced by the more expansive concept of work as a series of "projects." This restructuring allows people more freedom of movement, choice, and contact. Get rid of multiple managerial layers and sign-offs; those requirements are disabling and wasteful of time, money, talent, and motivation. They also lose customers.

In this dynamic global environment, only adaptive individuals and organizations will thrive. This means leaders must support more and greater individual discretion to meet the changing demands of customers, clients, suppliers, and other stakeholders. With this increased discretion comes an increased ability to use and expand one's talents, training, and experience. The payoff, as leaders like Grace Chan discovered, is improved performance.

As a program manager for Intel, Grace was leading a complex project requiring support from parties in Japan as well as the United States and input across several levels of management, functional partners, and suppliers. She understood the importance of making certain that job and specification requirements weren't so narrowly defined that people didn't have any room to maneuver. She made sure people had some latitude with their own choices and decisions and the chance to move across disciplines and boundaries. Grace's viewpoint was clear to all: "A healthy business relationship starts with reasonable compromises and mutual understanding from both sides, not by simply pressing hard on one side." She empowered team members to claim ownership of various parts of the program, and as the owner of their respective areas, they were held accountable for the outcome. She insisted on "providing some leeway to the suppliers, for example, on terms which were critical to them, and in turn we gained headroom on other terms essential to our business model. In the end, both parties were satisfied with the terms and conditions and there were absolutely no hard feelings.

In this dynamic global environment, only adaptive individuals and organizations will thrive.

"Empowering and strengthening all the members of the team to do their best," Grace told us, "really motivated them to strive for optimal results."

Foster Accountability

Grace understands something very fundamental about strengthening others. She knows that that the power to choose rests on the willingness to be held accountable. She knows that the more freedom of choice people have, the more personal responsibility they must accept. There's also a bonus: the more people believe that everyone else is taking responsibility for their parts of the job—and has the competence to do it—the more trusting and the more cooperative they're going to be. It's also true that people will be more confident in doing their part when they believe others will do theirs. This interconnectedness between choice and accountability takes on increasing importance in a virtually connected global workplace.

Unless people take personal responsibility and unless they are held accountable for their own actions, others are not very inclined to want to work

with them nor much inclined to cooperate in general. Individual accountability is a critical element of every collaborative effort. Everyone has to do
their part for a group to function effectively.

Structuring the situation so that people have to work collaboratively can
actually increase personal accountability. Why? Because when you know that
your colleagues are expecting you to be prepared and to do your job, these
peer expectations are a powerful force in motivating you to do well. The feeling of not wanting to let the rest of the group down strengthens people's resolve to do their best.

Some people believe that teams and other cooperative endeavors minimize individual accountability. They believe that if people are encouraged to
work collectively, somehow they'll take less responsibility for their own actions than if they are encouraged to compete or to do things on their own.
The evidence doesn't support this point of view.[8] It's true that some people
become social loafers when working in groups, slacking off while others do
their jobs for them. But this doesn't last for long, because their team members quickly tire of carrying the extra load. Either the slacker steps up to the
responsibility, or the team wants that person out. Leaders know that part of
their job is to set up conditions that enable each and every team member to
feel a sense of ownership for the whole job.

When Andy Gere was appointed to the new position of water treatment
supervisor at San Jose Water Company, an investor-owned water utility serving approximately one million people in Silicon Valley, his challenge was to
transform a fragmented, feuding group of individuals into a cohesive, cooperative workforce. In the end, this group developed a set of guidelines for communicating, problem solving, interacting, and performing critical functions
as a team. The guidelines were published in a manual (called *An Operator's
Guide to Making Teamwork Work*), and each person signed an agreement that
made the guidelines a contract for the way they would work with one another. Water quality improved dramatically, production increased by 8 percent, and plant-related overtime decreased by 12 percent.

This didn't happen instantly. Andy began by making the operators accountable. He gave them the authority to make plant process changes, including plant shutdowns, without first checking with a supervisor. "It took them awhile," Andy admitted, "to get used to the idea that as a licensed water treatment plant operator they not only had the authority but the responsibility to optimize the plant processes to the best of their ability, all the time." He made the operators own the new procedures by letting them establish their specific intergroup work rules (such as the protocol for deciding when to turn on a creek intake after a storm) rather than dictating them from management. Similarly, the operators developed working rules, relationship rules, and getting-along rules as a way to get beyond years of rivalry, grudges, and sour relationships.

Accountability was pushed by reminding the operators to "focus on the problem, not the person." And making each operator accountable was critical to the success of Andy's initiative. As Andy explained, "Asking the operators to write their own mission statements and goals gave them a new sense of purpose and created an opportunity for them to see an end product that went beyond the end of their shift. They could see how they were interconnected and how by working together they could accomplish more than by working alone." Pointing out individuals' success in the presence of their peers was one of the ways that Andy reinforced who was accountable for what. Not only did this reinforce team members' existing feelings of personal strength and capability but, Andy found, it "helped them to recognize just how competent their counterparts in other areas were."

Accountability results in feelings of ownership.

Accountability results in feelings of ownership, that you—not someone else—have the responsibility for what's going on around you. When there is no "they," then no one has to be told what to do or why it is important. We can all figure it out for ourselves. Leaders have created real owners en route to the extraordinary.

DEVELOP COMPETENCE AND CONFIDENCE

Options, latitude, and accountability fuel people's sense of power and control over their lives. Yet as necessary as enhancing self-determination is, it's insufficient. Without the knowledge, skills, information, and resources to do a job expertly, without feeling competent to skillfully execute the choices that it requires, people feel overwhelmed and disabled. Even if they have the resources, there may be times when people don't have the confidence that they're allowed to use them, or that they'll be backed up if things don't go as well as expected. And there may be times when they just lack the self-confidence to do what they need to do.

Developing competence and building confidence are essential to delivering on the organization's promises and maintaining the credibility of leaders and team members alike. To get extraordinary things done leaders must invest in strengthening the capacity and the resolve of everyone in the organization.

Educate, Educate, Educate

When you increase the latitude and discretion of your constituents, you also have to increase expenditures on training and development. Without education and coaching, people are reluctant to exercise their knowledge, in part because they don't know how to perform the critical tasks and in part out of fear of being punished for making mistakes. If you're going to promise customers quality products and superior customer service, you're going to have to equip employees with the skills and resources to do superior work. Successful quality or service programs, for example, all have in common the fact that the group members receive training in basic statistical measurement methods, group communication skills, and problem-solving techniques. The same goes for any improvement process, including the development of better leaders.

Strengthening others requires up-front investments in initiatives that develop people's competencies and foster their confidence. These investments in training and development produce profits: companies that spend more than the average amount on training have a higher return on investment than companies that are below average spenders.[9] Organizations that have invested more than the average amount of money on training enjoy higher levels of employee involvement and commitment and better levels of customer service, along with greater understanding of and alignment with company visions and values.

As director of product development with Vasconnect, a start-up medical device company, Gita Barry realized that building a new 3mm sterile delivery tool would be quite a stretch for her and her team. She had to challenge everyone, internal and external to the program, to meet some very aggressive deadlines and expand their competencies in the process. As she put it,

> They needed to extend themselves beyond their current comfortable skill sets. I ensured that team members were trained to complete each task rather than assuming that previous experience was sufficient. This ended up being very important to the success of the project because there were many significant gaps in previous training, which would have killed the project if they were not identified and addressed. With the additional training and individual attention, individuals felt like they were part of the team and poised, even eager, to make a contribution.

For leaders, developing the competence and confidence of their constituents (so that they might be more qualified, more capable, more effective, and leaders in their own right) is a personal and hands-on affair. Leaders are genuinely interested in those they coach, having empathy for and an understanding of each of their constituents.[10] Among sales managers, for example, developing others has been shown to be the competency most frequently found among those at the top of their field.[11] In today's world, if you're not growing and learning in a job, you'd better find a new one. Dan Warmenhoven, Network Appliance's CEO, told us that a critical hiring requirement for mid-level to senior managers has become "Can I learn from this person? We don't want to hire people that others don't believe can teach them and make them better in the process."

Be sure to tap the teachers in your midst. Schoolteachers have long realized that the learning of older children can be enhanced by having them tutor younger students. In this process, the learning by both parties is strengthened. This is equally true in organizations, as demonstrated by the experiences of Sanjay Bali, whose personal-best leadership story opened this chapter. The late Peter Drucker explained that "knowledge workers and service workers learn most when they teach."[12] He pointed out that the best way to improve a worker's productivity was to ask for him or her to give a presentation on "the secret of my success"; for example, your star salesperson could present at the company's sales conference, or your top surgeon could give a talk at the county medical society, or your top volunteer could speak to the board.

> Leaders are genuinely interested in those they coach.

Keep in mind that sometimes teaching can be informal and quite serendipitous. A study by Xerox's Palo Alto Research Center revealed that service personnel learn most about fixing copiers not from company manuals but from hanging around swapping stories.[13] Instead of busting up the gang by the water cooler, make opportunities for learning at informal get-togethers and loosely organized off-site meetings.

Organize Work to Build Competence

In our case studies of personal bests, people talked of confronting critical organizational issues—whether improving quality, reducing manufacturing start-up times, changing customer perceptions, raising literacy rates, reengineering core agency processes, or mobilizing legislative initiatives. Although it may seem obvious that people do their best when the work is critical to success, this principle is often lost in the day-to-day design of work.

Jack Stack, CEO of SRC Holdings, writes, "THE best, most efficient, most profitable way to operate a business is to give everybody in the company a voice in saying how the company is run and a stake in the financial outcome, good or bad. . . . Financial education of the workforce—we call it open-book management—is the key to extraordinary and sustained success. . . . Everyone at SRC . . . understands how they personally affect the income and profitability of the company."[14] At SRC at the time, 86 percent of the training budget was spent on educating everyone to be a businessperson. Jack believes that when everyone has the same information about what's happening in the business, then everyone starts thinking and acting like a CEO—regardless of their organizational position.

Your constituents can't act like owners and provide leadership if they fundamentally don't understand how your business, agency, company, product, or program operates. This goes way beyond clear visions and goals into the interior domains of operations. To really understand the critical organizational issues and tasks, they need to be able to answer such questions as Who are our most important customers, clients, suppliers, and stakeholders? How do they perceive us? How do we measure success? What has our track record been over the past five years? What new products or services will we initiate in the next six months?

Many other questions could be asked; come up with the ones that make the most sense in your context. If your constituents can't answer critical questions about your enterprise such as these, how can they work together to transform shared values and common purposes into reality? How can they know how their performance affects other teams, units, divisions, and ultimately the success of the entire enterprise or endeavor? How can they feel very strong or capable if they don't know the answers to the same questions every "owner" would know?

Another way leaders can help strengthen constituents is by understanding how the contextual factors of their jobs play out. Do people perceive themselves as lacking control over their immediate situation, or lacking the required capability, resources, or discretion needed to accomplish a task? If so, the most common reasons are excessive bureaucracy, authoritarian supervisory styles, nonmerit-based reward systems, and rigid or limiting job design.[15] Although you may have little or no control over the bureaucracy and reward systems, you certainly have control over your own leadership style and over the design of the jobs of your direct reports or team members.

Here's what to do: make certain that peoples' jobs are designed so that they know what is expected of them. Provide sufficient training and technical support so that people can complete their assignments successfully. Enrich their responsibilities so that they experience variety in their task assignments and opportunities to make meaningful decisions about how their work gets accomplished. Create occasions for them to network with others in the organization (including peers and senior managers). Involve them in programs, meetings, and decisions that have a direct impact on their job performance. Take a careful look at what your constituents are doing in their jobs and determine—best to include them—where you could be enriching their positions and consequently fostering greater self-confidence.

When he joined Datapro (India) as deputy manager, Raj Limaye found his group feeling "quite shy and unsuccessful." He immediately implemented regular meetings, with new themes and new chairs each week, and he made a concerted effort to get everyone to present their ideas. He met with each person and asked them what they wanted to do in their jobs. While their answers were not all the same, Raj made certain that he found challenging extensions to the tasks they were performing, and added variety to each job.

I tried removing unnecessary routine tasks where possible; and, if not, then these were put on rotation. In six months we had reduced the routine tasks to a minimum, as everyone shared ideas about how to improve these tasks or find alternatives. We helped everyone become more competent by creating a learning climate where people needed to look beyond their own job descriptions and organizational boundaries. People were assigned important tasks, and I made them accountable at the same time. We were able to complete a communications project at a critical moment in time that proved vital to the Border Security Force of India.

How did this group get transformed? I listened to them, asked for feedback, acted on the feedback, involved team members in the decisions, had them own the tasks, made them visible, and recognized their efforts for the success of the group. We acted together.

As Raj demonstrated, people's increased sphere of influence should be over something relevant to the pressing concerns and core technology of the business. Assess the critical tasks and issues in your organization and then make sure that your constituents are well represented on the task forces, committees, teams, and problem-solving groups dealing with them. If you're on one of these, make sure you take a key constituent or two along with you to meetings.

Foster Self-Confidence

Fostering the confidence to do well is critical in the process of strengthening others. Just because individuals know how to do something doesn't necessarily mean that they will do it. Enabling others to act is not just a practice or technique. It's a key step in a psychological process that affects individuals' intrinsic needs for self-determination. Each of us has an internal need to influence other people and life's events so as to experience some sense of order and stability in our lives. Feeling confident that we can adequately cope with events, situations, and people we confront puts us in a position to exercise leadership. Leaders take actions and create conditions that strengthen their constituents' self-esteem and internal sense of effectiveness.

Without sufficient self-confidence, people lack the conviction for taking on tough challenges. The lack of self-confidence manifests itself in feelings of helplessness, powerlessness, and crippling self-doubt. Building self-confidence is building people's inner strength to plunge ahead in uncharted terrain, to make tough choices, to face opposition and the like because they believe in their skills and in their decision-making abilities.[16]

Empirical studies document how self-confidence can affect people's performance. In one study, managers were told that decision making was a skill developed through practice. The more one worked at it, the more capable one became. Another group of managers was told that decision making reflected their basic intellectual aptitude. The greater one's underlying cognitive capacities, the better his or her decision-making ability. Working with a simulated organization, both groups of managers dealt with a series of production orders, requiring various staffing decisions and the establishment of different performance targets. When faced with difficult performance standards, those managers who believed that decision making was an acquirable skill continued to set challenging goals for themselves, used good problem-solving strategies, and fostered organizational productivity. Their counterparts, who believed that decision-making ability was latent (that is, you either have it or you don't), lost confidence in themselves over time as they encountered difficulties. They lowered their aspirations for the organization, their problem solving deteriorated, and organizational productivity declined.[17]

In a related set of studies, one group of managers was told that organizations and people are easily changeable. Another group was told, "Work habits of employees are not that easily changeable, even by good guidance. Small changes do not necessarily improve overall outcomes." Those managers with the confidence that they could influence organizational outcomes by their actions maintained a higher level of performance than those who felt they could do little to change things.[18] A study of entry-level accountants revealed that those with the highest self-confidence were rated ten months later by their supervisors as having the best job performance. Their level of self-confidence was a stronger predictor of job performance than the actual level of skill or training they had received before being hired.[19]

Experience tells us—and these studies underscore—that having confidence and believing in your ability to handle the job, no matter how difficult, is essential in promoting and sustaining consistent efforts. Fostering self-confidence is not a warmed-over version of the power of positive thinking.

By communicating to constituents that you believe that they—all of us—can be successful, you help people to extend themselves and to persevere.

Still, there is a direct connection between self-confidence and competence. You can't just tell people they can do it if they really can't. As founder of the Institute for Women's Leadership, Rayona Sharpnack, whom we discussed earlier, tackles the issues of competence and confidence head-on:

> I'll go around the room and ask people how many of them would like to have more confidence as a result of being in the class. Almost all of the hands go up. I say, "Okay, I'm going to make you a counteroffer. I'm not going to promise to give you more confidence. I'm going to promise to give you more competence. And I'm going to ask you to look and see where confidence comes from." Then I ask how many of them think of confidence as a prerequisite—how many of them will do something if they feel confident enough to attempt it. All of the hands go up. Then I ask them what they are confident about in their lives and how they got to be confident about those things. Whether it's horseback riding or shipping products or developing software code, they all got confidence by doing something over and over again. Oh, so then confidence is an aftermath, not a prerequisite. Bing, bing, bing, bing!
>
> Then it hits them: they've been spending their whole lives waiting to be confident before trying to do something new, when they couldn't possibly be confident until they're competent. That's transformational, because it suddenly sheds light on whole arenas of restriction and impediment that have nothing to do with anything other than the context from which they're viewing the situation or their lives or themselves.[20]

Leaders Coach

Leaders actively seek out ways to increase choice, providing greater decision-making authority and responsibility for their constituents. They also develop the capabilities of their team and foster self-confidence through the faith they demonstrate in letting other people lead. In taking these actions, leaders act as coaches, helping others learn how to use their skills and talents, as well as learn from their experiences.[21]

Brian Baker, family-practice physician and colonel in the U.S. Army, understood how important it is for leaders to coach. Upon his arrival as hospital commander he was told that the Raymond W. Bliss Army Health Center (located on Fort Huachuca near Tucson, Arizona) was the "most problematic hospital in the army." Brian found a group of talented people in disarray and an organization with low morale, a set of rigidly followed institutional rules, and a high degree of conflict between doctors and nurses. He also found a stunningly unfavorable accreditation report by the Joint Commission on Accreditation of Healthcare Organizations, a report that threatened to harm the military career of nearly everyone on staff. There was neither vision nor camaraderie—only fear, hostility, and conflict.

Leaders actively seek out ways to increase choice.

Yet within two years, under Brian's leadership, the hospital came "within inches" of receiving an exemplary rating—all without a single change in personnel. Brian didn't fire anyone, nor did he reassign anyone or significantly change anyone's job.

What Brian did do was coach. He listened, mentored, and fundamentally changed the culture and the decision-making process. Restoring his staff's sense of self-confidence was the first challenge. To that end, Brian held a series of meetings in rapid succession designed to allow him to meet and communicate openly with all of his constituents. No one's supervisor was allowed at these meetings because he wanted to ensure open and honest discussion. Brian promised that he would take no direct action as a result of the meetings, nor would he discuss what was said with anyone. He explained his philosophy of participatory and supportive (versus directive) management. These meetings set a tone of openness, genuine concern, and trust that was essential to ultimately restoring people's belief in their ability to succeed.

From Brian's perspective, his leadership challenge was just a matter of educating an already very bright and capable staff that wasn't fulfilling their potential:

> All I had to do was point them toward the data and explain how important it was that we did what the accreditation agency required. We're not here to tell people what to do but to make sure they understand what needs to be done and understand how to do it.
>
> You can't just tell them to go out and do a monumental task if you aren't sure they really know what exactly needs to be done. So you ask lots of questions to guide their thinking—you ask, "How are you going to do this and such"—but you never assume control of the issue. They own it, not you. You coach and you mentor, but you make them decide and act. If it's their plan, they're more likely to make it happen. I helped add what I consider the most important ingredient: mutual respect and a feeling of togetherness. After that, everything just came together.

When at their best, leaders, like Brian, never take control away from others. They leave it to their constituents to decide and to take responsibility for the decisions they make. When leaders coach, educate, enhance self-determination, and otherwise share power with others, they're demonstrating profound trust in and respect for others' abilities. When leaders help others to grow and develop, that help is reciprocated. People who feel capable of influencing their leaders are more strongly attached to those leaders and more committed to effectively carrying out their responsibilities. They own their jobs.

REFLECTION AND ACTION: STRENGTHENING OTHERS

Strengthening others is essentially the process of turning constituents into leaders—making people capable of acting on their own initiative. A virtuous cycle is created as power and responsibility are extended to others and as people respond successfully.

Leaders strengthen others when they make it possible for constituents to exercise choice and discretion, when they design in options and alternatives to the ways that work and services are produced, and when they foster accountability and responsibility that compels action. As more responsibility is assumed by constituents, leaders can expend more energy in other areas, enhancing their own sphere of influence and bringing additional resources back to their units to be distributed once again among the group members.

Leaders develop in others the competence, as well as the confidence, to act and to excel. They make certain that constituents have the necessary data and information to understand how the organization operates, gets results, makes money, and does good work. They create a learning climate, investing in people's continuing competence, and they coach people on how to put what they know into practice, stretching and supporting others to do more than they might have imagined possible. Exemplary leaders use their power in service of others because they know how well capable and confident people perform. As constituents increase their competencies, even further amounts of power and discretion can be extended.

Here are three action steps you can start taking today to Strengthen Others.

Increase Individual Accountability

Enhancing self-determination means giving people control over their own lives. Therefore you, the leader, have to give them something of substance to control and for which they are accountable. Here are some places to start:

- Make certain that everyone in your organization, no matter the task, has a customer. The customer can be internal or external, but each person needs to know who they are serving. And, by the way, the customer isn't you, the leader!
- Substantially increase signature authority at all levels.
- Remove or reduce unnecessary approval steps.

- Eliminate as many rules as possible.
- Decrease the amount of routine work.
- Automate routine work wherever possible.
- Assign nonroutine jobs.
- Support the exercise of independent judgment.
- Encourage creative solutions to problems.
- Define jobs more broadly—as projects, not tasks.
- Provide greater freedom of access, vertically and horizontally, inside and outside.

Remember to provide the necessary resources (for example, materials, money, time, people, and information) for people to perform autonomously. There's nothing more disempowering than to have lots of responsibility for doing something but nothing to do it with.

People's increased sphere of influence ought to be over something relevant to the pressing concerns and core technology of the business. Choosing the color of the paint may be a place to start, but you'd better give people influence over more substantive issues as well. For example, if quality is top priority, find ways to expand people's influence and discretion over issues of quality control. If innovation is a priority, increase people's influence over the development of new products, processes, or services.

Offer Visible Support

Power doesn't flow to unknown people; becoming powerful requires getting noticed. And getting noticed means getting the visible support of the leader. In strengthening your constituents ensure that they're highly visible and that individual and group efforts get noticed and recognized. Here are a few things you can do to offer more support to your constituents:

- Assign a key presentation to one of your team members. Offer coaching ahead of time. Introduce him or her to the group, and be there in the room to offer words of encouragement.

- Nominate one of your team members to address an industry conference.
- When someone asks you a question in a meeting, turn to a knowledgeable team member and say, "Tracy knows more about that than I do. What do you think, Tracy?"
- Ask a team member to accompany you on a sales call or important client visit. Introduce that person as your "valuable colleague and trusted adviser."
- Place people on task forces and committees whose members come from across the organization and encourage active participation in professional and community groups.
- Make sure that your constituents are well represented on the task forces, committees, teams, and problem-solving groups dealing with the critical issues that have to do with your part of the business. Take a key constituent or two with you to meetings.
- Provide team members with access to senior executives.
- Regularly brag about the accomplishments of your team members. Saying, "It wasn't me, it was us," or "It wasn't me, it was Byron," puts the spotlight on those who played a key role and also increases their esteem in the eyes of others.

These are just a few of the ways in which you can make others more visible. The point is, no one likes to be taken for granted, and everyone likes being noticed. By fostering outside contacts, and by developing and promoting people with promise, you help build a greater sense of personal power, increase confidence, and open doors for people so they can exercise more of their own influence.

Conduct Monthly Coaching Conversations

Why wait until that dreaded annual performance appraisal to talk with someone about how they are doing? By the time you get to them the feedback is often eleven months too late and long past the point of being helpful. Instead, you need to have monthly coaching conversations with each of your team members. Our colleague Marshall Goldsmith, a seasoned coach to some of the world's most senior executives, offered us the following suggestion on how to bolster the continuous improvement of individual players.

Schedule a once-a-month one-on-one dialogue with each of your direct reports. Have a two-way conversation on six key questions:

1. Where are *we* going?
   - I'll tell you where I think we're going.
   - You tell me where you think we're going.

2. Where are *you* going?
   - I'll tell you where I see you and your group going.
   - You tell me where you see you and your group going.

3. What are *you* doing well?
   - I'll give you my sense of what you're doing well.
   - You give me your sense of what you're doing well.

4. What suggestions for improvement do you have for *yourself*?
   - I'll tell you the suggestions I have.
   - You tell me what suggestions you have.

5. How can I help *you*?
   - I'll add anything else I think I can do.
   - You tell me what I can do to help and support you.

6. What suggestions do you have for *me*?
   - I'll tell you what I think I need to do.
   - You tell me what you think I need to do.

In this dialogue, both parties learn how they can be doing better than they are. Notice how the leader and the constituent are exchanging information about one another. You might want to adapt these questions to your situation, but the basic idea is to have regular, structured conversations about a person's direction and performance.

Coaching is not a once-a-year process. Do this at least every month and you'll be sure to notice continuous improvements as people become stronger and more capable as a result of being encouraged to learn from their experiences. The difference may well be extraordinary.

COMMITMENT NUMBER 8
Strengthen Others

Essentials of Strengthening Others

- Enhance self-determination
- Develop competence and confidence

Taking Action

- Increase individual accountability
- Offer visible support
- Conduct monthly coaching conversations

PART

ENCOURAGE THE HEART

- RECOGNIZE CONTRIBUTIONS
- CELEBRATE THE VALUES AND VICTORIES

RECOGNIZE
CONTRIBUTIONS

"Recognition is important, challenging, and easily forgotten—
so pay attention and don't forget to say 'thanks.'"
Mary Le, Intel Corporation

Amanda Turner of Intuit is a leader who understands the importance of believing in people and showing appreciation. She realizes that by expecting the best from people, they in turn expect the best from themselves. On one occasion she even gave her direct report Melissa Pierce a stuffed horse. That's because when Melissa started at the company the team affectionately teased her about being a "galloping horse, jumping at every challenge and opportunity to contribute and support the group." Melissa explains,

Before my first meeting with the CEO, I was extremely nervous, but Amanda encouraged me by reminding me that I was hired for my abilities and fearlessness, and she expressed her confidence in me by saying that she knew that I could win him over. She was right. During that meeting, I presented the CEO with my proposal for a crisis communication plan, assigning roles to all the executive staff members, and he thought it was great. He said he would present it to his staff at their next meeting. I was elated! After my successful first presentation, Amanda presented me with a small stuffed horse that made gallop sounds when it was squeezed, followed by proud neighing sounds. She put a sticker on the horse that read "Victory" and told me that was his name. I displayed the horse on my shelf, and every time I had a success, Amanda walked by and gave it a squeeze in my honor.

Amanda also understands the importance of recognizing the accomplishments of her team. For example, after completing several rounds of difficult consolidations, Amanda lifted the spirits of her team by taking everyone out for lunch and a movie—as a surprise. "None of us remembers what movie we saw or where we ate that day," relates one of her constituents. "All we remember is how cool we thought Amanda was for taking time out for us, for considering our feelings and improving our little corner of the world." Leaders realize that recognition needs to be well thought-out, purposeful, and genuine. When Amanda took the team out that day, she started a ritual of going to the movies whenever they accomplished a big project and exceeded requirements. They never went to the movies together at any other time, for any other reason—that would have undermined the purpose and made the outing less special. Amanda communicated how much she valued her relationships with her team through her actions, and these actions set an example for the rest of the team to follow to express appreciation for one another and to celebrate their achievements as a team.

Amanda also invested in everyone's professional development by finding classes, seminars, conferences—any learning or developmental experience that she thought would increase their competencies. Why? As Amanda explained, "I knew that I could only be as successful as my team. If I hindered their growth, I also hindered my own. My job is to create leaders to ensure future successes for the company." When Amanda eventually relocated to another area, Whitney, another team member, was immediately identified as her replacement due to the exposure Amanda had given her, the feedback she had received from Amanda on her performance, and the developmental opportunities that Amanda had encouraged her to pursue.

Recognition is about acknowledging good results and reinforcing positive performance. It's about shaping an environment in which everyone's contributions are noticed and appreciated. In high-performing organizations—and when people reported being at their personal best—people work quite intensely and often put in very long hours, but this doesn't mean they don't or can't enjoy themselves. To persist for months at a demanding pace, people need encouragement. They need emotional fuel to replenish their spirits. They need the will to continue and the courage to do something they have never done before and to continue with the journey. One important way that leaders accomplish this is by recognizing individual contributions.

Exemplary leaders understand this need to Recognize Contributions and are constantly engaged in these essentials:

- **Expect the best**
- **Personalize recognition**

By putting these essentials into practice to recognize constituents' contributions, leaders stimulate and motivate the internal drive within each individual—and fulfill their commitment to encouraging the heart.

EXPECT THE BEST

Successful leaders have high expectations of themselves and of their constituents. These expectations are powerful because they are the frames into which people fit reality. As human beings we tend to live up to—or down to—our leaders' (teachers', coaches', parents') expectations. And we don't mean "expect" as in "obligation"—I expect you to do this or else! Instead, we mean it in the sense of "consider likely"—I consider it highly likely that you'll do this. The high performance that exemplary leaders get is because they fundamentally *believe in* the abilities of their constituents. Exemplary leaders set high expectations, because they know that they're much more likely to get high performance if they expect high performance than if they expect low performance. Social psychologists have referred to this as the "Pygmalion effect," from the Greek myth about Pygmalion, a sculptor who carved a statue of a beautiful woman, fell in love with the statue, and appealed to the goddess Aphrodite to bring her to life. His prayers were granted.

Leaders play Pygmalion-like roles in developing their constituents. When we've asked people to describe the best leaders they've ever had, they consistently talked about individuals who brought out the best in them. They said things like, "She believed in me more than I believed in myself," or "He saw something in me even I didn't see." This exact point was underscored by Jon Schrader's personal-best leadership experience. At the time he was the sales business manager for worldwide sales operations with Sun Microsystems, and they were attempting to combine two distinct organizational structures and processes into one new entity. "It was my boss," Jon told us, "who asked me to take on the project and told me that he thought I was up to this challenge. . . . In many respects it was his encouraging me to do this that made me actually believe that I could do it!"

Exemplary leaders can, figuratively speaking, bring others to life. These leaders significantly improve others' performance quite dramatically because they care deeply for their constituents and have an abiding faith in their capacities. Constituents are able to respond positively to these expectations not only because they have the abilities; they also respond because leaders are more nurturing, supporting, and encouraging toward people in whom they believe. Research on the phenomenon of self-fulfilling prophecies provides ample evidence that people act in ways that are consistent with others' expectations of them.[1] If you expect people to fail, they probably will. If you expect them to succeed, they probably will. Consider how Denise Kiehm described the impact that her leader had on her and their team:

> *People act in ways that are consistent with others' expectations of them.*

> When Keith led our group, we were not short of ideas or opinions. What we lacked was trust and confidence in ourselves and our ability to achieve the lofty goals we set. But Keith pushed us hard and never let us once believe that he thought we could fail. He spent time with me and all his team members learning what made us tick. For some it was money or additional benefits, and for others it was recognition of a job well done. He figured out what drove each individual and used this information to encourage us and push us forward. He required us to spend time with our clients and partners so we developed relationships on our own and trust beyond our day-to-day tasks. His leadership style created such a strong team that we were committed to giving 100 percent of ourselves on the job. It was very clear how he was able to bring us all together to work as a team and reach above and beyond our goals. He did this through expecting us to be the best and then trusting and being open to each and every member of the team.

The best leaders bring out the best in their constituents. If the potential exists within us, leaders always find a way to bring it out of us.

High Expectations Lead to High Performance

The high expectations of leaders aren't just fluff that they hold in their minds to keep a positive outlook or to psych themselves up. Another person's belief in your abilities accomplishes much more than that. The expectations that successful leaders hold provide the framework into which people fit their own realities. Just as with Pygmalion, these frameworks play an important role in developing people. Maybe you can't turn a marble statue into a real person but you can draw out the highest potential of your constituents.

Patti Kozlovsky told us how she experimented with this principle in one of her recent team projects at a large telecommunications company:

> I let team members know that I really thought they could do the job and I trusted their judgment to find the information and extract what was needed in a timely manner. In our group meetings, as we reviewed the information team members were contributing, I made a conscious effort to thank members for what they had contributed rather than commenting on what had not been done. What impact did this have? First of all, there was less tension in the group and team members felt as though everyone was participating to their fullest capacity. Instead of sniping at each other over what was not done, people were generally supporting one other and sharing resources, letting their colleagues know what they had found and sharing ideas about where others might find critical data.
>
> It was also interesting that team members were genuinely interested in what others had discovered and how that connected with information they had gathered. Because the team had confidence in each other's abilities, this strengthened our respect for one another and made it easy to incorporate multiple perspectives into our final product. This experiment taught me that people live up to our expectations. If you express confidence in their abilities, they will put their heart into whatever project is on the table.

Patti acknowledged to us that she wasn't always comfortable giving control over to her teammates, but she had clearly learned that her expectations of high performance and motivation in others, along with recognizing them for their contributions, easily beat the alternative of command-and-control management. To be successful on a job, leaders make certain that people feel they belong, are accepted and valued, and have the skills and inner resources needed to be successful.

Jason Cha's experience affirms the importance of the leader's belief in constituents. He was challenged to reduce costs in the global industrial and commercial business unit of Tyco Electronics by reclaiming spool construction and bringing it in-house despite the limited available resources. Working with cross-functional teams in a matrix organizational environment, he discovered that "recognizing and rewarding individual contributions was one of the most effective ways to keep people focused and to foster innovation." He explained,

> Team members feel appreciated when their names are included in presentations about projects. Being recognized also raises a particular individual's commitment to excellence because his or her name is associated with a given project; each member of the team becomes part of the feedback loop for that project. It also creates a sense of community in that people feel they are part of a winning team.
>
> The encouraging feedback prompted people to seek out greater opportunities to work together as a team and to cooperate more in finding workable solutions to everyday problems and issues. This "Pygmalion Effect"—in which people respond to being treated in a pleasant, positive, and respectful fashion—gets perpetuated across many situations. The winner's attitude truly is one that is cultivated through positive expectations and perpetuated through meaningful feedback. It even works its magic by making me a better leader in return.

Believing in others is an extraordinarily powerful force in propelling performance. Feeling affirmed and appreciated increases a person's sense of self-worth, which in turn precipitates success in all areas of one's life. Research and everyday experience confirm that people with high self-esteem, of all ages and levels of education and socioeconomic backgrounds, "feel unique, competent, secure, empowered, and connected to the people around them."[2] If we have someone in our life who believes in us, and who constantly reinforces that belief when interacting with us, we're strongly influenced by that support.

Our research has shown that people are most often anxious or nervous when they are on the eve of going out and delivering their personal best. Spurred on by their leaders' high expectations and encouragement, they developed the self-confidence, courage, and volition to live up to their leaders' expectations. They took the initiative and did even more than was expected of them.

Clear Expectations and Goals Focus Our Attention

Being clear about what's expected of them, and what you're trying to accomplish, is essential to helping people stay the course, especially when the going gets tough. When you were a kid you might have read Lewis Carroll's *Alice's Adventures in Wonderland*. Remember the croquet match? The flamingos were the mallets, the playing card soldiers were the wickets, and the hedgehogs were the balls. Everyone kept moving and the rules kept changing all the time. Poor Alice. There was no way of knowing how to play the game or what it took to win. Besides, it was all rigged in favor of the Queen, no matter what Alice did.

You needn't have gone down the rabbit hole to know how Alice felt: we've all been Alice at one time or another in our lives. We've all been at a place where we're not sure where we're expected to be going, what the ground rules are that govern how we behave, how we're doing along the way, or when we'll be done. And just when we think we're getting the hang of it, the organization comes along and changes everything. This is a recipe for maddening frustration and pitiful performance.

Believing you can do it is only part of the equation for success. If leaders want people to give their all, to put their hearts and minds into it, they must also focus positive expectations on outcomes and make sure that there are some consistent norms about how the game is played. Goals and values provide people with a set of standards that concentrates their efforts. They both have to do with what's expected. Goals connote something shorter-term whereas values (or principles) connote something more enduring. Typically, values and principles serve as the basis for goals; they're your standards of excellence, your highest aspirations. They define the arena in which goals and metrics must be set. Values mediate the path of action. Goals release the energy.

> *Values mediate the path of action. Goals release the energy.*

The ideal state—on the job, in sports, in life generally—is often called "flow." "Flow experiences," as we described in Chapter Eight, are those times when you feel pure enjoyment and effortlessness in what you do.[3] To experience flow, it's necessary to have clear goals—because goals help you concentrate and avoid distractions. By having an intention to do something that is meaningful to you, by setting a goal, you take purposeful action. Action without goals, at least in an organizational context, is just busy-work. It's a waste of precious time and energy.

But what do goals have to do with recognition? They give it a context. People should be recognized for achieving something, for doing something extraordinary—like coming in first, breaking a record, doing something no one else has ever done before. Leaders should absolutely make sure they affirm the worth of every one of their constituents; that goes without saying. But for recognition to be meaningful and for it to reward appropriate behaviors, you have to have an end in mind. Goals help people keep their eyes on the vision. Goals and intentions keep them on track. They help people put the phone in do-not-disturb mode, shut out the noise, and schedule their time. Goal-setting affirms the person, and, whether you realize it or not, contributes to what people think about themselves.

Feedback and Goals Keep People Engaged

People need to know if they're making progress toward the goal or simply marking time. Having goals helps to serve that function, but that is not enough. People's motivation to increase their productivity on a task increases only when they have a challenging goal *and* receive feedback on their progress.[4] Goals without feedback, or feedback without goals, have little effect on motivation.

So just announcing that the idea is to reach the summit is not enough to get people to put forth more effort. They need information on whether they're still climbing in the right direction, making progress toward the top, or sliding downhill. With clear goals and detailed feedback, people can become self-correcting and can more easily understand their place in the big picture. With feedback they can also determine what help they need from others and who might be able to benefit from their assistance. Under these conditions they will be willing to put forth more productive effort. Without feedback, production will be less efficient and will exact a significant toll in the form of increased levels of stress and anxiety.

A study of the winningest high school and college athletic coaches reveals that they pay great attention to providing real-time feedback on their players' performance and will, as appropriate, recognize and reward outstanding contributions. As coaches explained, ongoing feedback "is a highly effective way to shape the behavior of the athletes so as to increase the team's ability to continue winning. Without immediate and precise feedback, the learning process ends and mediocrity is sure to emerge. Ongoing evaluation of the players' ability to play your game, to your expectations, is critical given the constant need to restock the team with younger athletes."[5] This viewpoint is echoed by twelve-year veteran and all-pro football player Brent Jones, now managing director of Northgate Capital, who told us, "Players, regardless of fame or fortune, need to hear when they do well and when they don't." What works for athletes also applies to those on the factory floor, behind the counter, in city hall, and in the corner office.

The importance of feedback was vividly demonstrated in a classic study involving soldiers who, after several weeks of intensive training, were competing for places in special units. The soldiers were divided into four groups, which were unable to communicate with one another. All the men marched twenty kilometers (about twelve-and-a-half miles) over the same terrain on the same day. The first group was told how far they were expected to go and were kept informed of their progress along the way. The second group was told only that "this is the long march you hear about." These soldiers never received any information about the total distance they were expected to travel, nor were they told how far they had marched. The third group was told to march fifteen kilometers, but when they had gone fourteen kilometers, they were told that they had to go six kilometers farther. The fourth group was told that they had to march twenty-five kilometers, but when they reached the fourteen-kilometer mark, they were told that they had only six more kilometers to go.

The groups were assessed as to which had the best performance and which endured the most stress. The results indicated that the soldiers who knew exactly how far they had to go and where they were during the march were much better off than the soldiers who didn't get this information. The next-best group was the soldiers who thought that they were marching only fifteen kilometers. Third best was the group told to march a longer distance, then given the good news at the fourteen-kilometer mark. Those who performed worst were the soldiers who received no information about the goal (total distance) or the distance that they had already traveled (feedback).[6]

In a study of the effects of feedback on self-confidence, M.B.A. students were praised or criticized, or received no feedback on their performance in a simulation of creative problem solving. They had been told that their efforts would be compared with how well hundreds of others had done on the same task. Those who heard nothing about how well they did suffered as great a blow to their self-confidence as those who were criticized.[7] Saying nothing about a person's performance doesn't help anyone—not the performer, not the leader, and not the organization. People hunger for feedback. They really do prefer to know how they are doing, and no news generally has the same negative impact as bad news.

When leaders provide a clear sense of direction and feedback along the way, they encourage people to reach inside and do their best. Information about goals and about progress toward those goals strongly influences people's abilities to achieve—and influences how well and how long they live.[8] Because encouragement is more personal and positive than other forms of feedback, it's more likely to accomplish something that other forms cannot: strengthening trust between leaders and constituents. Encouragement, in this sense, is the highest form of feedback.

Create Conditions for Success

When leaders expect the best of others, they get the best performance from others. But what happens in organizations when leaders have low expectations of others? And what happens when managers are constantly on the lookout for problems? Three things: they get a distorted view of reality; over time, production declines; and their personal credibility hits bottom. Wandering around with an eye for trouble is likely to get you just that. More trouble.

Put yourself in this situation. If you knew someone was coming around to check up on you, how would you behave? Conventional wisdom holds that as soon as they spot the boss coming people put on their best behavior. Wrong. They may put on different behavior, but it's not their best. In fact, it can be their worst because they get nervous and tense. In addition, when you know that people are coming around to look for problems, you're more likely to hide them than to reveal them. People who work for highly controlling managers are more likely to keep information to themselves, hide the truth, and be dishonest about what is going on.

No surprise, then, that controlling managers have low credibility. Highly controlling behaviors—inspecting, correcting, checking up—signal lack of trust. How do you respond to people who don't trust you? You don't trust them. And because trustworthiness is a key element of personal credibility, credibility diminishes. People are unlikely to believe someone who does not exhibit trust in them.[9]

> *People are unlikely to believe someone who does not exhibit trust in them.*

Can you imagine any right-thinking manager doing anything that would *not* help people to succeed? Surprisingly, European researchers' meticulous studies show that "bosses—albeit accidentally and usually with the best intentions—are often complicit in an employee's lack of success. How? By creating and reinforcing a dynamic that essentially sets up perceived underperformers to fail. If the Pygmalion effect describes the dynamic in which an individual lives up to great expectations, the set-up-to-fail syndrome explains the opposite."[10]

The set-up-to-fail syndrome may begin quite innocently. An employee seems to have a performance problem—a missed deadline, a lost account. Or it can even start when a manager is distant (figuratively or literally) from the employee for personal reasons. This triggers an increase in the manager's supervision and control of this individual, who then begins to believe that the manager lacks trust and confidence in him or her. Eventually, because of low expectations, the person withdraws, stops making independent decisions or taking initiative—and the problem intensifies.

Clearly, before you can lead, you have to believe in others, and you have to believe in yourself. This has positive benefits for leaders, positive benefits for their constituents, and positive benefits for the organizations they serve. Consider what Gary Garcia, as IT director at The Santa Cruz Operation, told us about how he made his team members feel:

My team members felt strong and capable because they were needed and important—and because I wouldn't let them fail. I wish I had some altruistic intent that caused me to say that "I wouldn't let them fail." The truth is less noble. I wouldn't let them fail because their failure would be my failure. I needed them to succeed, so I really couldn't let them fail. I would coach them, pair them up with buddies, ride along with them—whatever it took to make sure that the job got done.

High expectations matter—and they matter a lot. And the opposite is also true. Low expectations and negative stereotypes also matter, but in a direction that makes things worse. Everyone benefits when leaders hold the belief that people *can* change and people *can* develop new skills and abilities.

PERSONALIZE RECOGNITION

One of the more common complaints that we've heard about recognition is that far too often it's highly predictable, routine, and impersonal. A one-size-fits-all approach to recognition feels disingenuous, forced, and thoughtless. Over time it can even increase cynicism and actually damage credibility.

In contrast, when we ask people to tell us about their "most meaningful recognitions," one of the things they consistently tell us is that it's "personal." They go on to say that it feels special, and that it's not something that everyone else gets. That's why it's so important for leaders to pay attention to the likes and dislikes of each and every individual. By personalizing recognition, leaders send the message that someone took the time to notice the achievement, seek out the responsible individual, and personally deliver praise in a timely manner.

About a month after Linda Lewis arrived as senior vice president of learning and education at Charles Schwab & Company, she initiated the monthly Giraffe Award—given, naturally enough, for sticking your neck out, going above and beyond normal responsibilities and duties. Linda told the first person who received the award to select another deserving recipient within the company and present the award at the next meeting.

Giraffe Award winners received custody of a stuffed giraffe, plus a colored poster to commemorate the event. Cute, but maybe a bit predictable? Not necessarily—and that's the beauty of it. Linda and her associates found a way to take the potentially predictable and infuse it with surprise. They found a way to take something that might be impersonal and make it a personal, one-to-one experience. Recipient Paul Oknaian started it when he decided he'd add a little something extra, and he put a lei around the stuffed giraffe's neck. Pretty soon the giraffe had a cowboy hat, some shoes, and a shoulder bag. Then came the navel piercing that Linda Chan gave the giraffe before she passed it on to Denise Green, who'd jumped in above and beyond the call to assist Chan in facilitating some classes. What Linda initiated was a process that enabled everyone to get involved and make subsequent recognition personally special.

The extent to which recognition and rewards are applied to each individual in a personal (rather than an impersonal) manner explains a lot about how leaders and their organizations get a motivational bang for their buck (or not) from recognizing people's contributions. "A sincere word of thanks from the right person at the right time can mean more to an employee than a raise, a formal award, or a whole wall of certificates and plaques," Bob Nelson writes in *1001 Ways to Reward Employees*.[11] As he points out, "Part of the power of such rewards comes from the knowledge that someone took the time to notice the achievement, seek out the employee responsible, and personally deliver praise in a timely manner."

Leaders get the best from others not by building fires under people but by building the fire within them. As U.S. Postal Service district manager Mike Matuzek told us, "There's a fire that already burns inside of each person. My job is simply to stoke it." This explained Mike's own motivation in sending out personally addressed and personally signed birthday cards to all 13,567 postal employees in his district each year (that's thirty-seven a day, seven days a week!). This human touch and the few minutes it took to establish some personal connection with each person in the organization was certainly a reason Mike's district was consistently rated at the top.

Get Close to People

To make recognition personally meaningful, you first have to get to know your constituents. Daniela Maeder, of the Department of Economics and Labor, Switzerland, said to us, "Organizational diagrams don't matter at all. Be sure to treat employees as human beings and not as functional workers." If you're going to personalize recognition and make it feel genuinely special, you'll have to look past the roles people play and see the person inside. You need to get to know who your constituents are, how they feel, and what they think. And they want to get to know who you really are as well. They want to see you in living color. This is another reason why trust between leaders and their constituents plays an essential role.

Because proximity is the single best predictor of whether two people will talk to one another, you have to get near enough to people if you're going to find out what motivates them, what they like and don't like, and the kinds of recognition that are most appreciated. It means regularly walking the halls and plant floors, meeting often with small groups, and hitting the road for frequent visits with associates, key suppliers, and customers. It may even mean learning another language if a large portion of your workforce or customer base speaks it.

Paying attention, personalizing recognition, and creatively and actively appreciating others increases their trust in you. This kind of relationship is becoming more and more critical as workforces are becoming increasingly global and diverse. If others know that you genuinely care about them, they're more likely to care about you. This is how you bridge cultural divides.

Yet managerial myth says leaders shouldn't get too close to their constituents, that they can't be friends with people at work. Well, set this myth aside. Over a five-year period, researchers observed groups of friends and groups of acquaintances (people who knew each other only vaguely) performing motor-skill and decision-making tasks. The results were unequivocal. The groups composed of friends completed, on average, more than three times as many projects as the groups composed merely of acquaintances. In terms of decision-making assignments, groups of friends were over 20 percent more effective than groups of acquaintances were.[12]

People are just more willing to follow someone they like and trust. To become fully trusted you must trust. And that means being open: open to others, open with others. An open door is a physical demonstration of a willingness to let others in. So is an open heart. This means disclosing things about yourself. We don't mean tabloid-style disclosures. We mean talking about your hopes and dreams, your family and friends, your interests and your pursuits. We mean telling others the same things you'd like to know about them. "As a leader," said Anu Yamunan, technical leader at Hewlett-Packard, "I try to create a climate of trust not only within my team but also across teams. I realized that being open in these relationships is the way to go. I tell people what I stand for, what I value, what I hope for. When people see that I have taken the initiative in laying things out in the open and making myself vulnerable, they are willing to do so."

> *People are just more willing to follow someone they like and trust.*

Certainly, disclosing information about yourself can be risky. You can't be certain that other people will like you, appreciate your candor, agree with your aspirations, buy into your plans, or interpret your words and actions in the way you intend. But by demonstrating the willingness to take such risks, leaders encourage others to take a similar risk—and thereby take the first steps necessary to build *mutual* trust. Disclosing information about yourself is a start, as is asking for and encouraging feedback. When you're out there paying attention to what's happening, noticing the positive contributions people are making, stop and ask for feedback yourself. It's a demonstration that you appreciate your constituents and a way to encourage people to provide more information.[13]

Be Creative About Incentives

In getting close to her constituents, Anu Yamunan was able to find out what would be special for each of them. Armed with this information she was able to be more imaginative and creative in her approach to recognition and incentivizing people. As she told us,

> People love to do what they are recognized for, and they won't come to work with enthusiasm if they expect to be criticized, punished, or ignored. As a leader, I try to find out what my constituents care about. The rewards can then be used to reinforce outstanding performance. Some people in my team crave being recognized; others appreciate one-on-one time with senior leadership; some relish the opportunity to be in control of an aspect of their work; others care about bonuses or gifts. Whatever it is that motivates my team members, I try to give the rewards at the time of the achievement, not three or four months later. I also make the connection between the reward and the performance as direct, clear, and explicit as possible.

Leaders can't rely exclusively on the organization's formal reward system, which offers only a limited range of options. After all, promotions and raises are scarce resources. And don't make the mistake of assuming that individuals respond only to money. Although salary increases or bonuses are certainly valued, individual needs for appreciation and rewards extend much further than cash.

People respond to all kinds of rewards. At the vehicle repair business of the Whites Group in the southeast part of London, they do all kinds of things to recognize success. Each month twenty-five to fifty "Going the Extra Mile" awards are given throughout the organization. Get three and trade them in for a gold pin with a winged W. Get three in a row and you've earned a dinner certificate. These awards are generated by anyone in the organization, recognizing the contribution, the "extra mile" taken by someone else in pursuit of serving the customer. "It uplifts everyone's hearts," says Whites Group chairman Lindsay Levin, "to see what people are doing on their own: like traveling up to Scotland to help a customer whose car has broken down, delivering a car after midnight to a customer who was returning home from an overseas flight, or rearranging one's own schedule so that a teammate can attend a child's celebration at school." Lindsay herself writes lots of personal memos to congratulate people on achievement, signed with a smiley face. This has become a Lindsay trademark, and people talk about how many "smileys" they have received.

"We really try very hard at Whites," says Lindsay, "to make certain that we are giving people positive strokes—boosting their motivation by recognizing a job well done and giving them the confidence to push themselves further." She believes you need to stroke people on a regular basis. "If everyone is doing a great job, what's the problem in letting them know that?" Lindsay also appreciates that in difficult and challenging circumstances, sometimes all people need is to be supported and propped up. "This can be as simple as asking people how they are feeling or taking them out for a cup of coffee. Putting a bit of time aside to acknowledge the efforts they are making, and also that change can be difficult, makes a big difference to how people feel." Lindsay demonstrates that imagination may be the only thing in short supply when it comes to showing appreciation.

Verbal recognition of performance in front of one's peers and visible awards such as certificates, plaques, and other tangible gifts are powerful indeed and almost unlimited in their application. Spontaneous and unexpected rewards are often more meaningful than the expected formal ones. "The form of recognition that has the most positive influence on us, and that should be used most often is on-the-spot recognition," says Sonia Clark, Align Technology's vice president of human resources. "When something really terrific happens, I comment on it right away and to whomever may be close enough to hear. In a group setting, when one person really goes the extra mile to make sure the company delivers on its promises, we all really try to give that person public recognition."

Rewards are most effective when they're highly specific and given in close proximity to the appropriate behavior. One of the most important results of being out and about as a leader is that you can personally observe people doing things right and then reward them either on the spot or at the next public gathering.

In contrast, relying on an organization's formal reward system typically does a poor job of linking rewards to performance. That's because the lag time between the action and the recognition is too great. Our research found that the time lapse between performance and promotion is often more than six months.[14] It's tough to remember exactly what you did to earn the promotion when the feedback comes a half-year later. And while it's true that money may get people to do the job, it doesn't get them to do a good job.[15]

Instead of relying only or even primarily on formal rewards, effective leaders make tremendous use of intrinsic rewards—rewards that are built into the work itself, including such factors as a sense of accomplishment, a chance to be creative, and the challenge of the work—all directly tied to an individual's effort. These rewards are far more important than salary and fringe benefits in improving job satisfaction, commitment, retention, and performance.[16] Praise and coaching are significant forms of recognition as well. Often it's the simple, personal gestures that are the most powerful rewards.

Just Say "Thank You"

Not enough people make enough use of another powerful but inexpensive two-word reward—"thank you." Tsung-Chieh (T. C.) Lin, SoSIL manager, ground systems, at BAE Systems, has realized that "sometimes a 'thank you' is more important than a big victory party." He remembers with great fondness how he felt when one of his managers—ten years ago—"simply stopped by my office frequently and gave me praise on what a good job I had done. Furthermore, he called me to show appreciation when I worked late in the evening or on the weekend." T. C. gives personal testimony to what researchers have discovered: personal congratulations rank at the top of the most powerful nonfinancial motivators identified by employees.[17]

There are few if any more basic needs than to be noticed, recognized, and appreciated for one's efforts. It's true for every one of us, whether we're volunteers, teachers, doctors, priests, politicians, salespeople, customer service representatives, maintenance staff, or executives. There's little wonder, then, that a greater volume of thanks is reported in highly innovative companies than in low-innovation firms.[18] Recent studies show that work teams in which the ratio of positive to negative interactions is greater than three to one are *significantly* more productive than those teams that haven't achieved this ratio.[19]

Extraordinary achievements bloom more easily in climates in which performance is nurtured with a higher volume of appreciative comments.[20] Again, T. C. Lin's personal experience attests to these findings. His company had hired lots of new people as "contract employees because of uncertainties about future defense budgets." Under this hiring restriction, he explains,

> The incentive system has very little power, or should I say, has zero effect on most of the new hires. Without the formal recognition system, it has been a big challenge for me to motivate people to build long-term team commitment, and so I've relied upon intangible rewards to build my team. For example, I arranged a lunch party to celebrate and to say "thank you" to my team when we made a software release. I arranged a small birthday lunch gathering, while the company bought the lunch for the birthday person. Sometimes, I assigned a new "exploring" task to a person as a reward for a job well done (which enables them to buy a few books and maybe attend a training class on the topic).

Although T. C.'s team has the highest contractor-to-employee ratio in this department, he has had zero turnover, despite the fact that the company's turnover rate has been quite "significant."

Saying "thank
you" goes a
long way in sus-
taining high
performance.

Saying "thank you" is important, and can be accomplished in a variety of ways. Aimee Blum experienced the power of "thank you" in her new company, much to her initial surprise. "If a client sends a compliment to a manager," she told us, "the manager will forward it to the entire company to let everyone know about a job well done. Employees are also frequently recognized for their contributions to the company's success at all employee meetings." Aimee said that even in her short time with the company she had received several e-mails and positive comments about her performance:

At first it surprised me. At my previous company compliments were rarely given; it was expected that you would do a good job since you were being paid to work there. But once I got used to it, I found not only did I like receiving positive feedback, I like giving it as well. When someone has gone out of their way to help you out with a last-minute deadline, it seems the least you can do is take the time to show your appreciation; even a simple "thank you" can mean a lot. Going from a company that did not recognize contributions to one that makes a point of it on a regular basis has shown me how much of an impact simple gestures can have on the work environment and how they really instill a sense of community among coworkers.

Making a point of regularly saying "thank you" goes a long way in sustaining high performance.

Be Thoughtful

Personalized recognition comes down to being thoughtful. It means knowing enough about another person to answer the questions "What could I do to make this a memorable experience so that he always remembers how important his contributions are? and What would really make this special and unique for her?" For a model of this kind of thoughtfulness, take a lesson from Wayne Bennett, the founder and president of Glenn Valley Homes, a unique company set up to build computer-designed, precision-crafted custom homes in a small town northeast of Sacramento, California. Wayne knew how to give personalized recognition—and do it in a manner that acknowledged high expectations, focused on the positive, and reinforced clear standards; at the same time, his approach was creative, and clearly the result of his ability to get close to his constituents and their situations.

For example, when they first started up, Glenn Valley Homes was so successful that its new factory was faced with a backlog of home orders. When Wayne needed a highly skilled production manager to meet this extraordinary challenge, he selected Ray Freer, a veteran with fifteen years in the industry. Ray, whose talents and expertise had not been fully used in previous jobs, was energetic and eager to make a difference. Wayne believed in Ray and entrusted him with full responsibility to lead the crew.

Wayne's confidence in Ray was well placed. After several six- and seven-day weeks, they were ready to begin regular production. The plant was state-of-the-art, the previously inexperienced crew well-trained, and Ray had personally built and installed additional buffer stations to augment production during unexpected delays. The first house was successfully cut, sized, and shipped within three days of the start of production.

Wayne wanted to recognize Ray's accomplishments, so—during a barbecue party he was holding for all the workers and their families—he called the group over to one side of the factory and asked Ray to show how one of the buffer stations worked. When Ray threw the lever to operate the skate-wheel conveyor that he had designed and constructed, an automotive radio antenna popped up, displaying a flag with an envelope attached. Ray looked inside the envelope and found a $1,000 check and a personal letter from Wayne thanking him for his outstanding work. Wayne read the letter out loud to everyone else in the company—and their spouses and families—acknowledging the importance of Ray's innovativeness, dedication, and tireless work. Ray was clearly moved by Wayne's public display of appreciation, and the loud clapping and cheers of his coworkers and crew demonstrated their mutual support for his well-earned award.

Wayne obviously put a lot of thought into this recognition. He closely observed what Ray had done to contribute to the success of the factory, and he used equipment that Ray had constructed as an integral part of the celebration. Another leader might have just handed a check to Ray in private, without all the ceremony. Not Wayne. He knew that personalizing recognition was essential. He also knew that telling the story in public would create deeper meaning, go a long way toward thanking everyone for their hard work, and help build a strong sense of community.

REFLECTION AND ACTION: RECOGNIZING CONTRIBUTIONS

Leaders have high expectations of themselves and of their constituents. Their goals and standards are clear and help people focus on what needs to be done. Leaders provide clear directions, feedback, and encouragement. They expect the best of people and create self-fulfilling prophecies about how ordinary people can produce extraordinary actions and results. By maintaining a positive outlook and providing motivating feedback leaders stimulate, rekindle, and focus people's energies and drive.

Leaders recognize and reward what individuals do to contribute to vision and values. And they express their appreciation far beyond the limits of the organization's formal performance appraisal system. Leaders enjoy being spontaneous and creative in saying thank you, whether by sending notes, handing out personalized prizes, listening without interrupting, or trying any of a myriad number of other forms of recognition.

Personalizing requires knowing what's appropriate individually and culturally. Rather than assuming that they naturally know what's right for others, leaders take the time to inquire and observe. Leaders know that uncomfortable or embarrassing as it may seem at first to recognize someone's efforts, it's really not difficult to do. And it's well worth the effort to make a connection with each person. Leaders learn from many small and often casual acts of appreciation what works for each of their constituents and how best to personalize recognition.

Here are three actions that will help to build your competence and skill in Recognizing Contributions.

Find Out What's Encouraging

To get a sense of what will work for your constituents, discuss what they find encouraging themselves, and in what ways they prefer to encourage others. Here are some questions to get you started in your conversation with them:

- What types of encouragement make the most difference for you? Think of a time when you felt encouraged, supported, or cared about by this team. What happened? Who helped? Think about the best recognition you ever received. What happened? Who helped?
- How have you best encouraged other people? Name two abilities you have that can be tapped into for recognizing others. How can you be genuine, maintaining sincerity as well as spontaneity? Think about two abilities that your teammates have when it comes to recognition and encouragement. How can you tap into these capabilities?

Talk with coworkers to learn more about what their colleagues find meaningful and significant. Brainstorm with your teammates about ideas for meaningful recognition. Consider "Super Person of the Month" awards, employee photographs with the company president, verbal encouragement, pictures in annual reports and company newsletters, published thank-yous, contributions to employees' favorite charities, gift certificates and merchandise credits, embossed business cards, gifts for spouses and families, and banners displayed in the cafeteria.[21]

Obviously there are many, many ways to encourage people—just use your imagination and tap into your constituents' creativity. Leaders know that it's the human touch that makes a difference, and that requires not just learning what is meaningful to your constituents but showing you care by paying attention to the right things.

Stop By for a Visit

We all know from our own experience how much fun it is when a good friend drops by for a visit. The same principle applies to leaders. When you drop by for a visit you have the chance to uplift someone's spirit. People like to be noticed. People like to be paid attention to. People like to know that you care about them. Spending time with people sends the message to them that they are important to you. So make a commitment to start your day by chatting with your constituents.

Stop by your colleagues' offices or cubicles and ask them how they are doing. Ask what they did last night, or what good news they might have to share or what problems you might be able to help them with. With each person, find out something you didn't know before. Be self-disclosing yourself and let others know about the things that bring joy to your life.

Let's say you have fifty constituents you ought to see each week. That's ten each workday. At five minutes per person, that's just under one hour each day. If strengthening credibility is one of your goals, there is no more productive way to spend that hour than talking one-on-one. Fit some form of CBWA (Caring By Wandering About) into your daily routine. Reach out. Whether by foot, bus, plane, or train, reaching out sends a message that you're personally involved. It has the added benefit of giving you a better sense of what's happening outside the walls of your own office and building.

Develop a Winner's Attitude

Being a Pygmalion—someone who has a strong belief in the capacity of others and a confidence in his or her own ability to develop others—entails developing a winner's attitude in those around you. Only those who envision themselves as winners are likely to work hard, try new actions, and become leaders in their own right.

If you want a winning attitude you have to do two things. First, you have to *believe* that your constituents are already winners. It's not that they will be winners some day; they are winners right now! If you believe that people are winners, you will treat them that way. It's just a mental trick you play on yourself. Second, if you want people to be winners, you have to behave in ways that communicate to them that they are winners. And it's not just about your words. It's also about tone of voice, posture, gestures, and facial expressions. No yelling, frowning, cajoling, making fun of, or putting them down in front of others. Instead, it's about being friendly, positive, supportive, and encouraging.

Developing a winner's attitude in others means paying considerable attention to your constituents' successes. It means noticing what they're doing right, and pointing it out to them. You also have to give them more opportunity to participate. Ask for their opinions. Ask for their ideas. And when you are instructing them, offer suggestions, helpful hints, and practical tips. Treat them like winners, and you'll get winning performances.

Developing a winner's attitude also means providing training and development opportunities. People can't do what they say if they don't know how. You shouldn't be surprised that people aren't doing something that they don't know how to do—or go out of their way to avoid being in a position to be asked to do something they don't feel comfortable or skillful in accomplishing. If they stumble or fall, discuss this result with them as only a temporary lack of success. Raise the negative consequences of failure for inadequate performance and you can guarantee high levels of absenteeism, turnover, and poor morale. If criticism is necessary, comments should be restricted to behavior rather than character. Similarly, feedback—preferably extensive—should stress continuous progress rather than comparisons with other people. When the goal is reached, make certain that constituents understand that it happened because of what they did.

COMMITMENT NUMBER 9

Recognize Contributions

Essentials of Recognizing Contributions

- Expect the best
- Personalize recognition

Taking Action

- Find out what's encouraging
- Stop by for a visit
- Develop a winner's attitude

CELEBRATE THE VALUES AND VICTORIES

"Through appreciation and celebration we show people that they are significant and their contributions are vital to our overall success."
Soumya Mitra, EMC Corporation

To some a corporate celebration may seem like a wasteful distraction. You can almost hear the critics say in Scrooge-like voices, "We haven't got time for fun and games. After all, this is a business." Well, computer and materials science, and now biomedical and renewable energy research, make for a scientifically complex enterprise and a money-making business at PARC (Palo Alto Research Center), and leaders there understand that one of the most significant contributors to a strong and resilient workforce—and one that, in the long run, can get extraordinary things done—is a culture that builds and strengthens relationships.

"Celebrations at the organizational level play a critical role for us," Jennifer Ernst, PARC's director of business development, told us as she described one annual recognition event and why it was so important.

As people entered the auditorium, they knew it wasn't a typical meeting. Lights on the walls gave the look of theatrical sconces; twenty-foot high graphics of Oscar-like images framed the screen; and the sound of an orchestra warming up percolated through the audio system. Then the event started. The room went dark, a garish fanfare sounded, a spotlight hit the curtain, and our president, a quiet and understated man in most public appearances, strode out in a tux. The room exploded with laughter; the release of tension, pent-up since a year-end layoff, was tangible. The laughter continued when, for the first award, he proclaimed, "The envelope please." As the presenting manager walked to the stage, a member of the administrative staff, wearing a floor-length black gown and dripping with jewelry, delivered an oversized envelope on a golden platter.

For each award, senior managers told rich and personal stories about the research and its impact before calling individuals to the stage. Other members of the lab carried award plaques onto the stage, again on golden platters. When the recipients came down, triumphant music played in the background. Interspersed between the awards for major accomplishments, videos marked "special recognition" awards given for values such as exemplary service, "chipping-in," citizenship, and spirit. Each video featured people from different parts of the organization sharing how the award recipient had impacted them and expressing appreciation. By the end of the one-hour event, the room was on fire, creating a buzz that lasted for weeks.

Why was this so powerful? Certainly the theatrics assured it would be memorable. Stories were a key element in recalling the accomplishments (and sacrifices), showing how the honorees modeled the best in PARC. By stepping outside their comfort zones, the organization's leaders personally demonstrated that their expressions of respect and recognition were genuine. Between the on-stage volunteers, the presenters, and the people in the videos, nearly a fourth of PARC was actively visible in providing recognition to their peers. Finally, the messages of this event resonated with broadly held values of the organization—the senior managers' stories kept the scientific values at the forefront, while the other elements of the event connected to the sense of community within PARC.

Exemplary leaders know that promoting a culture of celebration fuels the sense of unity and mission essential for retaining and motivating today's workforce. Besides, who really wants to work for a place that has no ritual or ceremony—a boring place that neither remembers nor celebrates anything? David Campbell, senior fellow with the Center for Creative Leadership, says it well: "A leader who ignores or impedes organizational ceremonies and considers them as frivolous or 'not cost-effective,' is ignoring the rhythms of history and our collective conditioning. [Celebrations] are the punctuation marks that make sense of the passage of time; without them, there are no beginnings and endings. Life becomes an endless series of Wednesdays."[1]

What leaders like Jennifer and her colleagues at PARC know from practice is confirmed in our research. Performance improves when leaders bring people together to rejoice in their achievements and to reinforce their shared principles. If leaders are to effectively Celebrate the Values and Victories, they must master these essentials:

- **Create a spirit of community**
- **Be personally involved**

By bringing people together, sharing the lessons from success, and getting personally involved, leaders reinforce in others the courage required to get extraordinary things done.

CREATE A SPIRIT OF COMMUNITY

All over the world—in every country, in every culture—people stop working on certain days during the year and take the time to celebrate. We hold elaborate parades or gather in the city's main square to shower our championship teams with cheers of appreciation. We set off fireworks to commemorate great historic victories or the start of a new year. We convene impromptu ceremonies in the company conference room to rejoice in the award of a new contract. We attend banquets to show our respect for individuals and groups who've accomplished the extraordinary. We get together with colleagues at the end of a grueling work session and give each other high-fives for a job well done. Even in tragic times we come together in remembrance and song to honor those before us and to reaffirm our commitment.

Why? Why do we take time away from working to come together, tell stories, and raise our spirits? Sure, we all need a break from the hectic pace of our jobs, but celebrations are not trivial excuses to goof off. Celebrations are among the most significant ways we have to proclaim our respect and gratitude, to renew our sense of community, and to remind ourselves of the values and history that bind us together. Celebrations serve as important a purpose in the long-term health of our organizations as does the daily performance of tasks.

Research on corporate celebrations has found that: "Celebrations infuse life with passion and purpose. . . . They bond people together and connect us to shared values and myths. Ceremonies and rituals create community, fusing individual souls with the corporate spirit. When everything is going well, ritual occasions allow us to revel in our glory. When times are tough, ceremonies draw us together, kindling hope and faith that better times lie ahead."[2] In acknowledging the community ("common unity") that we share with one another, leaders create a sense of team spirit, and they build and maintain the social support we need to thrive, especially in the most stressful times.

Connect Celebration, Community, and Commitment

Community may not be the stuff of ordinary organizations, but it is the stuff of great ones, ones with strong cultures. The best leaders know that every gathering is a chance to renew commitment. They never let pass an opportunity to make sure that everyone knows why they're all there and how they're going to act in service of that purpose.

That's just what Prasad Kanneganti, quality operations director at Pfizer's pharmaceutical ingredients plant in Singapore, did when he was heading the Right First Time (RFT) initiative at this facility. The RFT initiative was started worldwide to transform the way Pfizer carried out its manufacturing operations. RFT is realized when processes are carried out correctly, as designed, the first time.

Every gathering is a chance to renew commitment.

There were many RFT champions and enthusiastic supporters in the Singapore plant but there were also the usual skeptics and others who waited for the initiative to fizzle out. So Prasad came up with the idea of an "RFT Carnival" to encourage commitment to the use of six sigma tools and statistical techniques to improve process understanding and achieve continuous improvement. "Carnivals are all about fun," Prasad observed, "and the message would be that learning about RFT and using six sigma tools can be fun too!"

The week-long RFT Carnival was held in the cafeteria, where participants solved puzzles, played games such as Target (mini-basketball), CTQ–Critical-to-Quality (mini golf), and CPK–Process Capability (darts), and saw presentations by recently trained colleagues. Teams that successfully completed their RFT projects were asked to invite their members and supporters to an RFT high tea and recognition ceremony. After everyone completed their RFT orientation, many were trained in continuous-improvement tools and awarded "Black Belt" and "Green Belt" certificates for completed process-improvement projects. Details of the RFT Carnival were published in the company's global newsletter, and requests to share information were received from Pfizer plants all over the world.

When asked to explain the carnival's success, Prasad said, "When we were young, we learned new things through games and fun together. There is no reason to abandon the fun part when we grow up. Even dry topics such as statistics and quality tools can be made interesting and engaging. Sharing success stories and celebrating contributions encourages all to come together and work towards the larger goal the company has set for itself. The experience of learning and celebrating together will give us a great sense of satisfaction at work."

Whether they're to honor an individual, group, or organizational achievement or to encourage team learning and relationship building, celebrations, ceremonies, and similar events offer leaders the perfect opportunity to explicitly communicate and reinforce the actions and behaviors that are important in realizing shared values and shared goals. These observances are to the culture of an organization "what the movie is to the script or the concert is to the score—they provide expression of values that are difficult to express in any other way."[3] Adding a sense of excitement or drama to the organization's rites and rituals, Prasad's experience reminds us, makes things even more memorable and more lasting.

Everything about a ceremony or celebration should be matched to its purposes. From the setting to the speeches, from the music to the mood, every little detail can have an impact on the lasting influence of the event. For organizational values to have an impact, leaders must make explicit connections between shared values and the actions that exemplify those values. These occasions are magnificent opportunities for leaders to expressly link principles to practices in a way that's memorable, motivating, and uplifting.

What leaders preach and what leaders celebrate must be one and the same. If they aren't, the event will come off as insincere and phony—and the leader's credibility will suffer. The celebration must be an honest expression of commitment to certain key values and to the hard work and dedication of those people who have lived the values. It's authenticity that makes conscious celebrations work.

Celebrate Accomplishments in Public

Although individual recognition increases the recipient's sense of worth, and improves performance, public celebrations have this effect and more: they add other significant and lasting contributions to the welfare of individuals and the organization. It's this added benefit that makes celebrating together so powerful.

Maybe you're reluctant to recognize people in public, fearing that to do so might cause jealousy or resentment. But private rewards do little to set an example—and often the recipient, not wanting to brag or appear conceited, has no opportunity to share the story with others. So tell your constituents that they've done well as soon as you find out about it, and let other people know about the accomplishment too.

Public events can also showcase real examples of what it means to "do what we say we will do." When the spotlight shines on your peers and stories are told about their actions, they become role models. It symbolically conveys a memorable message to everyone: "Here are people who are examples to all of us of what we stand for and believe in. You too can do this. You too make a significant contribution to our success."

Public celebrations of accomplishment build commitment, because they make people's actions visible to their peers and therefore difficult to deny or revoke. They also help to strengthen recipients by increasing their visibility. Military organizations make tremendous use of medals and insignias, which are almost always handed out at public ceremonies. Awards serve the same purpose.

Consider the experience of Mark Delucia, global account manager at Agilent Technologies, when he was pulling together a team responsible for the development of a new automated production test end-to-end solution for one of their most important customers. At one point, when milestones started to slip, and Mark feared that an atmosphere of complacency was developing, he decided to focus on the positives in a public spotlight. "I put up a 3 × 8-foot hardcopy of our project milestones and highlighted the commitments that were on time and the names associated with them," he told us. "Once a month we would review this data and vote on the most important team member and award them with a gift certificate for a 'date' with their significant other." While this was "hardly dramatic," Mark told us, in the same breath he said, "But it was highly effective. We were able to get everyone focused on what we individually and collectively needed to do, and were doing, and these monthly celebrations were excellent reminders of the progress we were making and what we were capable of doing."

Public ceremonies serve as a collective reminder of why people are there, of the values and visions that they share. The process of creating and building a sense of community ensures that people feel that they belong to something greater than just themselves. Not being alone or the only one who cares about the values and victories gives people a strong sense of team spirit.

Make Celebrations Part of Organizational Life

Putting celebrations on the organization's calendar is another way in which leaders create a sense of community. These scheduled celebrations serve as opportunities to get people together so that they see themselves as part of a bigger picture, of having a shared destiny and affirming shared values and victories.

Celebrations should always serve a dual purpose—one is to honor a principle or an achievement, and the other is to create community. In setting up your celebrations, the first task is to decide which organizational values, events of historical significance, or specific successes are of such importance that they warrant a special ritual, ceremony, or festivity. Perhaps you want to honor the group or team of people who created the year's important innovations, praise those who gave extraordinary customer service, or thank the families of your constituents for their support. Whatever you wish to celebrate, formalize it, announce it, and tell people how they become eligible to participate. At a minimum, you ought to have at least one celebration each year that involves everyone, though not necessarily at the same site, and one that draws attention to each of the key values of your organization.

Leaders make celebrations as much a part of their organization's life as they can. In their book *Corporate Celebration,* Professors Terrence Deal and M. K. Key provide a detailed framework to schedule or anticipate celebrations.[4] Here's a brief glimpse:

- *Cyclical celebrations.* Seasonal themes, key milestones, corporate anniversaries, individual birthdays, marriages, reunions, and other recurring events.
- *Recognition ceremonies.* Public applause and acknowledgment for a job well done, being best-in-class, attaining specific goals, achieving a special rank, getting a promotion, and other achievements that deserve broad attention.
- *Celebrations of triumph.* Special occasions for accentuating collective accomplishments, such as winning a championship; beating forecasts; beating the competition; launching a new product or strategy; founding a new company; and opening a new office, plant, or store.
- *Rituals for comfort and letting go.* Not all of organization life is about victory; sometimes there's calamity and loss. There's the loss of a contract, layoffs of employees, death of a colleague, an experiment that failed, and site closings. These occasions can be marked by ceremony and ritual to help people let go and move on.
- *Personal transitions.* Ways to celebrate entrances and exits, initiations, separations, and other life passages as people come and go in organizations.
- *Workplace altruism.* Celebrations of doing good for others, pulling together to help others, promoting social change, showing appreciation to customers and clients.
- *Events.* A company's anniversary, opening day, holidays, articulation of an organization's vision.

- *Play.* Energizing meetings and conventions, spoofing and poking fun, games and sporting events.

The point is that there really is no shortage of opportunities or occasions for which to bring people together. A word of caution: don't make everything that people accomplish a reason for celebrating. You don't want to replace people's intrinsic motivation with external motivators or justifications, nor do you want to trivialize recognition so that it's taken for granted. In our studies, however, overdoing recognition and celebration was not the problem; more typically, the concern was just the opposite.

Provide Social Support

Ceremonies and celebrations are opportunities to build healthier groups, to enable members of the organization to know and care about each other. And supportive relationships at work—relationships characterized by a genuine belief in and advocacy for the interests of others—are critically important to maintaining personal and organizational vitality.[5] Humans are social animals. We're hardwired to connect with others. If we weren't, we'd all be living the lives of hermits, working alone, eating alone, shopping alone, living alone, and avoiding contact with others. It's an absurd notion, but many organizations operate as if social gatherings are a nuisance.

Consider "the gift of the goose," one of the principles that Ken Blanchard and Sheldon Bowles write about in their book *Gung Ho!* about boosting enthusiasm and increasing performance.[6] In short, the gift of the goose is cheering others on. Wild geese fly thousands of miles each year, and they do it by cheering one another on every inch of the way, honking encouragement.

One of the significant lessons learned from an extensive ten-year study of service quality is that social support networks are essential for sustaining the motivation to serve. Service-performance shortfalls are highly correlated with the absence of social support and teamwork. As the researchers point out, "Coworkers who support each other and achieve together can be an antidote to service burnout. . . . Working with others should be rejuvenating, inspirational, and fun."[7]

This is just what Bob Branchi, as managing director of Western Australia's largest network of automobile dealerships, imparted to a delivery driver at a celebration he attended at a large parts supply facility. As he mingled with those applauding their recent accomplishments, Bob came across a fellow who held himself in low esteem. "I'm just a parts delivery driver," the man told Bob, "so I don't feel I made any real contribution." Bob replied that if hands-on involvement in the accomplishments being celebrated were the criterion, then Bob shouldn't have been there either. "Each of us makes an important contribution," he assured the driver, "and doing our best makes this company a success. We're in this together. It's important that you get involved in these celebrations so people know that you can be counted as part of this team." Bob made it a point to personally introduce the delivery driver to others at the celebration "as another important contributor to our team and to our success."

Social support enhances productivity, psychological well-being, and even physical health.

Investigations from a wide variety of disciplines consistently demonstrate that this kind of social support enhances productivity, psychological well-being, and even physical health. The California Department of Mental Health has stated the point strongly: "friends can be good medicine."[8] Studies have found that social support not only enhances wellness but also buffers against disease, particularly during times of high stress. This latter finding is true irrespective of an individual's age, gender, or ethnic group. Even after adjusting for such factors as smoking and histories of major illness, people with few close contacts were two to three times more likely to die during the study period than those who regularly had friends to turn to.[9]

What's true at home and in the community is just as true at work. Recent research indicates, for instance, that "If you have a best friend at work you are significantly more likely to engage customers, get more done in less time, have more fun on the job, have a safe workplace with fewer accidents, innovate and share ideas, feel informed and know that your opinion counts, and have the opportunity to focus on your strengths each day."[10] And if you report that your manager is a close friend, you are 2.5 times more likely to be satisfied with your job.[11] Friends are not only good for your health, they're good for your business. The sad fact is, however, that only 18 percent of people report that their organizations offer opportunities to develop friendships at work.[12]

Our files are full of personal-best leadership cases in which strong human connections produced spectacular results. Extraordinary accomplishments are achieved when everyone—leader and constituent alike—gets personally involved with the task and with other people. When people feel a strong sense of affiliation and attachment to their colleagues they're much more likely to have a higher sense of personal well-being, to feel more committed to the organization, and to perform at higher levels. When they feel distant and detached they're unlikely to get anything done at all.[13]

Leaders understand that what makes people most miserable is being alone. Celebrations create positive interactions among people, providing concrete evidence that people generally care about each other. Knowing that you aren't alone in your efforts and that you can count on others if necessary helps build the courage needed to continue in times of turmoil and stress.

Without group celebrations, people might all come to believe that the organization revolves around their individual work and that they're independent and not responsible to others. Social interactions remind people that they're in it together, that they need each other, that their work gets done because they're connected and caught up in each other's lives. They bring more joy to people's work lives. Celebrations reinforce the fact that it always takes a group of people working together with a common purpose in an atmosphere of trust and collaboration to get extraordinary things done. By making achievements public, leaders build a culture in which people know that what they do is not taken for granted and clearly feel that their efforts are appreciated and applauded.

Have Fun Together

Fun isn't a luxury, even at work. All the personal-best leadership experiences were a combination of hard work and fun. In fact, most people we spoke with agreed that without the enjoyment and the pleasure that they experienced with one another on the team, they wouldn't have been able to sustain the level of intensity and hard work required. "Make sure that you and the team are having fun," was the key lesson for Andy Mackenzie, vice president of engineering at Biocardia, Inc. from his personal-best leadership experience. "While every day won't be fun," he observed, "sharing in the struggles can bring the team together. If it's all drudgery than it's hardly worth getting out of bed for."

Similarly Mike Sawyer, when he was senior vice president of marketing at Aerocast, told us he "didn't want to consume the team's outside-of-work time with contrived activities, but I did want to have some fun." One thing they did was to change the character of department-wide planning meetings. "We set up an informal meeting area in the marketing department," Mike explained, "with couches, a TV, and other things that allowed both standing and ad-hoc meetings to seem more like a friendly environment. This area was in the middle of where everyone sat, so even if just a few people were meeting, it let everyone know what was going on and they could freely join others if they wanted. We also did group 'fun' dinners semi-regularly around milestones to encourage camaraderie as well as to reward progress."

Having fun sustains productivity, creating what researchers refer to as "subjective well-being." People simply feel better about the work they are doing when they enjoy a supportive network of close relationships.[14] We can see the importance of fostering a sense of connection in even everyday mundane affairs, as the experience of Doug Podzilni, president of Gourmet Source

Food Brokers, reveals. He simply brought a box of candy suckers to the office and placed them out in a common area. In no time at all, "everyone had a sucker sticking out of their mouth and a smile on their face," he says. Later that afternoon, during the break in a particularly tedious and combative meeting, he put another bunch of suckers in the middle of the table. Before he knew it, Doug says, people were reaching for their favorite flavors and smiling at one another, and the tone of the meeting got noticeably friendlier: "It's hard to be too combative or in a bad mood when you and everyone around you has a sucker in their mouth!"

Elizabeth James, chief information officer and vice chairman of financial services giant Synovus, came up with a fun way to launch a massive information-technology conversion at more than forty banks.

> The new system was called TIPS—Technology Improving Personal Service—and a TIPS troupe traveled to every bank to host a crazy casting call. The TIPS team recruited employees at each bank to play roles in a skit designed to teach everyone about the conversion, its timeline, and the reasons for doing it. There were executives in miniskirts, grandmas with pom-poms, and employees dancing in the aisles. TIPS chips were given out for attending these parties and could be cashed in for various prizes.[15]

The celebration didn't end there. At the conclusion of each bank's successful conversion, every employee received a $100 tip. Elizabeth explained, "We really wanted to look these folks in the eye at the end of this deal and say, 'Look, even $100 is not enough, but it's a token of our appreciation for everything you did.'" By eliciting laughs and spreading good will, Elizabeth and the TIPS team made a challenging assignment and the hard work that followed easier for them as well as for the people learning the new system.

When you witness Mike's merriment, Doug's lollipops, and Elizabeth's casting call you understand that these leaders—and hundreds of others we studied—are passionate about their purpose and care deeply for their team members. They understand that work in today's organizations is difficult and demanding, and in this climate people need to have a sense of personal well-being in order to sustain their commitment. And leaders set the tone. When key leaders openly demonstrate the joy and passion they have for their organizations, their team members, and their clients it sends a very loud message to others that it's perfectly acceptable for people to make public displays of playfulness; it's okay to show enthusiasm at work.

BE PERSONALLY INVOLVED

Remember: leadership is a relationship, and people are much more likely to enlist in initiatives led by those with whom they feel a personal attachment. It's precisely the human connection between leaders and constituents that ensures more commitment and more support. Saying thank you—and genuinely meaning it—and joining with others to celebrate accomplishments are very concrete ways of showing respect and enhancing personal credibility.

As we approach the end of our Five Practices of Exemplary Leadership story we've come full circle. We started our discussion of personal-best leadership with Model the Way—and here we are again. If you want others to believe in something and behave according to those beliefs, you have to set the example by being personally involved. You have to practice what you preach, put your money where your mouth is, and walk the talk. If you want people to stay true to shared values, you have to stay true to them as well. If you want people to aspire to be the best, you have to live and breathe that vision. If you want people to innovate, you have to innovate. If you want people to collaborate, you have to collaborate. If you want to build and maintain a culture of excellence and distinction, then you have to recognize, reward, reinforce, and celebrate exceptional efforts and successes. You have to get personally involved in celebrating the actions that contribute to and sustain the culture. And if you want people to have the courage to continue the quest in the face of great adversity, you have to encourage them yourself.

Celebration and community only work when they're genuine. Elaborate productions that lack sincerity are more entertainment than encouragement. Many people have told us that they don't need or want recognition from someone they don't respect, or in front of people they don't feel a connection with. It's a theme we've repeated over and over again: *credibility is the foundation of leadership.* When it comes to celebrating the values and the victories it's even more critical. You can't encourage the hearts of others unless your heart is encouraged. When you *feel* excited and upbeat, other people will know that it's for real.

When it comes to sending a message throughout the organization, nothing communicates more clearly than what the leaders do. You don't have to ride site-to-site on a bus, publish a CD-ROM of corporate tales, pass out lollipops, simulate the Academy Awards, or copy any particular method from our leadership stories. You might want to adopt a few of these inventive ideas for yourself, but the specific technique is not the point. The point is that by directly and visibly showing others that you're there to cheer them along, you're sending a positive signal. You're more likely to see others do it if you do it. It's that simple.

> Nothing communicates more clearly than what the leaders do.

When you set the example that communicates the message "Around here we say thanks, show appreciation, and have fun," others will follow your lead. The organization will develop a culture of celebration and recognition. Everyone becomes a leader, everyone sets the example, and everyone takes the time to celebrate the values and the victories. Although Karyn Bechtel may have been the official director for a national collegiate leadership development conference, she got the biggest "hoot," she told us, "from seeing everyone else being so appreciative of one another and what each person had contributed to the success of the conference. I kept telling everyone at the conference, it wasn't me, it was 'us' that made this all happen."

When leaders model encouragement and others follow their example, organizations develop a reputation for being great places to work. They're magnetic, attracting and retaining employees and customers far better than their competitors can. People form a strong bond with these institutions. They're proud to be affiliated. Employees want to excel, business partners want to delight, and customers want to stay loyal for a lifetime.

Wherever you find a strong culture built around strong values—whether the values are about superior quality, innovation, customer service, distinctiveness in design, respect for others, or just plain fun—you'll also find endless examples of leaders who personally live the values. The leader has to set the example of what's expected and what will be rewarded by being personally involved, which is precisely what Keon Yang Kim, accounting manager, described to us when telling how the new CEO at Pizza Hut Korea needed to change the company's culture and stem the high turnover and low employee morale:

> Mr. Lee started a monthly recognition party. Every month, all the employees gather together and vote for the best employee of the month. This party was the beginning of creating a recognition culture. He extended this culture to our customers. All the restaurants provided a recognition card, and customers could leave a note when they appreciated the service from employees. Mr. Lee was happy to reward employees who received recognition notes from customers. He brought these people to headquarters to join the monthly recognition party and gave them an award in front of the whole body of employees.
>
> Employees learned how to appreciate each other's excellent job and this became a habit among employees. Now employees were searching for someone to recognize. This culture certainly made the company a fun place to work. This recognition culture also attracted a lot of attention from other big companies, and they came to monitor this recognition party.
>
> However, to make this happen, Mr. Lee's personal leadership was needed. At first, employees did not understand what he was trying to do. But Mr. Lee was persistent. He was the first person to be at the party place

all the time and helped prepare for the party. He really enjoyed the party, and he was really happy when he was able to find things to appreciate from employees.

Show You Care

One of the most significant ways in which leaders, like the one that Keon Yang describes, show others that they care and that they appreciate the efforts of their constituents is to be out there with them. They walk the halls, meander around the corridors, eat in the cafeteria, listen to complaints, go to parties, attend organizational events (even when they are not on the program), and tell stories about successes.

This visibility makes them more real, more genuine, more approachable, and more human. It helps leaders stay "in touch" with what's really going on. And it puts their money where their mouths are about the values shared by them and their constituents. Believability goes up when leaders are personally involved.

Exemplary leaders are out and about all the time. They're attending meetings, visiting customers, touring the plants or service centers, dropping in on the labs, making presentations at association gatherings, recruiting at local universities, holding roundtable discussions, speaking to analysts, or just dropping by constituents' cubicles to say "Hello." Being mobile goes with the territory.

Consider Dick Pettingill's experience. When he was president and chief executive officer, California Division, Kaiser Foundation Health Plans and Hospitals, he wanted to cheer his constituents on and get them pumped up to meet industrywide challenges. He rented a bus so he could visit all of the facilities across the state—Dick was not only setting an example for his constituents but learning a lot in the process. "When I started out with this, it was really a talking tour," he said. "I expected to talk up the great success that we'd had and talk about what we still had to do. It became very apparent to me (probably by mid-morning on the first day of the bus trip) that this wasn't about talking, it was about listening. It was about me listening to our employees and physicians talk about what was important to them, about what they wanted me to hear."

One major lesson for Dick from this bus tour was that you have to believe that spending your own time listening to others is important. Another critical realization, he told us, was how important it is to open up to your constituents. "You have to make yourself vulnerable," Dick told us. "You have to have a willingness and a desire to be connected with the people of the organization. . . . I knew before I left that . . . 70 percent of the people didn't trust leadership. So I'm out there, trying to get people to have a sense of believability in what we're all about, recognizing that, again, it's not what I say, it's what I do that's going to make a difference."

Leaders are not wandering about purposelessly. Leaders are out-and-about with intentionality. One of the reasons is to focus people's attention, but another important reason is to personally demonstrate that they care. That's what Carolyn Borne makes it a point to do in her three leadership roles at the UCLA Medical Center: unit director of the General Clinical Research Center, program director of the Women's Health Initiative, and Magnet director. For example, after leading the Medical Center to Magnet status—sometimes called the "Nobel Prize for Nursing"—she intentionally keeps the pride and momentum going by constantly thinking about others and what she can do to make their lives more rewarding. "I don't want them to lose the power of what they felt when we finally got Magnet," she told us. "I am constantly deliberating with them, talking with them, sensing them, finding out where they are, what they want, how they are feeling about the organization, and what they want me to bring to them." Whether hard at work or over coffee, at lunch, or just "hanging out," Carolyn sees each encounter as an opportunity to show that she pays attention to each member of the team as an individual as well as a professional. As she sums it up, "I hope that at the end of the day I've given my staff, or any of the people that I'm in contact with, the feeling that I cared about them."

Perpetuate the Stories

Another benefit from celebrations, being out-and-about, and getting personally involved is that it is often at these exact moments that leaders are able to both find and spread the stories that put a human face on success. First-person examples are always more powerful and striking than third-party examples (the difference between "I saw for myself" and "Someone told me about"). Leaders are on the lookout for "catching people doing things right," and this can't be easily done sitting behind a desk.[16] They want to see and know firsthand what's being done right not only so that they can let that person know to "keep up the good work" but so that they can tell others about this and other examples of what it means to put into practice and live out shared values and aspirations.

Stories aren't meant to be kept private; they're meant to be told.

These are the stories they tell about someone just like you who made it happen. Leaders, in this way, create organizational role models that everyone can relate to. They put the behavior in a real context. They make standards more than statistics; they make standards come alive. By being able to tell a story in rich and personal detail, leaders illustrate what everyone needs to do to live by the organization's values and standards. Consider this practice by Lidia Kwiatkowska, Personal Banking Area Manager at Bank of Montreal/Harris, who says one of the most powerful activities is sharing success stories about building lasting relationships through exceptional service. "Weekly," she says, "we share these stories, and how individual team members exhibit the customer attributes. We don't just celebrate, but challenge each other as a team." Before Lidia's arrival her area hadn't achieved their revenue goals for several years, and within six months of her arrival they exceeded their targets for the entire year![17]

Stories by their nature are public forms of communication. Storytelling, as we discussed in Chapter Four, is how people pass along lessons from generation to generation, culture to culture. Stories aren't meant to be kept private; they're meant to be told. And because they're public, they're tailor-made for celebrations. In fact, stories are celebrations, and celebrations are stories.

Stories are better able to accomplish the objectives of teaching, mobilizing, and motivating than are bullet points on an overhead projection. Well-told stories reach inside people and pull them along. They simulate the actual experience of being there and give people a compelling way of learning what is really important about the experience. Angie Yim's experience at Hewlett-Packard underscored this point. "We all enjoy telling stories," she explained, and so as one crucial part of orienting a replacement for one of the key members of her multidisciplinary and transnational technical support teams

> We got together and told stories about how we worked together best on various projects in the past. For the newly hired person, he learned from our experience, whereas, for the veterans, they also shared some painful lessons we had learned together. The storytelling became very interactive when we talked about the same story, but from different perspectives. I noticed that we especially enjoyed this moment of sharing. This was an interesting and positive experience because I felt like we were somehow part of a family, where members kept coming in and out at different stages of the team's life.

As Dave Snowden, founder and chief scientific officer of Cognitive Edge, puts it, stories are "an integral part of defining what that organization is and what it means to work for it. Stories show, for example, whether employees are rewarded or punished for speaking up. A lack of stories may indicate heavy-handed controlling management."[18] Indeed, much about the culture of a company can be learned as a result of listening to and understanding the stories it tells about itself.

That's the approach Bob Phillips took when he became CEO of Guide Dogs for the Blind. Bob knew very little about the actual workings of the organization when he joined it. To find out, he asked people to tell him a story about some important organizational event or experience. He followed that up by asking them for one of their own personal stories, a time that they felt proud about what they had accomplished in the organization. Bob understood the importance of learning what has been, and is, going on with people and their organizations; as he puts it, you have to "say hi to the story, and that's how you find out about their history (hi-story)." In these stories—of innovation, of bravery, of service, of keeping commitments, of making tough choices—he learned important lessons about the real things that formed the core of this organization. In finding out about people's stories, Bob was able, even as a newcomer, to include rather quickly these stories and examples when he spoke with potential donors, trustees, media, and his constituents about what they believed in and where they needed to be heading in the future, building upon their rich traditions.

Leaders find other ways to perpetuate the important stories. For instance, publishing a story in the company newsletter or annual report, relating a story in a public ceremony, or making a video and broadcasting it on the internal television network. Leaders shine the spotlight on someone who's lived out an organizational value—and provide others in the organization with an example they can emulate.

Stories can be particularly helpful in providing inspiration to individuals facing challenging situations. "Telling the story gives the details and it helps people to be there, even though they weren't there," says Allison Babb of The MathWorks, a Massachusetts-based developer of engineering software. "It's real easy to find stories that are just like what somebody else is now encountering." The story can highlight "roadblocks that somebody else has had . . . people who've really struggled with the exact same issues, and here's what they did to get over it." Stories illustrating organizational values and practices are not only easier to remember and recall than policies, rules, and guidelines, they translate more quickly into action. Scientist Gary Klein studies how people make decisions under conditions of extreme emergency. He's taken a look at professionals in high-stakes environments in which a decision could mean life or death—people such as firefighters, critical care nurses, paramedics, pilots, nuclear plant operators, and battle planners. Klein has discovered that in an emergency, the rational model of decision making is not how people make decisions. Instead they use a more nonlinear approach that involves intuition, mental simulation, metaphors, analogies, stories, and other less rational means. In discussing his research, Klein says, "The method we found most powerful for eliciting knowledge is to use stories."[19] Klein points out that storytelling is an essential skill for passing along the lessons that people learn from highly complex, challenging situations. Leaders are great storytellers.

REFLECTION AND ACTION: CELEBRATING VALUES AND VICTORIES

Celebrating together reinforces the fact that extraordinary performance is the result of many people's efforts. By celebrating people's accomplishments visibly and in group settings, leaders create community and sustain team spirit; by basing celebrations on consistency with key values and attainment of critical milestones, leaders reinforce and sustain people's focus.

Social interaction increases people's commitments to the standards of the group and has a profound effect on people's well-being. Intimacy heals; loneliness depresses. When people are asked to go beyond their comfort zones, the support and encouragement of their colleagues enhances their resistance to the possible debilitating effects of stress. Make sure that your workplace is not the place where "fun goes to die."

Leaders set the example by getting personally involved in celebration and recognition, demonstrating that encouraging the heart is something everyone should do. Telling stories about individuals who have made exceptional efforts and achieved phenomenal successes provides role models for others to emulate. Stories make people's experiences memorable, often even profound in ways that they hadn't envisioned, and serve as a marker for future behaviors. Making personal connections with people in a culture of celebration also builds and sustains credibility. It reduces any we-they demarcations between leaders and constituents. Adding vitality and a sense of appreciation to the workplace is what encouraging the heart is all about.

Here are three actions you can start doing today to even more effectively Celebrate the Values and Victories.

Plan a Celebration Today

Set the example for celebrating by planning a celebration right now. You've got a meeting that's coming up. How can you use that opportunity to celebrate a milestone? Is there a regularly scheduled quarterly review on the books? How can you include in it a ceremony that calls attention to a special part of your culture? Perhaps you've got a training session at which you're going to give a presentation. How can you include a story about real people in your organization who exemplify one or more of your values?

Any time people gather there's the opportunity to create a spirit of community, to tell a story that reinforces a cultural standard or to model the behavior you expect of others. Exemplary leaders use every opportunity to celebrate the values and the victories. Do the same: view every occasion on which your constituents gather as a chance for some kind of celebration, big or small. If your organization isn't doing much celebrating, start an informal celebration task force. Or make it your job to liven up the place, borrowing where you can from the inventiveness of others and creating your own fun and games at work.

Encouraging the heart doesn't have to come at the end of a seminar or the conclusion of a project. It also doesn't have to come after you've done everything else a leader does. It's not the end of the process, it's a continuous part of the leadership journey. You can celebrate at any time, anywhere. So do it! Give courage, spread joy, and care about people, product, and process all along the way.

Reinforce Core Values in Your Celebrations

Be mindful of the messages you're sending when you celebrate. It's quite clear that celebrations are much more than parties. They're rituals that create meaning. And because celebrations are so visible and significant, it's vitally important to be clear about the statements you're making and the behaviors you're reinforcing. You should be fully aware that people are going to leave the event remembering and repeating what you say and what they see. You should always be personally prepared with the key messages you want to send. Constantly ask yourself,

- What values do we hold dear?
- What visions do we aspire to realize?
- What behaviors do we want to reinforce?

Be prepared for every public opportunity to reinforce the culture and the meaning you want to create.

If being fast and flexible is what's expected, for example, make sure that the individuals who got a customized product to market quickly are publicly acknowledged and rewarded. If an important agency objective is to obtain new sources of funding, celebrate when grants are signed. If the organization values loyalty, celebrate tenure with years-of-service dinners and recognition pins. If personalized service is what makes the business profitable, then make a big deal of publishing that special letter from a customer who expresses appreciation to the people who turned a potential nightmare into a delightful experience. If innovation is valued, then whenever a new patent is granted give out awards to those involved in creating new technology.

Enjoy Yourself

Celebrations should be a joyful experience for you, along with everyone else. What's most important is your genuine appreciation for the work of others; your constituents need to know that you are clear about what outstanding performance looks like and that you will recognize it fairly when it is achieved. Celebrations also give you the chance to demonstrate your credibility in the form of "putting your money (time, resources, and so on) where your mouth is." You ask others to reach certain achievement levels, and when they do so you let them know that you know what they've done and how much you sincerely appreciate it.

Being sincere really means being yourself. You don't have to cheerlead with pom-poms and elaborate routines to make your appreciation meaningful. You don't have to celebrate by getting up in front of others and leading a chant, shouting out loudly, or waving your arms and jumping around—if that's not you. But you do need to be present, and you do have to smile and put some personal energy into the pageantry.

Even so, you need to lighten up and not take yourself all that seriously. It may feel a little weird to appear in public dressed up in a costume that is appropriate only for Halloween, but you'll forget about your own embarrassment when you think about the message it sends about the lengths to which you will go to tell folks how much you appreciate them. People will remember it fondly, and even more so if this action is out of your everyday character. They'll probably take pictures and talk about it for months or years to come: "Remember when Frank put on that hula skirt and danced in front of everyone? Wasn't that a hoot? It's nice to know we work for an organization that can have some fun and show appreciation for all our hard work." Showing your strong commitment, enthusiasm, and appreciation will pay big dividends for a very long time.

COMMITMENT NUMBER 10

Celebrate the Values and Victories

Essentials of Celebrating the Values and Victories

- Create a spirit of community
- Be personally involved

Taking Action

- Plan a celebration today
- Reinforce core values in your celebrations
- Enjoy yourself

PART 7

LEADERSHIP FOR EVERYONE

- LEADERSHIP IS EVERYONE'S BUSINESS

LEADERSHIP IS EVERYONE'S BUSINESS

"Don't ever let anyone tell you that you can't make a difference. If we all work on our little parts of the planet we will change the world."
Tara Church, Quinn Emanuel Urquhart Oliver & Hedges LLP

Throughout this book we've told stories of ordinary people who've gotten extraordinary things done. We've talked about men and women from a variety of organizations, public and private, government and NGOs, high-tech and low-tech, small and large, schools and professional services. And we've talked with people from all over the globe, from all walks of life and ages. Chances are you haven't heard of most of them. They're not public figures, famous people, or mega-stars. They're people who might live next door or work in the next cubicle over.

We've focused on everyday leaders because leadership is not about position or title. Leadership is not about organizational power or authority. It's not about celebrity or wealth. It's not about the family you are born into. It's not about being a CEO, president, general, or prime minister. And it's definitely not about being a hero. Leadership is about relationships, about credibility, and about what you *do*.

YOU ARE THE MOST IMPORTANT LEADER IN YOUR ORGANIZATION

If you're a manager in an organization, to *your* direct reports *you* are the *most important* leader in your organization. *You* are more likely than any other leader to influence their desire to stay or leave, the trajectory of their careers, their ethical behavior, their ability to perform at their best, their drive to wow customers, their satisfaction with their jobs, and their motivation to share the organization's vision and values.

If you're a parent, teacher, coach, or community leader *you* are the person that's setting the leadership example for young people. It's not hip-hop artists, movie stars, or professional athletes they seek guidance from. *You* are the one they are most likely going to look to for the example of how a leader responds to competitive situations, handles crises, deals with loss, or resolves ethical dilemmas. It's not someone else. It's you.

The leaders who have the most influence on people are those who are the *closest* to them. You have to challenge the myth that leadership is about position and power. And, once challenged, people can come to see leadership in a whole new light. Yukari Huguenard, solutions product manager at KANA Software, told us how much she had changed her view of leadership after she had examined her assumptions:

I used to think leaders had to be at the top level of a large organization. With that view of leadership, the chasm between where I am and being a leader was uncrossable. Now, I see leaders leading a group of people of any size and leading at any level. You are a leader if you employ these five leadership practices because people around you want to follow. In that sense, I feel that I'm already a leader.

There's no escape. *Leadership is everyone's business.* No matter what your position is, you have to take responsibility for the quality of leadership your constituents get. You—and that means all of us—are accountable for the leadership you demonstrate. And, because *you* are the most important leader to those closest to you, the only choice you really have is whether or not to be the best leader you can be.

LEADERSHIP IS LEARNED

The notion that leadership is reserved for only a very few is reinforced every time someone asks, "Are leaders born or made?" Whenever we're asked this question—which is almost every time we give a speech or conduct a class or workshop—our answer, always offered with a smile, is this: "Yes, of course, all leaders are born. We've never met a leader who wasn't. So are all accountants, artists, athletes, parents, zoologists, you name it." We're all born. What we do with what we have before we die is up to us.

It's just pure myth that only a lucky few can ever understand the intricacies of leadership. Leadership is not a gene, and it's not a secret code that can't be deciphered by ordinary people. The truth is that leadership is *an observable set of skills and abilities* that are useful whether one is in the executive suite or on the front line, on Wall Street or Main Street, in any campus, community, or

> *It's just pure myth that only a lucky few can ever understand the intricacies of leadership.*

corporation. And any skill can be strengthened, honed, and enhanced, given the motivation and desire, along with practice and feedback, role models, and coaching.

It's very curious—and revealing—that no one has ever asked us, "Can management be taught? Are managers born or made?" Why is it that management is viewed as a set of skills and abilities, while leadership is typically seen as a set of innate personality characteristics? It's simple. People *assume* management can be taught. Because they do, hundreds of business schools have been established, and each year thousands of management courses are taught. By assuming that people can learn the attitudes, skills, and knowledge associated with good management practices, schools and companies have raised the caliber of managers. They've also contributed to the idea that good management skills are attainable.

The same can be said for leadership. In over twenty-five years of research, we've been fortunate to have heard and read the stories of thousands of ordinary people who've led others to get extraordinary things done. And there are millions more. It's not the absence of leadership potential that inhibits the development of more leaders, it's the persistence of the myth that leadership can't be learned. This haunting myth is a far more powerful deterrent to leadership development than is the nature of the person or the basics of the leadership process.

The experience of Juan Gonzalez, industry solution manager at IBM, is typical of that of the leaders we've worked with around the world. Juan told us that The Five Practices of Exemplary Leadership were a good start for understanding that leadership was everyone's business, and this approach offered him a new perspective on the world of human interaction by demystifying the notion of natural-born leaders and, if anything, making it more complex. The fact that leaders can learn to be leaders through self-awareness and effort opens the possibility that individuals have a choice about pursuing or ignoring the calling of leadership. Not everyone will be a leader of historical proportions; however, we all can and should assume leadership roles in our regular activities more often than not. The experience could be more rewarding and purposeful.

It's our collective task to liberate the leader in each and every one of us. Rather than view leadership as an innate set of character traits—a self-fulfilling prophecy that dooms society to having only a few good leaders—it's far healthier and more productive to assume that it's possible for everyone to learn to lead. By assuming that leadership is learnable, we can discover how many good leaders there really are. Somewhere, sometime, the leader within each of us may get the call to step forward—for the school, the congregation, the community, the agency, the company, the union, or the family. By believing in yourself and your capacity to learn to lead, you make sure you'll be prepared when that call comes.

Certainly, none of us should mislead people into believing that they can attain unrealistic goals. However, neither should we assume that only a few would ever attain excellence in leadership (or in any other human endeavor). Those who are most successful at bringing out the best in others are those who set achievable "stretch" goals and believe that they have the ability to develop the talents of others. Researchers note that effective leaders are constantly learning. They see all experiences as learning experiences, not just those sessions in a formal classroom or workshop. They're constantly looking for ways to improve themselves and their organizations. By reading this book and engaging in other personal development activities, you're demonstrating a predisposition to lead. Even if some people think that they're not able to learn to lead, *you* must believe that you and they can. That's where it all starts—with your own belief in yourself and in others.

LEADERS MAKE A DIFFERENCE

We regularly ask people in our classes and workshops to share a story about a leader they admire and whose direction they would willingly follow. Virtually everyone we've asked has been able to name at least one leader whose genuine influence they've felt. Sometimes it's a well-known figure—perhaps someone out of the past who changed the course of history. Sometimes it's a contemporary role model who serves as an example of success. Most often, however, it's someone personally close to them who's helped them learn—a parent, friend, member of the clergy, coach, teacher, manager.

When Verónica Guerrero of Winning Edge Research selected her father, José Luis Guerrero, as the leader she most admired, she underscored for us just how extraordinary those around us can be. She told the story of her father's leadership in the Unión Nacional Sinarquista (UNS) back in the early 1940s. She related in detail what her father did and then summed up his influence with this remembered observation from José Luis: "I think the work that I did back then helped me extend myself and others to levels that I didn't know I could reach. . . . If you feel strongly about anything, and it's something that will ultimately benefit your community and your country, don't hold back. Fear of failing or fear of what might happen doesn't help anyone. . . . Don't let anyone or anything push you back."

Verónica closed her description of her father (who was then dying of pancreatic cancer) with this observation: "As I heard his story and I saw a sick, tired, and weak man, I couldn't help thinking that our strength as humans and as leaders has nothing to do with what we look like. Rather, it has everything to do with what we feel, what we think of ourselves. . . . Leadership is applicable to all facets of life." That's precisely the point. If you are to become a better leader, you must first believe that leadership applies to you and that you can be a positive force in the world.

Yet there has never been universal acceptance of this proposition. Determinism and fatalism govern the minds of many. Some management scholars contend, in fact, that leaders have little impact on organizations, that other forces—internal or external to the organization—are the determinants of success.[1] Others claim that the role of the leader is largely symbolic, even romantic, but not substantive.[2] Our evidence, along with hundreds of other studies, suggests quite the contrary.[3] Managers, individual contributors, volunteers, pastors, government administrators, teachers, school principals, nurses, salespeople, students, and other leaders who use The Five Practices of Exemplary Leadership more frequently than their counterparts are more effective. For example, they

- More often meet job-related demands
- More successfully represent their units to upper management
- Create higher-performing teams
- Increase sales and customer satisfaction levels
- Foster renewed loyalty and greater organizational commitment
- Increase motivation and the willingness to work hard
- Facilitate high patient satisfaction scores and more effectively meet family member needs
- Promote high degrees of involvement in schools
- Enlarge the size of their congregations
- Increase fundraising results and expand gift-giving levels
- Extend the range of their agency's services
- Reduce absenteeism, turnover, and dropout rates
- Positively influence recruitment rates

People working with leaders who demonstrate The Five Practices of Exemplary Leadership are significantly more satisfied with the actions and strategies of their leaders; they feel more committed, excited, energized, influential, and powerful; and they are more productive. In other words, the more you engage in the practices of exemplary leaders, the more likely it is that you'll have a positive influence on others in the organization.

Person to person and over time, leaders make a difference. If you want to have a significant impact on people, on communities, and on organizations, you'd be wise to invest in learning to become the very best leader you can. But first you too must believe that a leader lives within each of us.

FIRST LEAD YOURSELF

Leadership development is self-development. Engineers have computers; painters, canvas and brushes; musicians, instruments. Leaders have only themselves. The instrument of leadership is the self, and mastery of the art of leadership comes from mastery of the self. Self-development is not about stuffing in a whole bunch of new information or trying out the latest technique. It's about leading out of what is already in your soul. It's about liberating the leader within you. It's about setting yourself free.

Leadership development is self-development.

The quest for leadership is first an inner quest to discover who you are. Through self-development comes the confidence needed to lead. Self-confidence is really awareness of and faith in your own powers. These powers become clear and strong only as you work to identify and develop them.

Learning to lead is about discovering what you care about and value. As you begin this quest toward leadership, you must wrestle with some difficult questions:

- How certain am I of my own conviction about the vision and values?
- What gives me the courage to continue in the face of uncertainty and adversity?
- How will I handle disappointments, mistakes, and setbacks?
- What are my strengths and weaknesses?
- What do I need to do to improve my abilities to move the organization forward?
- How solid is my relationship with my constituents?
- How can I keep myself motivated and encouraged?
- What keeps me from giving up?
- Am I the right one to be leading at this very moment? Why?

- How much do I understand about what is going on in the organization and the world in which it operates?
- How prepared am I to handle the complex problems that now confront my organization?
- What are my beliefs about how people ought to conduct the affairs of our organization?
- Where do I think the organization ought to be headed over the next ten years?

Honest answers to these questions (and to those that arise from them) tell you that you must open yourself to a more global view. The leader, being in the forefront, is usually the first to encounter the world outside the boundaries of the organization. The more you know about the world, the easier it is to approach it with assurance. Thus you should seek to learn as much as possible about the forces—political, economic, social, moral, or artistic—that affect the organization.

Honest answers tell you that to become as effective as possible you must improve your understanding of others and build your skills to mobilize people's energies toward higher purposes. To be a leader, you must be interpersonally competent, and you must be able to develop the trust and respect of others.

Honest answers to these questions tell you that sometimes liberation is as uncomfortable as intrusion, but in the end when you discover them for yourself you know that what's inside is what you found there and what belongs there. It's not something put inside you by someone else; it's what are your true gifts.

MORAL LEADERSHIP CALLS US TO HIGHER PURPOSES

Leadership practices per se are amoral. But leaders—the men and women who use the practices—are moral or immoral. There's an ethical dimension to leadership that neither leaders nor constituents should take lightly. This is why we began our discussion of leadership practices with a focus on clarifying your values—on finding your authentic voice in a set of principles and ideals.

These you have to find for yourself and test against others. Attending to moral values will always direct your eyes to higher purposes. As you work to become all you can be, you can start to let go of petty self-interests. As you give back some of what you've been given, you can reconstruct your community. As you serve the values of freedom, justice, equality, caring, and dignity, you can constantly renew the foundations of democracy. As each of us takes individual responsibility for creating the world of our dreams, we can all participate in leading.

All exemplary leaders have wrestled with their souls. Such personal searching is essential in the development of leaders. You must resolve those dissonant internal chords. Extensive knowledge of history and the outside world increases your awareness of competing value systems, of the many principles by which individuals, organizations, and states can choose to function. You can't lead others until you've first led yourself through a struggle with opposing values.

When you clarify the principles that will govern your life and the ends that you will seek, you give purpose to your daily decisions. A personal creed gives you a point of reference for navigating the sometimes-stormy seas of organizational life. Without such a set of beliefs, your life has no rudder, and you're easily blown about by the winds of fashion. A credo that resolves competing beliefs also leads to personal integrity. A leader with integrity has one self, at home and at work, with family and with colleagues. Leaders without integrity are putting on an act.

Leaders take people to places they've never been before. But there are no freeways to the future, no paved highways to unknown, unexplored destinations. There's only wilderness. To step out into the unknown, begin with the exploration of the inner territory. We continue to discover that the most critical knowledge for all of us—and for leaders especially—turns out to be self-knowledge.

HUMILITY IS THE ANTIDOTE TO HUBRIS

There's a catch, however. You can do all of these leadership practices perfectly and still get fired! There's absolutely no way that we can say that leadership will always work, all of the time, or with everyone. We know for certain that there's a much greater probability that it will, but there's no ironclad, money-back guarantee. In addition, you will never find, in historic or present times, even one example of a leader who controlled every aspect of the environment. And you'll never find an example of a leader who enlisted 100 percent of the possible constituency in even the most compelling of future possibilities.

And there's still another catch. Any leadership practice can become destructive. Virtues can become vices. There's a point at which each of The Five Practices, taken to extremes, can lead you astray.

Far more insidious than any of these potential problems, however, is the treachery of hubris. It's fun to be a leader, gratifying to have influence, and exhilarating to have scores of people cheering your every word. In many all-too-subtle ways, it's easy to be seduced by power and importance. All evil leaders have been infected with the disease of hubris, becoming bloated with an exaggerated sense of self and pursuing their own sinister ends. How then to avoid it?

Humility is the only way to resolve the conflicts and contradictions of leadership. You can avoid excessive pride only if you recognize that you're human and need the help of others. As Egon Zehnder, chairman emeritus of Egon Zehnder International, told us, "Listen to what your colleagues have to say. They know more than you do. Have the humility to step back and correct yourself." Humility. It comes up time and again.[4] Exemplary leaders know that "you can't do it alone," and they act accordingly. They lack the pride and pretense displayed by many leaders who succeed in the short term but leave behind a weak organization that fails to remain viable after their departure. Instead, with self-effacing humor and generous and sincere credit to others, humble leaders get higher and higher levels of performance.

Nothing in our research hints that leaders should be perfect. Leaders aren't saints. They're human beings, full of the flaws and failings of the rest of us. They make mistakes. Perhaps the very best advice we can give all aspiring leaders is to remain humble and unassuming—to always remain open and full of wonder.

LEADERSHIP IS IN THE MOMENT

Michele Goins, chief information officer for Hewlett-Packard's Imaging and Printing Group, spoke to our students at Santa Clara University. What she said resonated very loudly with them. "Leadership opportunities are presented to everyone," she observed. "What makes the difference between being a leader or not is how you respond *in the moment.*" Michele's observation and her own experiences of leadership in the moment are testimony to how important it is to approach every interaction and every situation as an opportunity to lead.

Sometimes we imagine leadership to be something majestic—about grand visions, about world-changing initiatives, about transforming the lives of millions. While all are noble possibilities, real leadership is in the daily moments. Sergey Nikiforov, cofounder and vice president of product development at Stack3, Inc., put it to us this way:

Where do I start becoming a better leader? This question has been nagging me for some time. Naively I assumed that to become a better leader meant to perform formidable tasks: moving mountains, saving lives, changing the world for the better. As you pointed out these noble, grandiose tasks are often insurmountable for a single person.

Then it occurred to me—I was thinking selfishly. What I envisioned was instant gratification, recognition for my skills and talent. Although the issues at work matched well with your book's materials, the way I dealt with them was far from ideal. In most cases, I used wrong tools and methods.

I found that every day I had an opportunity to make a small difference. I could have coached someone better, I could have listened better, I could have been more positive toward people, I could have said "thank you" more often, I could have . . . the list just went on.

At first, I was a bit overwhelmed with the discovery of how many opportunities I had in a single day to act as a better leader. But as I have gotten to put these ideas into practice I have been pleasantly surprised by how much improvement I have been able to make by being more conscientious and intentional about acting as a leader.

Sergey has nailed it. Each day provides countless chances to make a difference. The chance might come in a private conversation with a direct report or in a meeting with colleagues. It might come over the family dinner table. It might come when you're speaking at a conference on the future of your business, or it might come when you're listening to a friend talk about a current conflict with a peer. There are many moments each day, as leaders like Michele and Sergey point out, when you can choose to lead, and many moments each day when you can choose to make a difference. Each of these moments serves up the prospect of contributing to a lasting legacy.

Each day provides countless chances to make a difference.

THE SECRET TO SUCCESS IN LIFE

Constituents look for leaders who demonstrate an enthusiastic and genuine belief in the capacity of others, who strengthen people's will, who supply the means to achieve, and who express optimism for the future. Constituents want leaders who remain passionate despite obstacles and setbacks. In uncertain times, leaders with a positive, confident, can-do approach to life and business are desperately needed.

Leaders must keep hope alive, even in the most difficult of times. Without hope there can be no courage—and this is not the time or place for the timid. This is the time and place for optimism, imagination, and enthusiasm. Leaders must summon their will if they are to mobilize the personal and organizational resources to triumph against the odds. Hope is essential to achieving the highest levels of performance. Hope enables people to transcend the difficulties of today and envision the potentialities of tomorrow. Hope enables people to bounce back even after being stressed, stretched, and depressed. Hope enables people to find the will and the way to unleash greatness.[5]

And yet, hope is not all. There's still one more final leadership lesson that we have learned. It's the secret to success in life.

When we began our study of leadership bests we were fortunate to cross paths with then U.S. Army Major General John H. Stanford. We knew that he had grown up poor, that he failed sixth grade but went on to graduate from Penn State University on an ROTC scholarship, that he survived multiple military tours in both Korea and Vietnam, that he was highly decorated, and that the loyalty of his troops was extraordinary. John headed up the Military Traffic Management Command for the U.S. Army during the Persian Gulf War. When he retired from the Army he became county manager of Fulton County, Georgia, when Atlanta was gearing up to host the 1996 Summer Olympics, and then he became superintendent of the Seattle Public Schools, where he sparked a revolution in public education.[6]

When John Stanford wanted change, he didn't simply order it, as his longtime friend Billie Reilly explained.[7] For example, in Korea, John never told soldiers under his command that they couldn't stay out late. He just kept moving up the time of the morning physical training—to the point that it once started at 3 A.M. When he finally moved it back to 6 A.M., Reilly said, John got 100 percent attendance. "Have you ever met someone and immediately said, 'I need to listen to that person'? That's John," said Reilly. "Have you ever met someone and said, 'I like what he's doing and I want to follow him'? That's John. Have you ever met someone who can energize a group that's lethargic? That's John. We might call it character, we might call it leadership.

When you are in contact with John Stanford, you are immediately drawn to him. Where he's going, you want to go. And it's always the right place to go."

All that we learned of John's public service was impressive, but it was his answer to one of our interview questions that most influenced our own understanding of leadership. We asked John how he'd go about developing leaders, whether in colleges and universities, in the military, in government, in the nonprofit sector, or in private business. He replied,

> When anyone asks me that question, I tell them I have the secret to success in life. The secret to success is to stay in love. Staying in love gives you the fire to ignite other people, to see inside other people, to have a greater desire to get things done than other people. A person who is not in love doesn't really feel the kind of excitement that helps them to get ahead and to lead others and to achieve. I don't know any other fire, any other thing in life that is more exhilarating and is more positive a feeling than love is.

"Staying in love" isn't the answer we expected to get—at least not when we began our study of leadership. But after numerous interviews and case analyses, it finally dawned on us how many leaders used the word *love* freely when talking about their own motivations to lead.

Of all the things that sustain a leader over time, love is the most lasting. It's hard to imagine leaders getting up day after day, putting in the long hours and hard work it takes to get extraordinary things done, without having their hearts in it. The best-kept secret of successful leaders is love: staying in love with leading, with the people who do the work, with what their organizations produce, and with those who honor the organization by using its products and services.

Leadership is not an affair of the head. Leadership is an affair of the heart.

NOTES

The stories that we tell in this book bring the principles and practices of leadership to life. What gives credibility to these stories is our more than twenty-five years of extensive research—research that clearly indicates that if you do more of what we've described in this book you will get better results in your work, in your relationships, and in your life.

We invite you to explore the research by going to www.leadershipchallenge.com/research. Our "Guide to the Research" includes a description of how we conducted the research underlying The Five Practices of Exemplary Leadership, the data supporting the model, the reliability and validity of that data, and summaries of key findings on the effects of exemplary leadership.

In addition to the reports on our data, the Guide section of our leadershipchallenge.com Web site includes executive summaries of over 350 doctoral dissertations and other research projects based on The Five Practices of Exemplary Leadership framework. You'll also be able to link to other resources and product information on the Web site, including the *Leadership Practices Inventory* (LPI) and other assessment instruments, information for college and university instructors, tips, and answers to frequently asked questions. Most important, we update the Guide regularly, and from time to time we ask readers to participate in exploring leadership issues with us.

We invite you to join us on the Web and to continue your own adventure in leadership and learning.

PREFACE: GETTING EXTRAORDINARY THINGS DONE IN ORGANIZATIONS

1. The Five Practices of Exemplary Leadership® is a registered trademark of J. M. Kouzes and B. Z. Posner.

CHAPTER ONE: THE FIVE PRACTICES OF EXEMPLARY LEADERSHIP

1. Unless otherwise noted, all quotations are taken from personal interviews or from personal-best leadership case studies written by the respondent leaders. The titles and affiliations of the leaders may be different today from what they were at the time of their case study or publication of this volume. We expect that many have moved on to other leadership adventures while we were writing, or will do so by the time you read this.

2. The SG Group is being recognized for the difference that it is making. What began out of necessity has grown into something that others now look to for ideas that will help them grow their businesses and retain their staffs. In 2004 Stopgap was listed as number ten on the Sunday *Times* "50 Best Small Companies to Work For" list, and in 2005 was named number five. Claire Owen was declared the "Best for Leadership" by the Sunday *Times* two years in a row.

3. Telephone interview with Jodi Taylor, Center for Creative Leadership, Colorado Springs, Colorado, April 1998. See also V. I. Sessa and J. J. Taylor, *Executive Selection: Strategies* for Success (San Francisco: Jossey-Bass, 2000).

4. "FC Roper Starch Survey: The Web," *Fast Company* (October 1999): 302.

5. Public Allies, *New Leadership for a New Century* (Washington, D.C.: Public Allies, 1998).

CHAPTER TWO: CREDIBILITY IS THE FOUNDATION OF LEADERSHIP

1. For more information about the original studies, see B. Z. Posner and W. H. Schmidt, "Values and the American Manager: An Update," *California Management Review* 26, no. 3 (1984): 202–216; and B. Z. Posner and W. H. Schmidt, "Values and Expectations of Federal Service Executives," *Public Administration Review* 46, no. 5 (1986): 447–454.

2. A point often made by respondents about the checklist is that leadership is not about following a person per se but following a person who embodies for them a purpose (vision) that they believe is worthy and makes it possible for them to be leaders themselves.

3. Our own research is supported by a study by the Corporate Leadership Council, an organization that provides best practices to human resource executives in leading global corporations. They found exactly what we did—that honesty is at the top of the list of what people look for in their leaders. Sixty-one percent of their respondents said this was an important leadership attribute. See *Voice of the Leader* (Washington, D.C.: Corporate Leadership Council, 2001).

4. There is one significant finding about the quality of being forward-looking that's important to note. When we survey individuals at the most senior levels in organizations, the percentage of people who select "forward-looking" as a desired leader characteristic is around 95 percent. When we administer our checklist to people in frontline supervisory roles, the percentage of people selecting "forward-looking" is around 60 percent. This wide gap indicates an important difference in expectation that's clearly tied

to the breadth, scope, and time horizon of the job. More senior people see the need for a longer-term view of the future than do those at the front lines of operations. This also suggests a major developmental need for individuals as they move into roles that are more strategic in nature.

5. For more on the role of positive emotions and leadership, see D. Goleman, R. Boyatzis, and A. McKee, *Primal Leadership: Realizing the Power of Emotional Intelligence* (Boston: Harvard Business School Press, 2002); and B. L. Fredrickson, "The Role of Positive Emotions in Positive Psychology: The Broaden-and-Build Theory of Emotions," *American Psychologist* 56 (2001): 218–226.

6. The classic study on credibility goes back to C. I. Hovland, I. L. Janis, and H. H. Kelley, *Communication and Persuasion* (New Haven, CT: Yale University Press, 1953); and early measurement studies include J. C. McCroskey, "Scales for the Measurement of Ethos," *Speech Monographs* 33 (1966): 65–72 and D. K. Berlo, J. B. Lemert, and R. J. Mertz, "Dimensions for Evaluating the Acceptability of Message Sources," *Public Opinion Quarterly* 3 (1969): 563–576. However, even further back, Aristotle (384–322 B.C.), writing in the *Rhetoric*, suggested that Ethos, the Trust of a speaker by the listener, or what some have referred to as "source credibility," was based on the listener's perception of three characteristics of the speaker: the intelligence of the speaker (correctness of opinions, or competence), the character of the speaker (reliability—a competence factor—and honesty—a measure of intentions), and the good will of the speaker (positive energy and favorable intentions toward the listener). These three characteristics (competence, honesty, and inspiration) have consistently emerged in factor-analytic investigations of communicator credibility (D. J. O'Keefe, *Persuasion: Theory and Research* [Thousand Oaks, CA: Sage, 2002]). Another contemporary perspective is provided in R. Cialdini, *Influence: The Psychology of Persuasion* (New York: Collins, 2007).

7. F. F. Reichheld with T. Teal, *The Loyalty Effect: The Hidden Force Behind Growth, Profits, and Lasting Value* (Boston: Harvard Business School Press, 1996), 1.

8. F. F. Reichheld, *Loyalty Rules: How Today's Leaders Build Lasting Relationships* (Boston: Harvard Business School Press, 2001), 6. See also F. F. Reichheld, *The Ultimate Question* (Boston: Harvard Business School Press, 2006).

9. F. F. Reichheld and P. Schefter, "E-Loyalty: Your Secret Weapon on the Web," *Harvard Business Review* 78, no. 4 (July-August 2000): 107. See also Bain & Company and Mainspring, "Bain/Mainspring Online Retailing Survey" (joint survey of 2,116 online shoppers in the categories of apparel, groceries, and consumer electronics) (Boston: Bain & Company, December 1999); and Reichheld, *Loyalty Rules*, 8. For additional information on Web credibility, see B. J. Fogg and others, "What Makes Web Sites Credible? A Report on a Large Quantitative Study," *Proceedings of ACM CHI 2001 Conference on Human Factors in Computing Systems*, v. 1 (New York: ACM Press, 2001), 61–68. For more insight on customer focus and business results, see F. F. Reichheld, *The Ultimate Question* (Boston: Harvard Business School Press, 2006) and the discussion and blogs at www.theultimatequestion.com and www.netpromoter.com.

CHAPTER THREE: CLARIFY VALUES

1. M. De Pree, *Leadership Jazz* (New York: Currency Doubleday, 1992), 1–3.

2. De Pree, *Leadership Jazz*, 5.

3. *Merriam-Webster's Collegiate Dictionary*, 10th ed., s.v. "care."

4. M. Rokeach, *The Nature of Human Values* (New York: Free Press, 1973), 5.

5. Rokeach, *The Nature of Human Values*, 14–15.

6. R. Basu, Santa Clara University Leadership Lecture, Leavey School of Business, Santa Clara University, May 30, 2006.

7. B. Z. Posner and W. H. Schmidt, "Values Congruence and Differences Between the Interplay of Personal and Organizational Value Systems," *Journal of Business Ethics* 12 (1993): 171–177.

8. A. Lamott, *Bird by Bird: Some Instructions on Writing and Life* (New York: Pantheon, 1994), 199–200.

9. L. Gunning, remarks at Unilever Foods Asia "Journey to Greatness: Sri Lanka," March 6–11, 2005. For additional information on Gunning's leadership philosophy and practices, see P. Mirvis and L. Gunning, "Creating a Community of Leaders," *Organizational Dynamics* 35, no. 1 (2006): 69–82; available online at www.sciencedirect.com; P. Mirvis, K. Ayas, and G. Roth, *To the Desert and Back: The Story of One of the Most Dramatic Business Transformations on Record* (San Francisco: Jossey-Bass, 2003); and K. Hazelton, "Rethinking Business at Unilever," Business as an Agent of World Benefit Innovation Bank; available online at http://worldbenefit.cwru.edu/inquiry/feature_unilever.cfm.

10. See, for example, B. Z. Posner and W. H. Schmidt, "Values Congruence and Differences Between the Interplay of Personal and Organizational Value Systems," *Journal of Business Ethics* 12 (1993): 171–177; and B. Z. Posner, "Person-Organization Values Congruence: No Support for Individual Differences as a Moderating Influence," *Human Relations* 45, no. 2 (1992): 351–361.

11. B. Z. Posner and R. I. Westwood, "A Cross-Cultural Investigation of the Shared Values Relationship," *International Journal of Value-Based Management* 11, no. 4 (1995): 1–10; J. W. Haas, B. D. Sypher, and H. E. Sypher, "Do Shared Goals Really Make a Difference?" *Management Communication Quarterly* 6, no. 2 (1992): 166–179.

12. See, for example, R. I. Westwood and B. Z. Posner, "Managerial Values Across Cultures: Australia, Hong Kong and the U.S." *Asia Pacific Journal of Management* 14 (1997): 31–66; B. Z. Posner, J. M. Kouzes, and W. H. Schmidt, "Shared Values Make a Difference: An Empirical Test of Corporate Culture," *Human Resource Management* 24, no. 3 (1985): 293–310; B. Z. Posner and W. H. Schmidt, "Demographic Characteristics and Shared Values," *International Journal of Value-Based Management* 5, no. 1 (1992): 77–87.

13. Posner and Westwood, "A Cross-Cultural Investigation of the Shared Values Relationship."

14. R. V. Lee, L. Fabish, and N. McGaw, "The Value of Corporate Values," *Strategy+Business* 39 (2006): 11.

15. J. P. Kotter and J. L. Heskett, *Corporate Culture and Performance* (New York: Free Press, 1992).

16. R. Roi, *Leadership Practices, Adaptive Corporate Culture & Company Financial Performance: 2005 Study Results.* Crawford International, 2005; available online at www.crawfordinternational.com/research.

17. B . Z. Posner and W. H. Schmidt, "Values and Expectations of Federal Service Executives," *Public Administration Review* 46, no. 5 (1986): 447–454.

18. Our colleague David Caldwell (Santa Clara University) shared this example with us originally. See also C. A. O'Reilly and D. F. Caldwell, "The Power of Strong Corporate Cultures in Silicon Valley Firms," presentation to the Executive Seminar in Corporate Excellence, Santa Clara University, February 13, 1985; see also C. A. O'Reilly, "Corporations, Culture, and Commitment: Motivation and Social Control in Organizations," *California Management Review* 23 (1989): 9–17.

19. J. C. Collins and J. I. Porras, *Built to Last: Successful Habits of Visionary Companies* (New York: HarperCollins, 1994).

20. C. A. O'Reilly and J. Pfeffer, *Hidden Value: How Great Companies Achieve Extraordinary Results with Ordinary People* (Boston: Harvard Business School Press, 2000).

21. R. A. Stevenson, "Clarifying Behavioral Expectations Associated with Espoused Organizational Values," Ph.D. dissertation, Fielding Institute, 1995.

22. Having a voice and giving voice to your deeply held beliefs requires competence. Words alone do not make a leader credible. Before you can do the right things, you have to know how to do them. Leaders must be aware of the degree to which they actually have the capabilities to do what they say. And if they lack the competence they must dedicate themselves to continuously learning and improving. Acquiring competence is a necessary part of becoming genuine. Your value as a leader is determined not only by your guiding beliefs but also by your ability to act on them. To strengthen credibility you must continuously assess your existing abilities and devote time and energy to learning new ones. The same is true for your organization. This applies to all ten commitments.

CHAPTER FOUR: SET THE EXAMPLE

1. T. Simons, "The High Cost of Lost Trust," *Harvard Business Review* 80, no. 9 (September 2002): 19. See also T. Simons, "The Integrity Dividend, *Harvard Business Review,* forthcoming.

2. This discussion draws upon T. J. Peters and N. Austin, *A Passion for Excellence* (New York: Random House, 1985); E. H. Schein, *Organizational Culture and Leadership,* 3rd ed. (San Francisco: Jossey-Bass, 1997); and E. H. Schein, *The Organizational Culture Survival Guide* (San Francisco: Jossey-Bass, 1999).

3. S. Zuboff, *In the Age of the Smart Machine: The Future of Work and Power* (New York: Basic Books, 1988), 394.

4. Additional information on DaVita's culture and language can be found in J. Pfeffer, "Kent Thiry and DaVita: Leadership Challenges in Building and Growing a Great Company," Stanford Graduate School of Business, Case OB-54, February 23, 2006.

5. F. A. Blanchard, T. Lilly, and L. A. Vaughn, "Reducing the Expression of Racial Prejudice," *Psychological Science* 2, no. 2 (1991): 101–105.

6. See, for example, D. Goleman, *Social Intelligence: The New Science of Human Relationships* (New York: Bantam, 2006) and his landmark *Emotional Intelligence: Why It Can Matter More Than IQ* (New York: Bantam, 1995). See also D. Goleman, *Working with Emotional Intelligence* (New York: Bantam, 1998) and D. Goleman, A. McKee, and R. E. Boyatzis, *Primal Leadership: Realizing the Power of Emotional Intelligence* (Boston: Harvard Business School Press, 2002).

7. Troy Hansen appears in J. M. Kouzes and B. Z. Posner, *The Leadership Challenge DVD Revised* (San Francisco: Jossey-Bass, 2006).

8. S. Denning, *The Springboard: How Storytelling Ignites Action in Knowledge-Era Organizations* (Boston: Butterworth-Heinemann, 2001), 10.

9. Denning, *The Springboard,* 14, xiii.

10. D. G. Kolb, "Seeking Continuity Amidst Organizational Change: A Storytelling Approach," *Journal of Management Inquiry* 12 (2003): 180–183.

11. D. M. Armstrong, *Managing by Storying Around: A New Method of Leadership* (New York: Doubleday, 1992), 7–8. See also D. M. Armstrong, *Once Told, They're Gold: Stories to Enliven and Enrich the Workplace* (Stuart, Fla.: Armstrong International, 1998); and D. M. Armstrong, *Chief Storytelling Officer: More Tales from America's Foremost Corporate Storyteller* (Stuart, Fla.: Armstrong International, 2002).

12. Armstrong, *Managing by Storying Around,* 10.

13. J. Martin and M. E. Power, "Organizational Stories: More Vivid and Persuasive Than Quantitative Data," in B. M. Staw (ed.), *Psychological Foundations of Organizational Behavior* (Glenview, Ill.: Scott, Foresman, 1982), 161–168. For additional evidence that storytelling improves a leader's ability to communicate, see also M. Bennett, *Once Upon a Time in Leadership: Inspiring a Shared Vision Through Storytelling,* masters thesis, College of Business and Public Management, University of La Verne, March 2005.

14. A. L. Wilkens, "Organizational Stories as Symbols Which Control the Organization," in L. R. Pondy and others (eds.), *Organizational Symbolism* (Greenwich, Conn.: JAI Press, 1983), 81–92; also Kolb, "Seeking Continuity."

15. R. P. Bagozzi and S. K. Kimmel, "A Comparison of Leading Theories for the Prediction of Goal-Directed Behaviors," *British Journal of Social Psychology* 34 (December 1995): 437–461.

16. "Brian Coleman, Manager, Tool and Dies, Ford Motor Co., Dagenham, England," *On Achieving Excellence* 8, no. 8 (1993) (newsletter from TPG Communications, Palo Alto, California).

17. J. Conger, *Winning 'Em Over: A New Model for Management in the Age of Persuasion* (New York: Simon & Schuster, 1998). See also J. Conger, "Inspiring Others: The Language of Leadership," *Academy of Management Executive* 5, no. 1 (1991): 31–45.

18. S. Taylor and L. Novelli Jr., "Some Basic Concepts of Innovation and Story Telling," *Issues & Observation* 11, no. 1 (1991): 6–9. For more about being a storyteller, see J. Maguire, *The Power of Personal Storytelling: Spinning Tales to Connect with Others* (New York: Tarcher, 1998); D. Lipman, *Improving Your Storytelling:*

Beyond the Basics for All Who Tell Stories in Work and Play (Little Rock, Ark.: August House, 1999); and C. Wortmann, *What's Your Story? Using Stories to Ignite Performance and Be More Successful* (Chicago: Kaplan Publishing, 2006).

CHAPTER FIVE: ENVISION THE FUTURE

1. Pam credits the early advice and counsel of Dr. Gary Dahl, Dr. Steve Cole, Dennis Fong (a.k.a. Thresh), Dr. Ellen Goldberg, Dr. Pamela Kato, Luis Meija, Mike Mohr, and Dr. Brad Pollock in enabling her to marry her love of science and her desire to alleviate children's suffering when she founded HopeLab. Pam also credits HopeLab president Pat Christen for her exemplary leadership, which has allowed the organization to thrive. To learn more about HopeLab and Re-Mission, visit www.hopelab.org.
2. D. Gilbert, *Stumbling on Happiness* (New York: Knopf, 2006), 5 and 6.
3. See G. Hamel, *Leading the Revolution* (Boston: Harvard Business School Press, 2000). Hamel observes, "One of the reasons many people fail to fully appreciate what's changing is because they're down at ground level, lost in the thicket of confusing, conflicting data. You have to make time to step back and ask yourself, 'What's the big story that cuts across all these little facts?'" (p. 128).
4. For extensive research on intuitive decision making under conditions of extreme uncertainty, see G. Klein, *The Sources of Power: How People Make Decisions* (Cambridge, Mass.: MIT Press, 1998). Envisioning and intuiting aren't logical activities, and they're extremely difficult to explain and quantify. Alden M. Hayashi, a senior editor of *Harvard Business Review* who has studied executive decision making, reports, "In my interviews with top executives known for their shrewd business instincts, none could articulate precisely how they routinely made important decisions that defied any logical analysis. To describe that vague feeling of knowing something without knowing exactly how or why, they used words like *professional judgment, intuition, gut instinct, inner voice,* and *hunch,* but they couldn't describe the process much beyond that." Yet, as he points out, the leaders he studied agreed that these hard-to-describe abilities were crucial to effectiveness. They even went so far as to say that it was the "X-Factor" that separated the best from the mediocre. See A. M. Hayashi, "When to Trust Your Gut," *Harvard Business Review* 79, no. 2 (February 2001): 59–65. In fact, by definition, intuition and vision are directly connected. Intuition has as its root the Latin word meaning "to look at"—see E. Partridge, *A Short Etymological Dictionary of Modern English* (New York: Macmillan, 1977), 359, 742.
5. O. A. El Sawy, "Temporal Perspective and Managerial Attention: A Study of Chief Executive Strategic Behavior," unpublished doctoral dissertation, Stanford University, 1983. Also see O. A. El Sawy, "Temporal Biases in Strategic Attention," research paper, November 1988, Marshall School of Business, University of Southern California.
6. El Sawy, "Temporal Perspective," vii–35.
7. J. Naisbitt, *Mindset: Reset Your Thinking and See the Future* (New York: Harper Collins, 2006), 20.
8. G. Hamel and C. K. Prahalad, *Competing for the Future: Breakthrough Strategies for Seizing Control of Your Industry and Creating the Markets of Tomorrow* (Boston: Harvard Business School Press, 1994).
9. See E. L. Deci with R. Flaste, *Why We Do What We Do: Understanding Self-Motivation* (New York: Penguin, 1995). For another excellent treatment of this subject, see K. W. Thomas, *Intrinsic Motivation at Work: Building Energy and Commitment* (San Francisco: Berrett-Koehler, 2000); and for an extensive academic treatment, see C. Sansone and J. M. Harackiewicz (eds.), *Intrinsic and Extrinsic Motivation: The Search for Optimal Motivation and Performance* (New York: Academic Press, 2000).
10. E. L. Deci with R. Flaste, *Why We Do What We Do,* 25.
11. J. Barker, "21st Century Scouting," 2006. Available online at www.strategicexploration.com/i-wheel/scouting4.htm; accessed on July 7, 2006.

12. A. Deering, R. Dilts, and J. Russell, *Alpha Leadership: Tools for Business Leaders Who Want More from Life* (London: Wiley, 2002).

13. B. L. Kaye and S. Jordon-Evans, *Love 'Em or Lose 'Em* (San Francisco: Berrett-Koehler, 1999).

14. Telephone interview with Dave Berlew, November 14, 1994. See D. E. Berlew, "Leadership and Organizational Excitement," *California Management Review* 17, No. 2 (1974): 21–30. Also see B. Nelson, *What Do Employees Want? Employee Recognition Practices Inventory.* Available online at www.nelson-motivation.com/bobsarticles.cfm; accessed on November 12, 2006.

15. Responses have been amazingly consistent over the years. For example, see C. Caggiano, "What Do Workers Want?" *Inc.,* November 1992, 101–102; S. Caudron, "Motivation?" *Industry Week,* November 15, 1993, 33; E. Galinsky, J. T. Bond, and D. E. Friedman, *The National Study of the Changing Workforce* (New York: Families and Work Institute, 1993); F. L. Branham, *Keeping the People Who Keep You in Business* (New York: Amacom, 2000); B. N. Pfau and I. T. Kay, *The Human Capital Edge* (New York: McGraw-Hill, 2001); and C. Coffman and G. Gonzalez-Molina, *Follow This Path* (New York: Warner Books, 2002). For discussions of related issues, see also R. B. Freeman and J. Rogers, *What Workers Want (Updated)* (Ithaca, NY: Cornell University Press, 2006); R. Wagner and J. K. Harter, *12:The Elements of Great Managing* (New York: Gallup Press, 2006); and L. Branham, *The Seven Hidden Reasons Employees Leave: How to Recognize the Subtle Signs and Act Before It's Too Late* (New York: AMACOM, 2005).

16. See, for example, M. Novak, *Business as a Calling: Work and the Examined Life* (New York: Free Press, 1996); R. J. Leider and D. A. Shapiro, *Whistle While You Work: Heeding Your Life's Calling* (San Francisco: Berrett-Koehler, 2001); R. J. Palmer, *Let Your Life Speak* (San Francisco: Jossey-Bass, 2000); D. Zohar and I. Marshall, *Spiritual Capital* (San Francisco: Berrett-Koehler, 2004); and R. Barrett, *Building a Values-Driven Organization* (Burlington, MA: Butterworth-Heinemann, 2006).

17. See, for example, H. Mintzberg and R. A. Norman, *Reframing Business: When the Map Changes the Landscape* (New York: Wiley, 2001); C. Handy, *The Hungry Spirit: Beyond Capitalism* (New York: Broadway Books, 1999); and G. Hamel, *Leading the Revolution* (Boston: Harvard Business School Press, 2000).

18. H. Mintzberg, "The Rise and Fall of Strategic Planning," *Harvard Business Review* 72, no. 1 (January–February 1994): 109.

19. J. M. Burns, *Leadership* (New York: HarperCollins, 1978), 20. See also J. M. Burns, *Transforming Leadership* (New York: Atlantic Books, 2003).

20. As quoted in L. Ioannou, "Make Your Company an Idea Factory," *Fortune,* June 12, 2000, F264N–F264R.

CHAPTER SIX: ENLIST OTHERS

1. Market researcher and author Doug Hall has found that "dramatically different" levels in a new product or service increase the idea's probability of success in the marketplace from 15 percent to 53 percent. That's a 253 percent greater chance of success. The same is true for a vision; the more unique it is the higher the probability of success in getting people to buy in. See D. Hall, *Jump Start Your Business Brain: Win More, Lose Less, and Make More Money with Your New Products, Services, Sales and Advertising* (Cincinnati: Brain Brew Books, 2001).

2. "'I Have a Dream' Leads Top 100 Speeches of the Century," press release from the University of Wisconsin, December 15, 1999. Available online at www.news.wisc.edu/releases/3504.html; accessed on June 13, 2006. Also often seen on international lists of great speakers from recent history are Winston Churchill, Mahatma Gandhi, Vaclav Havel, Nelson Mandela, Chuba Okadigbo, Mother Teresa, and Margaret Thatcher.

3. M. L. King Jr., "I Have a Dream," in C. S. King (ed.), *The Words of Martin Luther King, Jr.* (New York: Newmarket Press, 1983), 95–98. Reprinted by permission of Joan Daves, copyright © 1963 by Martin Luther King Jr.

4. See, for example, www.americanrhetoric.com/speeches/Ihaveadream.htm; accessed on on September 22, 2006.

5. R. Semler, *The Seven-Day Weekend: Changing the Way Work Works* (New York: Penguin, 2004), 1.

6. Semler, *The Seven-Day Weekend,* viii, 74, 217.

7. T. Oberlechner and V. Mayer-Schönberger, "Through Their Own Words: Towards a New Understanding of Leadership Through Metaphors," *Working Papers,* Center for Public Leadership, John F. Kennedy School of Government, Harvard University, 2003, p. 170. Available online at www.ksg.harvard.edu/leadership/pubs/papers/index.php?year=2003; accessed on September 24, 2006.

8. Oberlechner and Mayer-Schönberger, "Through Their Own Words," p. 170.

9. D. Goleman, *Social Intelligence: The New Science of Human Relationships* (New York: Bantam, 2006).

10. B. M. Bass, *Leadership and Performance Beyond Expectations* (New York: Free Press, 1985), 35. See also B. M. Bass, *Bass and Stogdill's Handbook of Leadership: Theory, Research, and Managerial Applications,* 3rd ed. (New York: Free Press, 1990) and B. M. Bass and R. E. Riggio, *Transformational Leadership,* 2nd ed. (Mahwah, N.J.: Lawrence Erlbaum Associates, 2005).

11. See, for example, H. S. Friedman, L. M. Prince, R. E. Riggio, and M. R. DiMatteo, "Understanding and Assessing Nonverbal Expressiveness: The Affective Communication Test," *Journal of Personality and Social Psychology* 39, no. 2 (1980): 333–351; D. Goleman, R. Boyatzis, and A. McKee, *Primal Leadership: Realizing the Power of Emotional Intelligence* (Boston: Harvard Business School Press, 2002); J. Conger, *Winning 'Em Over: A New Model for Management in the Age of Persuasion* (New York: Simon & Schuster, 1998); and M. Greer, The Science of Savoir Faire," *APA Monitor* 36, no. 1 (2005): 28.

12. B. L. Halpren and K. Lubar, *Leadership Presence: Dramatic Techniques to Reach Out, Motivate, and Inspire* (New York: Gotham Books, 2003), 141.

13. J. L. McGaugh, *Memory and Emotion* (New York: Columbia University Press, 2003), 90.

14. McGaugh, *Memory and Emotion,* 93.

15. McGaugh, *Memory and Emotion,* 92.

CHAPTER SEVEN: SEARCH FOR OPPORTUNITIES

1. R. M. Kanter, *The Change Masters: Innovation for Productivity in the American Corporation* (New York: Simon & Schuster, 1983), 125.

2. T. S. Bateman and J. M. Crant, "The Proactive Component of Organizational Behavior: Measures and Correlates," *Journal of Organizational Behavior* 14 (1993): 103–118; T. S. Bateman and J. M. Crant, "Proactive Behavior: Meaning, Impact, Recommendations," *Business Horizons* 42, no. 3 (May-June 1999): 63–70; and J. M. Crant, "Proactive Behavior in Organizations," *Journal of Management* 26, no. 3 (2000): 435–463.

3. J. M. Crant and T. S. Bateman, "Charismatic Leadership Viewed from Above: The Impact of Proactive Personality," *Journal of Organizational Behavior* 21, no. 1 (2000): 63–75.

4. J. M. Crant, "The Proactive Personality Scale and Objective Job Performance Among Real Estate Agents," *Journal of Applied Psychology* 80, no. 4 (August 1995): 532–537.

5. See J. A. Thompson, "Proactive Personality and Job Performance: A Social Capital Perspective," *Journal of Applied Psychology* 90, no. 5 (2005), 1011–1017. See also S. E. Seibert and M. L. Braimer, "What Do Proactive People Do? A Longitudinal Model Linking Proactive Personality and Career Success," *Personnel Psychology* 54 (2001): 845–875; D. Goetsch, *Effective Leadership: Ten Steps for Technical Professions* (Englewood Cliffs, N.J.: Prentice-Hall, 2004); and D. J. Brown, R. T. Cober, K. Kane, P. E. Levy, and J. Shalhoop, "Proactive Personality and the Successful Job Search: A Field Investigation of College Graduates," *Journal of Applied Psychology* 91, no. 3 (2006), 717–726.

6. Our sample involved managers from both the United States and Switzerland. See B. Z. Posner and J. W. Harder, "The Proactive Personality, Leadership, Gender and National Culture," paper presented to the Western Academy of Management Conference, Santa Fe, New Mexico, April 2002.

7. See A. Bandura, *Self-Efficacy: The Exercise of Self-Control* (New York: Freeman, 1997). Bandura offers a detailed discussion of ways to increase self-efficacy. He points out that there's a critical difference between self-efficacy and self-esteem. Self-efficacy is a belief in one's abilities, whereas self-esteem is a belief in one's worth. We prefer the concept of self-efficacy to self-esteem, because it's easier to offer suggestions on how to increase self-efficacy than to increase self-esteem. However, it is true that high self-esteem is positively correlated with speaking up. See also J. A. LePine and L. V. Dyne, "Predicting Voice Behavior in Work Groups," *Journal of Applied Psychology* 83, no. 6 (1998): 853–868.

8. For detailed information on mental simulation, see G. Klein, *Sources of Power: How People Make Decisions* (Cambridge, Mass.: MIT Press, 1998), 45–77; see also G. Klein, *The Power of Intuition: How to Use Your Gut Feelings to Make Better Decisions at Work* (New York: Currency, 2004).

9. Blum's stirring account of this highly acclaimed adventure is chronicled in A. Blum, *Annapurna: A Woman's Place,* Twentieth Anniversary Edition (San Francisco: Sierra Club Books, 1998). Leadership lessons from Arlene Blum were also gathered from personal conversations and correspondence between Arlene and the authors.

10. Blum, *Annapurna,* 3.

11. Blum, *Annapurna,* 6.

12. P. LaBarre, "How to Make It to the Top," *Fast Company,* September 1998, 72.

13. The finding that how we deal with challenge comes from the inside was dramatically reported by V. E. Frankl in *Man's Search for Meaning: An Introduction to Logotherapy* (New York: Touchstone, 1984) [first published in 1946].

14. See E. L. Deci with R. Flaste, *Why We Do What We Do: Understanding Self-Motivation* (New York: Penguin, 1995).

15. See A. Kohn, *Punished by Rewards* (New York: Houghton Mifflin, 1993). For a discussion of myths and truths about financial incentives, see J. Pfeffer and R. I. Sutton, *Hard Facts, Dangerous Half-Truths & Total Nonsense: Profiting from Evidence-Based Management* (Boston: Harvard Business School Press, 2006), 109–134.

16. See R. Foster and S. Kaplan, *Creative Destruction: Why Companies That Are Built to Last Underperform the Market—and How to Successfully Transform Them* (New York: Currency Doubleday, 2001); C. M. Christensen, *The Innovator's Dilemma: When New Technologies Cause Great Firms to Fail* (Boston: Harvard Business School Press, 1997); and C. M. Christensen, S. D. Anthony, and E. A Roth, *Seeing What's Next: Using the Theories of Innovation to Predict Industry Change* (Boston: Harvard Business School Press, 2004).

17. See, for example, C. M. Christensen and S. D. Anthony, "Cheaper, Faster, Easier: Disruption in the Service Sector," *Strategy and Innovation* 2, no. 1 (January-February 2004); J. Ettlie, *Managing Innovation,* 2nd ed. (Burlington, Mass.: Butterworth-Heineman, 2004); E. von Hippel, *Democratizing Innovation* (Boston: MIT Press, 2005); and T. Davila, M. J. Epstein, and R. Shelton, *Making Innovation Work: How to Manage It, Measure It, and Profit from It* (Upper Saddle River, N.J.: Wharton School Publishing, 2006). Also, go to www.innovationwatch.com for a revealing look at the multitude of sources and places around the world that give us hints about where our future new products and services will come from. It's a fascinating, and fun, look at the past, present, and future of innovation and change.

18. IBM, *Expanding the Innovation Horizons: The Global CEO Study 2006* (Somers, N.Y.: IBM Global Services, 2006).

19. R. Katz, "The Influence of Group Longevity: High Performance Research Teams," *Wharton Magazine* 6, no. 3 (1982): 28–34; and R. Katz and T. J. Allen, "Investigating the Not Invented Here (NIH) Syndrome:

A Look at the Performance, Tenure, and Communication Patterns of 50 R&D Project Groups," in M. L. Tushman and W. L. Moore (eds.), *Readings in the Management of Innovation,* 2nd ed. (Cambridge, Mass.: Ballinger, 1988), 293–309.

20. Katz, "The Influence of Group Longevity," 31.

21. L. Huston and N. Sakkab, "Connect and Develop: Inside Procter & Gamble's New Model for Innovation," *Harvard Business Review* 84, no. 2 (March 2006): 60.

22. Huston and Sakkab, "Connect and Develop," 60.

23. Huston and Sakkab, "Connect and Develop," 66.

24. See "A New Era Thinking," Chef Allen's. Available online at www.chefallens.com/philosophy.cfm; accessed on June 20, 2006. See also S. Greco, "Letting Workers Play Customers," *Inc.,* October 1994, 119.

CHAPTER EIGHT: EXPERIMENT AND TAKE RISKS

1. Patricia Maryland appears in J. M. Kouzes and B. Z. Posner, *The Leadership Challenge DVD Revised* (San Francisco: Jossey-Bass, 2006).

2. "Too Many Interruptions at Work?" Interview with Gloria Mark, *Gallup Management Journal,* p. 1. Available online at http://gmj.gallup.com/content/23146/Too-Many-Interruptions-at-Work.aspx; accessed on June 8, 2006. See also G. Mark, V. Gonzalez, and J. Harris, "No Task Left Behind? Examining the Nature of Fragmented Work." *Proceedings of ACM CHI'05,* Portland, Oregon, April 2005, pp. 321–330. See also the classic study on the subject of how managers spend their time: H. Mintzberg, *The Nature of Managerial Work* (New York: Prentice Hall, 1980).

3. C. Dahle, "Natural Leader," *Fast Company,* December 2000, 270–280. Copyright © 2000 by Mansueto Ventures LLC. Reproduced with permission of Mansueto Ventures LLC via Copyright Clearance Center.

4. A. Muoio, "Mint Condition," *Fast Company,* December 1999, 330–348.

5. Business volume per the U.S. Mint Web site; see www.usmint.gov/about_the_mint.

6. S. Hollander, *The Success of Increased Efficiency: A Study of DuPont Rayon Plants* (Cambridge, Mass.: MIT Press, 1965). See also D. Ulrich, S. Kerr, and R. Ashkenas, *The GE Work-Out* (New York: McGraw-Hill, 2002).

7. H. Mintzberg, *The Rise and Fall of Strategic Planning* (New York: Free Press, 1994), 134.

8. K. M. Eisenstadt and B. N. Tabrizi, "Accelerating Adaptive Processes: Product Innovation in the Global Computer Industry," *Administrative Science Quarterly* 40 (1995): 84–110.

9. D. Meyerson, *Tempered Radicals: How People Use Difference to Inspire Change at Work* (Boston: Harvard Business School Press, 2001).

10. M. Maidique, "Why Products Succeed and Why Products Fail," presentation to the Executive Seminar in Corporate Excellence, Santa Clara University, May 29, 1985; see also M. Maidique and B. J. Zinger, "The New Product Learning Cycle," *Research Policy* 14 (1985): 299–313; G. A. Moore, *Crossing the Chasm: Marketing and Selling High-Tech Products to Mainstream Customers* (New York: HarperBusiness, 1999); and C. M. Christensen, S. D. Anthony, and E. A Roth, *Seeing What's Next: Using the Theories of Innovation to Predict Industry Change* (Boston: Harvard Business School Press, 2004). See also J. McGregor, "How Failure Breeds Success." *Business Week,* July 10, 2006, pp. 42–50. McGregor writes, "The best companies embrace their mistakes and learn from them."

11. T. L. O'Brien, "Are U.S. Innovators Losing Their Competitive Edge?" *New York Times,* November 13, 2005, 3.

12. P. J. Schoemaker and R. E. Cunther, "The Wisdom of Deliberate Mistakes," *Harvard Business Review* 84, no. 6 (June 2006): 108–115.

13. D. H. Freedman, "When Your Company Screws Up, Don't Hide It," *Inc.*, October 2006, pp. 65–66. Copyright © 2000 by Mansueto Ventures LLC. Reproduced with permission of Mansueto Ventures LLC via Copyright Clearance Center.

14. R. J. Kriegel and L. Patler, *If It Ain't Broke . . . Break It!* (New York: Warner Books, 1991).

15. L. M. Brown and B. Z. Posner, "Exploring the Relationship Between Learning and Leadership," *Leadership & Organization Development Journal* (May 2001): 274–280.

16. M. Dalton, S. Swigert, E. Van Velsor, K. Bunker, and J. Wachholz, *The Learning Tactics Inventory: Facilitator's Guide* (San Francisco: Jossey-Bass/Pfeiffer, 1999).

17. See, for example, J. Collins, *Good to Great: Why Some Companies Make the Leap and Others Don't* (New York: HarperBusiness, 2001), 27–30.

18. A. C. Edmondson and M. D. Cannon, "Failing to Learn and Learning to Fail (Intelligently): How Great Organizations Put Failure to Work to Improve and Innovate," *Long Range Planning* 38, no. 3 (June 2005): 299–320.

19. S. R. Maddi and S. C. Kobasa, *The Hardy Executive: Health Under Stress* (Chicago: Dorsey Press, 1984); and S. R. Maddi and D. M. Khoshaba, "Hardiness and Mental Health," *Journal of Personality Assessment* 67 (1994): 265–274.

20. It may be difficult to overcome a habitual pattern of avoidance, but it is possible to learn to cope assertively with stressful events through counseling and educational programs. See Maddi and Kobasa, *The Hardy Executive*, 59; D. M. Khoshaba and S. R. Maddi, "Early Experiences in Hardiness Development," *Consulting Psychology Journal* 51 (1999): 106–116; S. R. Maddi, S. Kahn, and K. L. Maddi, "The Effectiveness of Hardiness Training," *Consulting Psychology Journal* 50 (1998): 78–86; and S. R. Maddi and D. M. Khoshaba, *Resilience at Work: How to Succeed No Matter What Life Throws at You* (New York: American Management Association, 2005).

21. A. Lashinsky, "Chaos By Design," *Fortune*, October 2, 2006, p. 88.

22. Lashinsky, "Chaos By Design," 88.

23. Lashinsky, "Chaos By Design," 88.

24. B. Breen, "What's Your Intuition?" *Fast Company*, September 2000, pp. 290–300.

CHAPTER NINE: FOSTER COLLABORATION

1. For detailed analyses of alliances and partnerships in the competitive marketplace, see Y. L. Doz and G. Hamel, *Alliance Advantage: The Art of Creating Value Through Partnering* (Boston: Harvard Business School Press, 1998); J. K. Conlon and M. Giovagnoli, *The Power of Two: How Companies of All Sizes Can Build Networks That Generate Business Opportunities* (San Francisco: Jossey-Bass, 1998); and, W. C. Kim and R. Mauborgne, *Blue Ocean Strategy* (Boston: Harvard Business School Press, 2005). For a discussion of collaboration and its importance to innovation, see IBM, *Expanding the Innovation Horizons: The Global CEO Study 2006* (Somers, NY: IBM Global Services, 2006).

2. Throughout this book we use *cooperate* and *collaborate* synonymously. Their dictionary definitions are very similar. In *Merriam-Webster's Collegiate Dictionary*, Tenth Edition (2001), the first definition of *cooperate* is "To act or work with another or others: act together" (p. 254). The first definition of *collaborate* is "To work jointly with others or together esp. in an intellectual endeavor" (p. 224).

3. For a variety of examples from organizations ranging from the United States Marine Corps to the Montreal-based Cirque du Soleil, see the "Secrets of Greatness: Teamwork!" features, *Fortune*, June 12, 2006, pp. 64–152. See also A. M. Brandenburger and B. J. Nalebuff, *Co-Opetition: A Revolution Mindset That Combines Competition and Cooperation: The Game Theory Strategy That's Changing the Game of Business* (New York: Currency, 1997); R. Wright, *The Logic of Human Destiny* (New York: Vintage, 2000); and Kim and Mauborgne, *Blue Ocean Strategy*.

4. Two classic empirical studies are D. E. Zand, "Trust and Managerial Problem Solving," *Administrative Science Quarterly* 17, no. 2 (1972): 229–239; and W. R. Boss, "Trust and Managerial Problem Solving Revisited," *Group & Organization Studies* 3, no. 3 (1978): 331–342. See also R. B. Shaw, *Trust in the Balance: Building Successful Organizations on Results, Integrity, and Concern* (San Francisco: Jossey-Bass, 1997); A. R. Ciancutti and T. L. Steding, *Built on Trust: Gaining Competitive Advantage in Any Organization* (New York: McGraw-Hill, 2000); K. Patterson, J. Grenny, R. McMillan, and A. Switzler, *Crucial Conversations: Tools for Talking When Stakes Are High* (New York: McGraw-Hill, 2002); H. Bracey, *Building Trust: How to Get It! How to Keep It!* (Taylorville, Ga.: HB Artworks, 2003); and S. M. Covey, R. R. Merrill, and S. R. Covey, *The SPEED of Trust: The One Thing That Changes Everything* (New York: Free Press, 2006).

5. *Innovation Survey* (London: PricewaterhouseCoopers, 1999), 3.

6. See M. B. Gurtman, "Trust, Distrust, and Interpersonal Problems: A Circumplex Analysis," *Journal of Personality and Social Psychology* 62 (1992): 989–1002. See also G. D. Grace and T. Schill, "Social Support and Coping Style Differences in Subjects High and Low in Interpersonal Trust," *Psychological Reports* 59 (1986): 584–586.

7. G. Colvin. "Why Dream Teams Fail," *Fortune*, June 8, 2006, available online at http://money.cnn.com/magazines/fortune/fortune_archive/2006/06/12/8379219/index.htm.

8. Boss, "Trust and Managerial Problem Solving Revisited," 338.

9. Boss, "Trust and Managerial Problem Solving Revisited," 338.

10. Boss, "Trust and Managerial Problem Solving Revisited," 338.

11. J. W. Driscoll, "Trust and Participation in Organizational Decision Making as Predictors of Satisfaction," *Academy of Management Journal* 21, no. 1 (1978): 44–56. See also R. M. Kramer, "Trust and Distrust in Organizations: Emerging Perspectives, Enduring Questions," *Annual Review of Psychology* 50 (1999): 569–598; and T. Simons and R. S. Peterson, "When to Let Them Duke It Out," *Harvard Business Review* 84, no. 6 (May–June 2006): 23–24.

12. C. A. O'Reilly and K. H. Roberts, "Information Filtration in Organizations: Three Experiments," *Organizational Behavior and Human Performance* 11 (1974): 253–265; and Boss, "Trust and Managerial Problem Solving Revisited."

13. Zand, "Trust and Managerial Problem Solving," and Driscoll, "Trust and Participation in Organizational Decision Making as Predictors of Satisfaction."

14. R. Axelrod, *The Evolution of Cooperation* (New York: Basic Books, 1984). See also W. Poundstone, *Prisoner's Dilemma: John Von Neumann, Game Theory, and the Puzzle of the Bomb* (New York: Doubleday, 1992).

15. Axelrod, *The Evolution of Cooperation*, 20, 190.

16. R. B. Cialdini, "Harnessing the Science of Persuasion," *Harvard Business Review,* October 2001, pp. 72–79. For a discussion of the principle of reciprocity, see R. B. Cialdini, *Influence: Science and Practice*, 4th ed. (Needham Heights, Mass.: Allyn & Bacon, 2001), 19–51; J. K. Butler Jr. "Behaviors, Trust, and Goal Achievement in a Win-Win Negotiating Role Play," *Group & Organization Management* 20, no. 4 (1995): 486–501; and W.E.D. Creed and R. E. Miles, "Trust in Organizations: A Conceptual Framework Linking Organizational Forms, Managerial Philosophies, and the Opportunity Costs of Controls," in R. M. Kramer and T. R. Tyler (eds), *Trust in Organizations: Frontiers of Theory and Research* (Thousand Oaks, Calif.: Sage, 1996): 16–39. See also G. Kohlrieser, *Hostage at the Table: How Leaders Can Overcome Conflict, Influence Others, and Raise Performance* (San Francisco, CA: Jossey-Bass, 2006).

17. R. Putnam, *Bowling Alone: The Collapse and Revival of American Community* (New York: Simon & Schuster, 2000), 134.

18. J. Vesterman, "From Wharton to War," *Fortune,* June 12, 2006, p. 106.

19. Vesterman, "From Wharton to War," p. 106.

20. D. W. Johnson and R. T. Johnson, *Cooperation and Competition: Theory and Research* (Edina, Minn.: Interaction, 1989), 63.

21. A. Van de Ven, A. L. Delbecq, and R. J. Koenig, "Determinants of Coordination Modes Within Organizations," *American Sociological Review* 41, no. 2 (1976): 322–338.

22. D. Cohen and L. Prusak, *In Good Company: How Social Capital Makes Organizations Work* (Boston: Harvard Business School Press, 2001), 20.

23. G. Homans, *The Human Group* (New York: Harcourt Brace Jovanovich, 1950).

CHAPTER TEN: STRENGTHEN OTHERS

1. R. M. Kanter, *The Change Masters: Innovation for Productivity in the American Corporation* (New York: Simon & Schuster, 1983). For more recent studies by Kanter on power, see R. M. Kanter, *When Giants Learn to Dance: Mastering the Challenges of Strategy, Management, and Careers in the 1990s* (New York: Simon & Schuster, 1989); and R. M. Kanter, *e-Volve!: Succeeding in the Digital Culture of Tomorrow* (Boston: Harvard Business School Press, 2001). For a study of how organizations create a culture of employee confidence, see R. M. Kanter, *Confidence: How Winning Streaks & Losing Streaks Begin and End* (New York: Crown Business, 2004).

2. A. Bandura, *Self-Efficacy: The Exercise of Control* (New York: Freeman, 1997); K. A. Karl, A. M. Leary-Kelly, and J. J. Martocchio, "The Impact of Feedback and Self-Efficacy on Performance in Training," *Journal of Organizational Behavior* 14, no. 4 (1993): 379–394; C. M. Shea and J. M. Howell, "Charismatic Leadership and Task Feedback: A Laboratory Study of Their Effects on Self-Efficacy and Task Performance," *Leadership Quarterly* 10, no. 3 (1999): 375–396; and A. Bandura, "Social Cognitive Theory: An Agentic Perspective," *Annual Review of Psychology* 52 (2001): 1–26.

3. See, for example, J. Borda, "Great Expectations," *Fast Company,* November 1999, pp. 212–222; S. R. Williams and R. L. Wilson, "Group Support Systems, Power, and Influence in an Organization: A Field Study," *Decision Sciences* 28, no. 4 (1997): 911–937; and A. Tannenbaum and others, *Hierarchy in Organizations: An International Comparison* (San Francisco: Jossey-Bass, 1974).

4. J. Thackray, "Feedback for Real," *Gallup Management Journal* 1, no. 1 (Spring 2001): 12–17. For a more detailed description, see M. Buckingham and C. Coffman, *First, Break All the Rules* (New York: Simon & Schuster, 1999).

5. R. Wagner and J. K. Harter, *12: The Elements of Great Managing* (New York: Simon & Schuster, 2006).

6. L. A. Schlesinger and K. L. Heskett, "Enfranchisement of Service Workers," *California Management Review* (Summer 1991): 83–100; J. L. Heskett and others, "Putting the Service-Profit Chain to Work," *Harvard Business Review,* March-April 1994, pp. 164–174; and J. L. Heskett, W. E. Sasser Jr., and L. A. Schlesinger, *The Service Profit Chain: How Leading Companies Link Profit and Growth to Loyalty, Satisfaction, and Value* (New York: Free Press, 1997).

7. As quoted in "Winners," *Sibson & Company* 1, no. 7 (October 1991): 2.

8. Evolutionary psychology demonstrates that in ecosystems, collaboration is what assists species to survive rather than become extinct; the group ends up eradicating bad or inefficient behavior. See R. Wright, *The Moral Animal: Why We Are the Way We Are: The New Science of Evolutionary Psychology* (New York: Vintage, 1995). For another interesting look at the origins of social cooperation, see A. Fields, *Altruistically Inclined?: The Behavioral Sciences, Evolutionary Theory, and the Origins of Reciprocity* (Ann Arbor, MI: University of Michigan Press, 2004).

9. See, for example, MICA Executive Survey, "Training Impact on Corporate Competitiveness," Toronto, Canada: MICA Management Resources, April 1991; *America and the New Economy* (Alexandria, Va.: American Society for Training and Development, 1990); and B. Sugrue and R. J. Rivera, *2005 State of the Industry Report* (Alexandria, Va.: ASTD Press, 2005).

10. R. Boyatzis and A. McKee, *Resonant Leadership* (Boston: Harvard Business School Press, 2004); M. M. Hughes, L. B. Patterson, and J. B. Terrell, *Emotional Intelligence in Action: Training and Coaching Activi-*

ties for Leaders and Managers (San Francisco: Jossey-Bass, 2005); V. U. Druskat, G. Mount, and F. Sala (eds.), *Linking Emotional Intelligence and Performance at Work: Current Research Evidence with Individuals and Groups* (Mahwah, N.J.: Lawrence Erlbaum Associates, 2005); and D. Goleman, *Social Intelligence: The New Science of Human Relationships* (New York: Bantam Books, 2006).

11. L. M. Spencer Jr. and S. M. Spencer, *Competence at Work: Models for Superior Performance* (New York: Wiley, 1993).

12. P. F. Drucker, "The New Productivity Challenge," *Harvard Business Review* 69, no. 6 (November-December 1991): 69–79.

13. T. A. Stewart, "Brainpower," *Fortune*, June 3, 1991, p. 50.

14. J. Stack with B. Burlingham, *The Great Game of Business* (New York: Currency Doubleday, 1994), 3. For a more recent account of Stack's philosophy, see J. Stack and B. Burlingham, *A Stake in the Outcome: Building a Culture of Ownership for the Long-Term Success of Your Business* (New York: Currency, 2002).

15. J. A. Conger, "Leadership: The Art of Empowering Others," *Academy of Management Executive* 3, no. 1 (1989): 17–24.

16. Psychologists often refer to this as self-efficacy. See, for example, Bandura, *Self-Efficacy*; and R. M. Steers, L. W. Porter, and G. A. Bigley, *Motivation and Leadership at Work*, 6th ed. (New York: McGraw-Hill, 1996).

17. R. E. Wood and A. Bandura, "Impact of Conceptions of Ability on Self-Regulatory Mechanisms and Complex Decision Making," *Journal of Personality and Social Psychology* 56 (1989): 407–415. Managers in this study who lost confidence in their own judgments tended to find fault with their people. Indeed, they were quite uncharitable about their employees, regarding them as unmotivatable and unworthy of supervisory effort; given the option, they would have fired many of them.

18. A. Bandura and R. E. Wood, "Effects of Perceived Controllability and Performance Standards on Self-Regulation of Complex Decision Making," *Journal of Personality and Social Psychology* 56 (1989): 805–814.

19. A. M. Saks, "Longitudinal Field Investigation of the Moderating and Mediating Effects of Self-Efficacy on the Relationship Between Training and Newcomer Adjustment," *Journal of Applied Psychology* 80 (1995): 211–225.

20. C. Dahle, "Natural Leader," *Fast Company*, November 2000, available online at www.fastcompany.com/magazine/41/sharpnack.html.

21. For more on how coaches coach, see M. M. Goldsmith and L. Lyons (eds.), *Coaching for Leadership: The Practice of Leadership Coaching from the World's Greatest Coaches*, 2nd ed. (San Francisco: Pfeiffer, 2006).

CHAPTER ELEVEN: RECOGNIZE CONTRIBUTIONS

1. Hundreds of research studies have since been conducted to test this notion, and they all clearly demonstrate that people tend to act in ways that are consistent with the expectations they perceive. See, for example, D. Eden, *Pygmalion in Management: Productivity as a Self-Fulfilling Prophecy* (Lexington, Mass.: Lexington Books, 1990); D. Eden, "Leadership and Expectations: Pygmalion Effects and Other Self-Fulfilling Prophecies in Organizations," *Leadership Quarterly* 3, no. 4 (1992): 271–305; and A. Smith, L. Jussim, J. Eccles, M. Van Noy, S. Madon, and P. Palumbo, "Self-Fulfilling Prophecies, Perceptual Biases, and Accuracy at the Individual and Group Levels," *Journal of Experimental Social Psychology* 34, no. 6 (1998): 530–561.

2. R. J. Blitzer, C. Petersen, and L. Rogers, "How to Build Self-Esteem," *Training and Development Journal* (February 1993): 59.

3. For a discussion of "flow," see M. Csikszentmihalyi, *Finding Flow: The Psychology of Engagement with Everyday Life* (New York: Basic Books, 1997).

4. See, for example, J. E. Sawyer, W. R. Latham, R. D. Pritchard, and W. R. Bennett Jr., "Analysis of Work Group Productivity in an Applied Setting: Application of a Time Series Panel Design," *Personnel Psychology* 52 (1999): 927–967; and A. Gostick and C. Elton, *Managing with Carrots: Using Recognition to Attract and Retain the Best People* (Layton, Utah: Gibbs Smith, 2001).

5. A. E. Schnur and C. Butz, *The Best Finish First: Top Coaches Talk About Winning* (San Francisco: Towers Perrin, 1994).

6. Blood tests taken during the march and again twenty-four hours later showed similar patterns. Blood levels of cortisol and prolactin (chemicals whose levels rise as stress increases) were, as expected, highest for the group that knew the least about the march and lowest for those soldiers who knew exactly where they were and how much farther they were expected to go. D. Eden and G. Ravid, "Pygmalion vs. Self-Expectancy: Effects of Instructor and Self-Expectancy on Trainee Performance," *Organizational Behavior and Human Performance* 30 (1982): 351–364; and D. Eden and A. B. Shani, "Pygmalion Goes to Boot Camp: Expectancy, Leadership and Trainee Performance," *Journal of Applied Psychology* 67 (1982): 194–199.

7. P. A. McCarty, "Effects of Feedback on the Self-Confidence of Men and Women," *Academy of Management Journal* 20 (1986): 840–847.

8. See, for example, R. M. Ryan and E. L. Deci, "Self-Determination Theory and the Facilitation of Intrinsic Motivation, Social Development, and Well-Being," *American Psychologist* 55, no. 1 (2000): 68–78.

9. For a more in-depth discussion of personal credibility, see J. M. Kouzes and B. Z. Posner, *Credibility: How Leaders Gain and Lose It, Why People Demand It* (San Francisco: Jossey-Bass, 1993).

10. J-F. Manzoni and J-L. Barsoux, "The Set-Up-to-Fail Syndrome," *Harvard Business Review* 76, no. 2 (March–April 1998): 102. See also J-F. Manzoni and J-L. Barsoux, *The Set-Up-to-Fail Syndrome: How Good Managers Cause Great People to Fail* (Boston: Harvard Business School Publishing, 2002).

11. B. Nelson, *1001 Ways to Reward Employees,* 2nd ed. (New York: Workman Publishing Company, 2005).

12. J. A. Ross, "Does Friendship Improve Job Performance?" *Harvard Business Review* 54, no. 2 (March-April 1977): 8–9. See also K. A. Jehn and P. P. Shah, "Interpersonal Relationships and Task Performance: An Examination of Mediating Processes in Friendship and Acquaintance Groups," *Journal of Personality and Social Psychology* 72, no. 4 (1997): 775–790. There is an important caveat, however. Friends have to be strongly committed to the group's goals. If not, then friends may not do better. This is precisely why we said earlier that it is absolutely necessary for leaders to be clear about standards and to create a condition of shared goals and values. When it comes to performance, commitment to standards and good relations between people go together.

13. D. Jamieson and J. O'Mara, *Managing Workforce 2000: Gaining the Diversity Advantage* (San Francisco: Jossey-Bass, 1991); and R. Goffee and G. Jones, *Why Should Anyone Be Led by YOU?* (Boston: Harvard Business School Press, 2006).

14. J. L. Hall, B. Z. Posner, and J. W. Harder, "Performance Appraisal Systems: Matching Theory with Practice," *Group and Management Studies* 14, no. 1 (1989): 51–69.

15. J. Pfeffer and R. I. Sutton, *Hard Facts, Dangerous Half-Truths and Total Nonsense: Profiting from Evidence-Based Management* (Boston: Harvard Business School Publishing, 2006).

16. See, for example, J. T. Bond, E. Galinsky, and J. E. Swanberg, *The 1997 National Study of the Changing Workforce* (New York: Families and Work Institute, 1998); F. L. Branham, *Keeping the People Who Keep You in Business* (New York: Amacom, 2000); and B. N. Pfau and I. T. Kay, *The Human Capital Edge* (New York: McGraw-Hill, 2001).

17. B. Nelson, "The Power of Rewards and Recognition," presentation to the Consortium on Executive Education, Leavey School of Business, Santa Clara University, September 20, 1996.

18. R. M. Kanter, "The Change Masters," presentation to the Executive Seminar in Corporate Excellence, Leavey School of Business, Santa Clara University, March 13, 1984.

19. See T. Rath and D. O. Clifton, *How Full Is Your Bucket? Positive Strategies for Work and Life* (New York: Gallup Press, 2004), 57. Original research: M. Losada, "The Complex Dynamics of High Performance Teams," *Mathematical and Computer Modeling* (1999): 30.

20. M. Buckingham and D. O. Clifton, *Now, Discover Your Strengths* (New York: Free Press, 2001). We can go overboard, however. At a thirteen-to-one ratio, productivity declines. Most of us don't have to worry about this upper limit; it's the three-to-one that we usually have trouble with.

21. Eric Harvey suggests lots and lots of creative ways to recognize people in his handbook *180 Ways to Walk the Recognition Talk* (Dallas: Walk the Talk Company, 2000). Also see B. Nelson, *1001 Ways to Energize Employees* (New York: Workman, 1997); and L. Yerkes, *Fun Works: Creative Places Where People Love to Work* (San Francisco: Berrett-Koehler, 2001).

CHAPTER TWELVE: CELEBRATE THE VALUES AND VICTORIES

1. D. Campbell, *If I'm in Charge Here, Why Is Everybody Laughing?* (Greensboro, N.C.: Center for Creative Leadership, 1984), 64.

2. T. Deal and M. K. Key, *Corporate Celebration: Play, Purpose, and Profit at Work* (San Francisco: Berrett-Koehler, 1998), 5.

3. T. E. Deal and A. A. Kennedy, *Corporate Cultures: The Rites and Rituals of Corporate Life* (Reading, Mass.: Addison-Wesley, 1982), 63. Deal and Kennedy have updated their original work in *The New Corporate Cultures: Revitalizing the Workplace After Downsizing, Mergers, and Reengineering* (Cambridge, Mass.: Perseus Books, 2000).

4. Deal and Key, *Corporate Celebration*, 28.

5. See, for example, K. J. Fenlason and T. A. Beehr, "Social Support and Occupational Stress: Effects of Talking to Others," *Journal of Organizational Behavior* 15, no. 2 (1994): 157–175; and J. S. Mulbert, "Social Networks, Social Circles, and Job Satisfaction," *Work & Occupations* 18, no. 4 (1991): 415–430.

6. S. Bowles and K. Blanchard, *Gung Ho! Turn on the People in Any Organization* (New York: William Morrow, 1998).

7. L. L. Berry, A. Parasuraman, and V. A. Zeithaml, "Improving Service Quality in America: Lessons Learned," *Academy of Management Executive* 8, no. 2 (1994): 32–45, quote on p. 41.

8. California Department of Mental Health, *Friends Can Be Good Medicine* (San Francisco: Pacificon Productions, 1981); and E. M. Hallowell, *Connect: Twelve Vital Ties That Open Your Heart, Lengthen Your Life, and Deepen Your Soul* (New York: Pocket Books, 2001).

9. L. F. Berkman and S. L. Syme, "Social Networks, Host Resistance, and Mortality: A Nine-Year Follow-Up Study of Alameda County Residents," *American Journal of Epidemiology* 109, no. 2 (1979): 186–204. See also S. Cohen, "Psychosocial Models of the Role of Social Support in the Etiology of Physical Disease," *Health Psychology* 7 (1988): 269–297.

10. T. Rath, *Vital Friends: The People You Can't Afford to Live Without* (New York: Gallup Press, 2006), 52. See also R. Wagner and J. K. Harter, *12: The Elements of Great Managing* (New York: Simon & Schuster, 2006) for a follow-up report on the Gallup engagement research, including discussion of the importance of having friends in the workplace.

11. Rath, *Vital Friends*, 62.

12. Rath, *Vital Friends*, 51.

13. R. F. Baumeister and M. R. Leary, "The Need to Belong: Desire for Interpersonal Attachment as a Fundamental Human Motivation," *Psychological Bulletin* 117 (1995): 497–529; H. W. Perkins, "Religious Commitment, Yuppie Values, and Well-Being in a Post-Collegiate Life," *Review of Religious Research* 32

(1991): 244–251; D. G. Myers, "The Funds, Friends, and Faith of Happy People," *American Psychologist* 55, no. 1 (2000): 56–67; and S. Crabtree, "Getting Personal in the Workplace: Are Negative Relationships Squelching Productivity in Your Company?" *Gallup Management Journal,* June 10, 2004, available online at www.govleaders.org/gallup_article_getting_personal.htm.

14. See, for example, Myers, "The Funds, Friends, and Faith of Happy People"; M. Csikszentmihalyi, "If We Are So Rich, Why Aren't We Happy?" *American Psychologist* 54 (1999): 821–827; D. G. Myers and E. Diener, "The Pursuit of Happiness," *Scientific American* 274 (1996): 54–56; and D. Gilbert, *Stumbling on Happiness* (New York: Knopf, 2006).

15. K. Freiberg and J. Freiberg, *Guts! Companies That Blow the Doors Off Business-As-Usual* (New York: Currency, 2004), 250.

16. K. Blanchard and S. Johnson, *The One-Minute Manager* (New York: Morrow, 1982).

17. BMO+Harris@Work (internal company publication), August/September 2006: 9.

18. P. J. Gill, "Once Upon an Enterprise," *Knowledge Management* (May 2001), available online at www.destinationcrm.com/km/dcrm_km_article.asp?id=823.

19. G. Klein, *The Sources of Power: How People Make Decisions* (Cambridge, Mass.: MIT Press, 1998).

CHAPTER THIRTEEN: LEADERSHIP IS EVERYONE'S BUSINESS

1. See, for example, D. C. Hambrick and S. Finkelstein, "Managerial Discretion: A Bridge Between Polar Views of Organizational Outcomes," *Research in Organizational Behavior* 9 (1987): 369–406; R. G. Lord and K. J. Maher, *Leadership and Information Processing: Linking Perceptions and Performance* (Boston: Unwin-Hyman, 1991); and P. E. Connor, L. K. Lake, and R. W. Stackman, *Managing Organizational Change,* 3rd ed. (Westport, Conn.: Praeger Publishers, 2003).

2. See, for example, J. Pfeffer, "The Ambiguity of Leadership," *Academy of Management Review* 2 (1977): 104–112; J. R. Meindl, S. B. Ehrlich, and J. M. Dukerich, "The Romance of Leadership," *Administrative Science Quarterly* 30 (1985): 78–102; J. R. Meindl, J. C. Pastor, and M. Mayo, "Romance of Leadership," in G. R. Goethals, G. J. Sorenson, and J. M. Burns (eds.), *Encyclopedia of Leadership,* Vol. 3 (Thousand Oaks, Calif.: Sage, 2004): 1347–1351; and M. C. Bligh and J. R. Meindl, "The Cultural Ecology of Leadership: An Analysis of Popular Leadership Books," in D. M. Messick and R. M. Kramer (eds.), *The Psychology of Leadership: New Perspectives and Research* (Mahwah, N.J.: Lawrence Erlbaum Associates, 2004).

3. See our Web site, www.leadershipchallenge.com, for more information about empirical studies using The Five Practices of Exemplary Leadership framework.

4. For more on the importance of humility in organizational success, see J. Collins, *Good to Great: Why Some Companies Make the Leap ... and Others Don't* (New York: HarperCollins, 2002), and J. Porras, S. Emery, and M. Thompson, *Success Built to Last: Creating a Life that Matters* (Upper Saddle River, N.J.: Wharton School Publishing, 2006).

5. C. R. Snyder and S. J. Lopez (eds.), *Handbook of Positive Psychology* (Oxford: Oxford University Press, 2002); C. R. Snyder, *Handbook of Hope: Theory, Measures, and Applications* (San Diego: Academic Press, 2006); and A. Raveghi, *Hope: How Triumphant Leaders Create the Future* (San Francisco: Jossey-Bass, 2006).

6. J. H. Stanford, *Victory in Our Schools: We CAN Give Our Children Excellent Public Education* (New York: Bantam Books, 1999).

7. As quoted in "Telling Moments from His Life," *Seattle Times.* Available online at http://seattletimes.nwsource.com/stanford/stories/anecdotes.html; accessed January 29, 2007.

ACKNOWLEDGMENTS

The making of a book is a highly collaborative effort, especially for the two of us who've been a research, writing, and teaching team for twenty-five years. This is the fourth edition of *The Leadership Challenge,* and we estimate there've been well over four hundred people who've contributed to these pages in one way or another. If it weren't for *every one* of them, there'd be no book at all, let alone one that has stood the test of time.

No book emerges whole from the minds of its authors. Throughout the years many scholars and students of leadership have strongly influenced our thinking. Their ideas have found their way onto the pages you read. We owe an immense continuing intellectual debt of gratitude to these very special colleagues and friends: James MacGregor Burns, Warren Bennis, Ken Blanchard, André Delbecq, John Gardner, Daniel Goleman, Rosabeth Moss Kanter, Tom Peters, Jeff Pfeffer, and Warren Schmidt.

Over the years, we continue to be moved to laughter and tears, awe and inspiration, as we listen in on the uplifting experiences of hundreds of men and women who accepted the leadership challenge. They're the ones who taught us what it really means to get extraordinary things done in organizations; they're the true heroes and heroines of this book, and of organizations. You'll meet lots of these courageous folks as you read *The Leadership Challenge.* We're forever grateful to them for sharing their lives with us, and we hope that we've represented them well.

One of the ways we've tested our ideas about leadership is through workshops and seminars. Our Master Facilitators continuously uplift our spirits with their faith in and commitment to *The Leadership Challenge Workshop*™.

We deeply appreciate their years of stimulation, support, and encouragement. Some of the many talented professionals who dedicate themselves to liberating the leader in everyone are Peter Alduino, Jo Bell, Hugh Blane, Lily Cheng, Peter Cheng, Kim Chesky, Steve Coats, Ron Crossland, Helen Green, Craig Haptonstall, Renee Harness, Dick Heller, Stephen Hoel, Steve Houchin, Dianne Kenny, Richard King, Sharon Landes, Madeleine McGrath, Michael Neiss, Chris Nel, David Pilbeam, L. J. Rose, Charles St. John, Robert Thompson, Valerie Willis, and Nancy Winship. Daren Blonski, Cheryl Boys, Lauren Parkhill, Amy Savage, and Carol Wolper have been critical to making sure our programs run smoothly. And the continuing growth of our workshop business is attributable largely to Jeni Nichols. She has taken more initiative and assumed more risk than anyone else, making sure that customers are delighted by their experience with our programs.

Moving from the realm of testing ideas to committing them to paper is always a test of teamwork. The first edition made it from ideas to print with the marvelous assistance of Liz Caravelli, Joy Congdon, Liz Currie, Judy Kasper, and Michael Malone. For the second edition, we relied heavily on Joan Carter for research assistance and case writing and Kathy Dalle-Molle for factchecking, permissions work, and attention to detail. We couldn't have written the third edition without the research and dedicated assistance of Ellen Peterson, Leigh Gillen, JoAnn Johnson, Donna Perry, Hilary Powers, and Leslie Tilley. Jan Hunter worked with us as developmental editor for both the second and third editions, and she was superb. Leslie Stephen took over the reins as our developmental editor on this edition, and with her wonderful wit and wise counsel she kept us keenly focused on the essentials, challenged us to be more global, contributed important stories, diplomatically resolved differences, gently moved us forward, and astutely strengthened our prose. All errors, of course, remain our responsibility!

The community of professionals at Jossey-Bass and Pfeiffer, both Wiley imprints, masterfully practices the true art of editing and publishing. Their confidence and patience have been overwhelming. Over the years and now through four editions we acknowledge the steadfastness, imagination, and encouragement of all the gracious folks at John Wiley & Sons. We especially want to thank current members of our creative, editorial, production, sales, and marketing teams: Walt Anthony, Rob Brandt, David Brightman, Leah Campbell, Carolyn Carlstroem, Janis Chan, Cedric Crocker, Rich Crucitt, Christine Dunn, Jessica Egbert, Paul Foster, Mary Garrett, Marc Gendron, Sheri Gilbert, Julianna Gustafson, David Horne, Mary Ann Hudson, Debra Hunter, Mark Karmendy, Marisa Kelley, Dawn Kilgore, Louise Koh, Adeline Lim, Neal Maillet, Cathy Mallon, Kasi Miller, Adrian Morgan, Erin Null, Amy Packard, Terry Palmer, Jeanenne Ray, Yvo Riezebos, Byron Schneider, Eric Thrasher, Serene Vannoy, Bernadette Walter, Jesse Wiley, Peter Wiley, Susan Williams, and Amie Wong. We offer a very special thanks to Lisa Shannon, *The Leadership Challenge* champion within the Wiley family. Lisa has taken risks on new ventures, shepherded all our projects, and been unwavering in her support.

Our families are constant sources of love and warmth, inspiration and insight, energy and resolve. We had to literally close the door on them on countless evenings and weekends, and still they were, and are, always there for us. Our parents, Tom and Thelma Kouzes and Delores and Henry Posner, were early role models of leadership and their examples forever fill our hearts. Jackie Schmidt-Posner continues to provide perspective and balance as well as imaginative advice and a sense of humor to a loving partnership that spans nearly four decades. Amanda Posner has grown into a talented, compassionate person who lives life to its fullest and brings out the best in others. Tae Kouzes is the love of Jim's life and his muse of leadership. With her astute counsel, sensitive coaching, and practical wisdom she always finds a way to broaden awareness and expand insights into even the most elusive of ideas. And she's a whole lot of fun to be with. Nicholas, Jim and Tae's son, gives meaning and purpose to the future of leadership. Participating in the blossoming of his talents and the strengthening of his character brings great joy and wonder. We are forever grateful for our families' sacrifices, their steadfastness, and their support. They embody what it means to love and to care about others.

As so many extraordinary leaders have told us, "You can't do it alone." We couldn't have done it without all of these folks, and the many others who have shared this journey along the way. *You* made this book possible.

We love you all.

James M. Kouzes

Barry Z. Posner

ABOUT THE AUTHORS

Jim Kouzes and Barry Posner are coauthors of the award-winning and best-selling book, *The Leadership Challenge*. *The Leadership Challenge* was the winner of the James A. Hamilton Hospital Administrators' Book Award and the Critics' Choice Award, was a *BusinessWeek* best-seller, and has sold over 1.4 million copies in more than twelve other languages. Jim and Barry have coauthored more than a dozen other leadership books, including *Credibility: How Leaders Gain It and Lose It, Why People Demand It*—chosen by *Industry Week* as one of its year's five best management books—*Encouraging the Heart*, and *A Leader's Legacy*, selected by *Soundview Executive Book Summaries* as one of the top thirty books of the year. They also developed the highly acclaimed *Leadership Practices Inventory* (LPI), a 360-degree questionnaire for assessing leadership behavior, which is one of the most widely used leadership assessment instruments in the world. More than three hundred fifty doctoral dissertations and academic research projects have been based on the Five Practices of Exemplary Leadership model.

Jim and Barry were named Management/Leadership Educators of the Year by the International Management Council. This honor puts them in the company of Ken Blanchard, Stephen Covey, Peter Drucker, Edward Deming, Frances Hesselbein, Lee Iacocca, Rosabeth Moss Kanter, Norman Vincent Peale, and Tom Peters, who are all past recipients of the award. In the book *Coaching for Leadership* they were listed among the nation's top leadership educators. Jim and Barry are frequent conference speakers, and each has conducted leadership development programs for hundreds of organizations, including Apple, Applied Materials, ARCO, AT&T, Australia Post, Bank of America, Bose, Charles Schwab, Cisco Systems, Community Leadership Association, Conference Board of Canada, Consumers Energy, Dell Computer, Deloitte Touche, Dorothy Wylie Nursing Leadership Institute, Egon Zehnder International, Federal Express, Gymboree, Hewlett-Packard, IBM, Jobs DR-Singapore, Johnson & Johnson, Kaiser Foundation Health Plans and Hospitals, L. L. Bean, Lawrence Livermore National Labs, Lucile Packard Children's Hospital, Merck, Mervyn's, Motorola, Network Appliance, Northrop Grumman, Roche Bioscience, Siemens, Standard Aero, Sun Microsystems, 3M, Toyota, the U.S. Postal Service, United Way, USAA, Verizon, VISA, and The Walt Disney Company.

Jim Kouzes is the Dean's Executive Professor of Leadership, Leavey School of Business, at Santa Clara University. Not only is he a highly regarded leadership scholar and an experienced executive, the *Wall Street Journal* has cited him as one of the twelve best executive educators in the United States. In 2006 Jim was presented with the Golden Gavel, the highest honor awarded by Toastmasters International.

Jim served as president, CEO, and chairman of the Tom Peters Company from 1988 through 1999, and prior to that led the Executive Development Center at Santa Clara University (1981–1987). Jim founded the Joint Center for Human Services Development at San Jose State University (1972–1980) and was on the staff of the School of Social Work, University of Texas. His career in training and development began in 1969 when he conducted seminars for Community Action Agency staff and volunteers in the "war on poverty" effort. Following graduation from Michigan State University (B.A. degree with honors in political science), he served as a Peace Corps volunteer (1967–1969). Jim also received a certificate from San Jose State University's School of Business for completion of the internship in organization development. Jim can be reached at jim@kouzesposner.com.

Barry Posner is dean of the Leavey School of Business and professor of leadership at Santa Clara University (Silicon Valley, California), where he has received numerous teaching and innovation awards. An internationally renowned scholar and educator, Barry is author or coauthor of more than a hundred research and practitioner-focused articles. He currently serves on the editorial review boards for *Leadership and Organizational Development, Leadership Review,* and *The International Journal of Servant-Leadership.* Barry is a warm and engaging conference speaker and dynamic workshop facilitator.

Barry received his baccalaureate degree with honors from the University of California, Santa Barbara, in political science, his master's degree from The Ohio State University in public administration, and his doctoral degree from the University of Massachusetts, Amherst, in organizational behavior and administrative theory. Having consulted with a wide variety of public and private sector organizations around the globe, Barry currently sits on the boards of directors of Advanced Energy (NASDAQ: AEIS), the San Jose Repertory Theatre, and EMQ Family & Children Services. He has served previously on the board of the American Institute of Architects (AIA), Junior Achievement of Silicon Valley and Monterey Bay, Public Allies, Big Brothers/Big Sisters of Santa Clara County, the Center for Excellence in Nonprofits, Sigma Phi Epsilon Fraternity, and several start-up companies. Barry can be reached at bposner@scu.edu.

More information about Jim and Barry, their work, and their services can be found at their Web site: www.leadershipchallenge.com.

INDEX

meaning, 120–121; forward-looking in times of change, 124–125; linking commitment to purpose, 121–123; role of listening in, 118–120, 126

Communication: expanding skills in, 155–156; practicing positive, 147–148; promoting external and internal, 177–179; required for innovation, 177; speaking from heart, 151–152; symbolic language in storytelling, 144–145; values communicated in words, 58–60, 80–83

Community, 310–321; connecting celebration with commitment and, 311–313; having fun together, 319–321; including celebration as part of organizational life, 314–316; leadership as everyone's business, 338–339; providing social support, 316–319; publicly celebrating accomplishments, 313–314

Competence and confidence, 260–269; buddy systems to improve, 249–250; developing winner's attitude, 304–305; education for developing, 260–262; fostering self-confidence, 265–267; leader competence, 29–31, 35–36; leaders as constituent coaches, 267–269; organizing work to build competence, 262–265

CompUSA, 181

Conducting postmortems, 212–213

Confidence. *See* Competence and confidence

Confronting critical incidents, 88–89

Constituents: coaching by leaders, 267–269; connecting to visions of, 134–136; empowering, 6–7; expectations of leaders, 28–36; getting people interacting, 246–247; leadership characteristics prized by, 36–38; offering visible support, 271–272; perception of control, 263–264; providing with sense of control, 209; putting them first, 11; reciprocity with leaders, 28; reinforcing behavior of, 92–94; role in developing common purpose, 117–118; routines for questioning, 96–97; surveying about aspirations, 128–129; value credible behavior by leaders, 40–41

Contributions. *See* Recognition

Control: constituents perception of, 263–264; feeling powerful and, 253; giving over, 251; noting feelings of being in, 210; providing constituents with sense of, 209; stress and sense of, 206

Cook, Scott, 180–181

Cooperation: cooperative goals and roles, 233–234; project structures promoting, 237–240. *See also* Collaboration; Teamwork

Corporate Celebration (Deal and Key), 315–316

Coughlin, Brian, 229–230

Coven, Andrew, 144–145

Crant, J. Michael, 168–169

Credibility: How Leaders Gain and Lose It, Why People Demand It (Kouzes and Posner), 109

Credibility, 27–41; behavioral aspects of, 40–41; feedback as way to establish, 86; forward-looking leaders and, 29–31, 33–34; foundation of leadership, 36–41, 322; honesty and, 29–33; importance of leadership, 38–40; inspirational qualities of leaders, 29–31, 34–35; leadership competency and, 29–31, 35–36; loyalty and, 39–40

Credo: dialogue about, 71–72; writing personal, 70, 72

Cross-cultural leadership characteristics, 28–32

Csikszentmihalyi, M., 211

Customers: gathering ideas from, 186–187; soliciting feedback, 162–163

D

Dalin International Trading Corporation, 254

D'Arcangelo, Mark, 17

Datapro, 264–265

Davis, Evelia, 17

DaVita, 80–82

De Pree, Max, 48–49

Deal, Terrence, 315–316

Decision making under stress, 328–329

Delucia, Mark, 313–314

Denning, Steve, 90–91

Deogirikar, Arvind, 165–167

words, 58–60, 80–83; wise use of, 78, 80–83

Passion: envisioning future with, 113–116, 125; expressing emotions, 148–150; inspirational leaders and, 132–133; performance and, 130–131; speaking from heart, 151–152

Past: clarity of vision based on, 125; reflecting on themes of, 107–108

Pepe, Mike, 19

Perepelitsky, Leon, 236–237

Performance: adding passion and pride for, 130–131; confidence and, 266–267; effect of feedback on, 288–290; optimal levels of, 210–211; reflecting expectations, 284–286; shared values and improved, 62–64

Personal audits for leaders, 95–96, 98

Personal involvement, 321–329; leadership and, 321–324; storytelling, 326–329

Personal journal writing, 51–52

Personal recognition, 292–302; creative incentives for, 296–298; getting close to people with, 294–296; showing you care, 324–325; thank you as, 298–300; thoughtfulness and, 300–302

Pettingill, Dick, 324–325

Pfizer, 311

Phillips, Bob, 327–328

Pickett, Siobhan, 232–233, 238

Pierce, Melissa, 279–280

Pitts, Jim, 103

Pizza Hut Korea, 323

Planning celebrations, 330

Plantronics, 240

Podzilni, Doug, 319–320

Positive communication, 147–148, 202–203

Posner, Barry, 109

Postmortems, 212–213

Powell, Stephanie, 240

Powerful times, 252–253

Powerlessness: ability to thrive under stress and, 206; conditions leading to, 251–252

Pre-mortems, 213–214

PricewaterhouseCoopers, 225

Pride: performance and, 130–131; uniqueness and, 136–137

PRIDE acronym, 7–8

Priest, Michael, 175–176

Prisoner's Dilemma puzzle, 235–236

Proactivity, 168–169

Procter & Gamble, 179

Psychological hardiness, 206–207; advantage of, 212; fostering, 208–211

Public Allies, 24–25

Public celebrations of accomplishments, 313–314

Purpose. *See* Common purpose

Putnam, Robert, 236

Q

Questions: asking, 244–246; asking purposeful, 78, 83–84; questioning status quo, 185–186; routines asking constituents, 96–98

Quinn Emanuel Urquhart Oliver & Hedges LLP, 337

R

Ravix Group, 120–121

Ravizza, Stephen, 170–172

Raymond W. Bliss Army Health Center, 268

Razouk, Laila, 151–152

Reagan, Ronald, 155

Reciprocity: as nature of leadership, 28; norms of, 234–237

Recognition, 279–306; action for, 302–306; clarifying expectations, 286–288; creating culture of, 323–324; developing winner's attitude, 304–305; encouraging the heart through, 22; essential keys to, 281; establishing conditions for success, 290–292; finding out what is encouraging, 303–304; importance of, 7; incentives for, 296–298; reinforcing values with, 93; stopping by for visit, 304; thank you as, 298–300; thoughtfulness and, 300–302; using feedback and goals, 288–290; within SG Group, 13

Recognition events, 308

Recording shared vision, 153–154, 156

Red Cross, 20

Reichheld, Frederick, 39

Reilly, Billie, 350–351

Reinforcing: behavior, 92–94; core values with celebrations, 331

A NOTE FROM THE PUBLISHER

We hope that you enjoyed this latest edition of *The Leadership Challenge* from Jim Kouzes and Barry Posner. If you are looking for those everyday opportunities to make a small difference in your world or if you are in need of the tools to get started or a community to keep inspired, we can help. Whether you would like to read more of the inspirational words of Jim Kouzes and Barry Posner, get some feedback on how you are doing, or implement a leadership development program within your organization, there are a variety of resources that will help as you begin or continue your leadership journey. These include:

Books—Jim and Barry have written several books, including *Credibility*, *Encouraging the Heart*, *Christian Reflections on The Leadership Challenge*, *The Jossey-Bass Academic Administrator's Guide to Exemplary Leadership*, and *A Leader's Legacy*.

Workbooks—Jim and Barry believe that an important part of the learning process is practice, practice, practice, so they have created *The Leadership Challenge Workbook* and *The Encouraging the Heart Workbook*. These interactive tools are designed to be used during that proverbial Monday morning when you are back at your desk, faced with a problem or situation, and would like to resolve the issue using Jim and Barry's framework.

Assessment—All leaders need feedback on how they are doing if they want to improve. *The Leadership Practices Inventory (LPI)* and *LPI Online* (www.lpionline.com) is the 360-degree assessment instrument designed by Jim and Barry that has helped develop the leadership skills of nearly one million people worldwide. The *Student LPI* is also available for high school and undergraduate classroom settings.

Videos—These visual aids to *The Leadership Challenge* program bring inspiring, real-life examples to the leadership development process.

Workshop—*The Leadership Challenge® Workshop* is a unique intensive program that consistently receives rave reviews from attendees. It has served as a catalyst for profound leadership transformations in organizations of all sizes and in all industries. The program is highly interactive and stimulating. Participants experience and apply Jim and Barry's leadership model through video cases, workbook exercises, group problem-solving tasks, lectures, and outdoor action learning. Quite often we hear workshop attendees describe how *The Leadership Challenge* is more than a training event. In many cases they talk about how it changed their lives. It's a bold statement, we know, but we've watched it happen time after time, leader after leader.

Combined, these offerings truly make Jim and Barry the most trusted sources on becoming a better leader. To find out more about these products, please visit www.leadershipchallenge.com. Or if you would like to speak to a leadership consultant about bringing *The Leadership Challenge* to your organization or team, call toll free (866) 888–5159.